D0561132

Signed by the Author

Glen de Vries

THE
PATIENT
EQUATION

GLEN DE VRIES
WITH JEREMY BLACHMAN

THE
PATIENT
EQUATION

THE **PRECISION MEDICINE REVOLUTION** IN THE AGE
OF **COVID-19** AND **BEYOND**

Published by John Wiley & Sons, Inc., Hoboken, New Jersey.
Published simultaneously in Canada.

For general information on our other products and services or for technical support, please contact our Customer Care Department within the United States at (800) 762-2974, outside the United States at (317) 572-3993 or fax (317) 572-4002.

Wiley publishes in a variety of print and electronic formats and by print-on-demand. Some material included with standard print versions of this book may not be included in e-books or in print-on-demand. If this book refers to media such as a CD or DVD that is not included in the version you purchased, you may download this material at http://booksupport.wiley.com. For more information about Wiley products, visit www.wiley.com.

Library of Congress Cataloging-in-Publication Data is available

ISBN 9781119622147(Hardback)
ISBN 9781119755760 (epdf)
ISBN 9781119755753 (ePUB)

Cover Design: Wiley
Cover Image: © teekid/Getty Images

Printed in the United States of America

10 9 8 7 6 5 4 3 2 1

Contents

Introduction

About a decade ago, I met Jack Whelan. An investment researcher working in the world of finance, Jack power-walked from the train to his office every day for years . . . until he noticed that walk getting more and more difficult, along with occasional nosebleeds that prompted him to see his doctor. He was diagnosed with a rare blood cancer—Waldenstrom macroglobulinemia (WM)—and his world changed completely. WM was (and is) incurable, with no FDA-approved treatments and an expected survival of just five to seven years. Wanting to extend his life, Jack sought out clinical trial after clinical trial. The first three trials failed, and then his fourth finally got him on a drug that stopped the cancer's progression for years.

Throughout his experience, Jack became an expert—and, more important for our story here, a tracker. Jack demanded weekly blood tests and charted a range of biomarkers—hematocrit, immunoglobulin, and others—hoping to find answers in the numbers, to be able to know if he was responding to treatment even before the doctors did. From physician to physician, from trial to trial, he brought these numbers with him in Excel spreadsheets. He hoped this growing collection of data about his body would uncover new and valuable information that could keep him alive.

Jack's diligence and initiative is rare, but he's not alone. Ray Finucane, a 75-year-old mechanical engineer with Parkinson's disease, built an app to track his symptoms and to try to optimize the dosing of his levodopa medication.[1] Dr. David Fajgenbaum used his own blood samples and software to find a new plausible biological explanation for Castleman disease that led him to try a drug never before applied to the condition—which has led him into remission for the past six years. Millions of people around the world—sick or not—wear fitness trackers or carry smartphones that are able to track massive amounts of data at a far more granular level than we could have ever conceived of just a few years ago.

Imagine a world where this data was harvested, analyzed, and combined with all of the medical records that are collected over the course of our lives and assembled into something useful, something to extend longevity, enhance the quality of life, and even help alter the arc of a pandemic.

Imagine if a patient like Jack didn't need to track his own body in an Excel spreadsheet because there were systems and devices that were doing it for him. What if he could do this while harnessing the collective wisdom of all of the research and real-world experience of the scientists, physicians, and patients who came before him to produce recommendations for the most effective treatments, the most critical behaviors, and the most valuable things he needed to know to beat his cancer and optimize his health?

Imagine a world where as soon as something useful could be detected, be it a data point we can track with conventional medical measurements or a misbehaving molecule or behavioral pattern that we may not even fully appreciate today (something about our sleep, our cognition, what we eat or drink, or an aspect of our environment, as just a few examples), we would be prompted to take action, use a medical device or drug, or change some aspect of how we live.

Instead of being limited to waiting for a scan to show an increased tumor volume or a blood value concentration rising to a level detectable by a relatively crude chemical medical test, imagine real-time, population-tested, scientifically-valid, difference-making, actionable recommendations—whether you're fighting cancer or just trying to maintain a healthy, high-quality life.

This is the future, and the analysis behind the scenes that will produce—and is already producing—these types of information are the "patient equations" that inspired the title of this book. Jack was ahead of his time because he knew that the numbers and his careful tracking of them mattered. His engineering intuition told him that within those numbers were the mathematical keys to unlocking extended life, and making sure he got the right treatments at the right time.

The world may not have been quite ready to put those numbers to use, but Jack was truly a trailblazer in realizing that many factors were relevant to his diagnosis and treatment, from his behavioral patterns (such as how tired he was when power-walking) to otherwise insignificant medical events (like a nosebleed). He understood that tracking his biology more proactively and frequently than would be done in standard-of-care medicine could make a difference, and that his own patient equation encompassed far more variables and inputs than many of us would suspect.

Jack passed away in late 2017, almost 10 years after his initial diagnosis, and spent the last years of his life as a speaker, a research advocate, and a fighter pushing for greater patient involvement in clinical trials and greater collaboration between the life sciences industry, the doctors on the front lines of treatment, and the patients ultimately receiving care. He knew that collaboration would be critical for achieving the future state of patient care that I'm describing, and for uncovering the business models that would make it all possible.

We are in a race to the holy grail of precision medicine—bringing the right treatments to the right patients at the right time. Progress is being made on so many fronts—life sciences companies are developing cell therapies in cancer, artificial pancreas device systems in diabetes, apps that help battle neurodegenerative diseases and optimize nutrition, and wearables that can track everything from heart disease to fertility.

Technology companies are creating algorithms to select cancer treatments. Hospital systems are implementing decision support systems to help physicians and patients evaluate options for therapy. But it's a disjointed landscape, and so much of what we're aiming for is still in a black box.

We know intuitively—like Jack—that the answers are there, and, more and more, we are amassing the data and developing the analyses to fill in the gaps of our knowledge and make that black box transparent. It's in many different places (from the phones in our pockets to the medical records at hospitals and the clinical trial data used to approve drugs and devices by the FDA). It's not always well-organized, standardized, or easy to work with. But it exists. And for the first time in history, we're organizing it, making it accessible, learning how to analyze it, and creating new benefits from it every day.

The magic is in the algorithms behind the scenes, and how they translate all of those inputs and all of that data into actionable information. These are the equations that will impact us all, mapping every condition that affects or could affect our lives (and every therapy that exists along with those yet to be invented), with unprecedented accuracy.

When the smartest and most well-informed patients get sick, they look for experts—doctors who have seen their condition before, and who have vast stores of wisdom and experience to apply. They put together care teams, hoping that someone's intuition will combine with the particulars of their disease, an understanding of the treatments out there, and, perhaps, a bit of luck, to lead them to the best path forward. Patient equations are going to turn that intuition into mathematically-reliable insights—and bring those insights from the halls of major medical centers and top life sciences companies to patients of all demographics around the world.

We are at the intersection of biological and technological revolution, at a point where the digitization of health and medicine is becoming a reality. The next breakthrough cure—or treatment that turns a fatal condition into a chronic disease—will come from computers and algorithms working in concert with patients, physicians, and scientists. And the COVID-19 pandemic will catalyze this change at an even faster rate.

Very soon, if you're a life sciences executive, you won't just be launching your clinical trials to develop your next drug or device, but you'll be tapping into a set of data never before available to help you ensure that what you're developing is best equipped to help patients and improve your bottom line. If you're a health care provider, you'll be relying on more than just broadly applied standards of care to find the best treatments for individual patients. And if you're a patient yourself, you'll have so much more insight into your health, now and into the future, than ever before.

In the chapters that follow, I'll dive into the world of precision medicine, driven by data and analytics, from an individual patient level all the way to our global population:

In Section 1 (From Hippocrates to Epocrates), I'll set the stage and explain the landscape of precision medicine and data analysis, looking at how we got to where we are today. I'll also set a baseline for what everyone needs to understand about medical data and the fundamentals of patient equations, looking at the kinds of data streams that exist, which of them seem to offer the most promise, and the surprising connections between variables that research is starting to uncover. I'll also look at some of the devices, wearables, apps, and approaches making headlines today with a critical eye, to start to understand how to separate the glitz from the truly meaningful developments that will make it possible to impact patients and consumers at a whole new level.

In Section 2 (Applying Data to Disease), I'll introduce you to some of the individuals and companies already making headway in applying data and analytics to help solve a range of conditions, from acute (bacterial infection and sepsis) to chronic (asthma and diabetes), and from relatively simple, closed-loop individual issues (like infertility) to more complex conditions (like cancer and rare diseases), and then to population-level concerns (like predicting the flu). These case studies will highlight the range of opportunities out there, and how patient equations can make an impact on so many different levels.

In Section 3 (Building Your Own Patient Equations), I'll talk about collecting good data, and putting that data into action. From inputs—ensuring that we start with high-quality, analyzable, and interoperable data that avoid the garbage-in/garbage-out problem that can plague so many systems—to outputs—useful, actionable insights presented in forms that patients can actually benefit from—I'll explain the ways the life sciences industry is changing, and how medicine needs to change to fully leverage these emerging ideas. I'll talk about the changing world of clinical trials—instrumenting patients and creating smarter research programs that constantly adapt and evolve to produce the maximum amount of evidence from every piece of data collected . . . which in turn yield more bang for the buck for the companies and governments who invest in them, and more quickly bring new treatments to patients who are waiting for them. I'll also discuss disease management platforms that will put information into the hands of the people—the patients and caregivers—who need it, and at the same time create virtuous cycles where as we prevent and treat various diseases, new data and insights will continuously be generated.

In Section 4 (Scaling Progress to the World), I'll look at how all of this can work together to effect real global change, and how COVID-19 has brought many of these issues to the forefront and increased the urgency with which we all need to act. Beyond the practice of medicine and the health of a single patient, evolving reimbursement models, better-aligned incentives, and genuine collaboration have to emerge to create huge worldwide impact. The biggest improvements to health around the world will come from these combined efforts, the evolution of health care's business models, and attention paid to the needs of every participant across the care continuum: patients, physicians, payers, researchers, and regulators.

Finally, I'll conclude with real hope about the limitless, data-driven future ahead of us, and how a bright future for health care businesses and greater good for patients are convergent outcomes that are both within our reach. At the intersection of biological and technological revolutions there is an incredible opportunity for creating patient value—healthier, happier lives—at the same time as realizing huge economic value across the industry as patient equations continue to transform the way treatments are developed, delivered, and applied.

This book comes from over two decades of real-world experience and leadership in the life sciences industry, as well as a personal passion for data and data-driven medicine. I'm the co-founder and co-CEO of Medidata, a company I helped start in 1999 and the world's leader in providing technology and analytics to power clinical research, drug development, and medical device companies across the globe. Until our $5.8 billion purchase by French industrial design software manufacturer Dassault Systèmes SE in 2019, we were New York City's largest publicly traded technology company, and we continue to work with over 1,500 pharmaceutical manufacturers and life sciences companies across the globe as they develop and launch their drugs and devices.

This book is built on the conversations I have day after day with executives about how we can use the latest devices to take their clinical trials to the next level, how we can navigate the complexity of ever-changing guidance and regulations from the FDA, how we can arm doctors with the tools that can transform how effectively they can treat their patients, how we can discover, test, and market new breakthrough drugs more quickly and at lower cost, and how we can thrive in a world changed by pandemic threat.

It wasn't long ago that I opened many of the talks I give around the world with a bit of a trick. I would ask how many people in the audience were walking around with a medically-relevant device on them, some piece of telemetry that was helping them or their doctors manage a condition or disease. People would think insulin pump or heart monitor, and not too many hands would go up. And then I'd ask how many people had a smartphone in their pocket. Because, of course, that was the reveal, at least until my audiences started to get savvier about our future. We're all walking around instrumented with hugely powerful machines that can improve our medical futures, and these machines and the data they produce are upending health care.

Understanding patient equations is so very critical for everyone across the industry spectrum—from life sciences executives and researchers who need to understand how to create, test, deploy, and market digital therapies, and how technology can help them iterate and deliver new treatments faster and more efficiently; to doctors and other health care providers hoping to understand how a new set of tools is on the horizon that can help them provide improved care to their patients; to hospital executives and others based at institutions looking for new approaches that can help them achieve greater impact with lower cost and bring breakthrough advances to their teams; to biotech entrepreneurs and tech pioneers looking to create the next generation of drugs and devices, and who need to understand how data and the algorithms working in the background are helping us understand disease at a level never before possible; to insurers looking to understand how data may be able to power new payment and reimbursement models, as well as provide opportunities to find new, cost-effective ways to improve the health of their policyholders and their own bottom line; to regulators and policymakers needing to understand this space and the implications that private-sector development may have on public health, including opportunities to make health care expenditures in a far smarter and more productive way than currently; to patient advocates, nonprofit groups in the health care space, and academic thinkers and researchers looking at new developments in disease management and how data is affecting cures and treatments coming soon to patients across a huge range of conditions; to informed readers interested in the biotech space, particularly as the biggest tech players—Apple, Google, Amazon—take steps into the health care market and attempt to disrupt the industry from all sides; and, finally, to patients who want to understand how technology can give them more control over their care and allow them to partner with their doctors and utilize the breakthroughs coming from pharma and biotech to improve their health and longevity.

This book was about to go to press just before COVID-19 became a reality. In the midst of the pandemic, I realized the ideas here not only still mattered, but they mattered even more. Patient equations can inform everything we do in life sciences—and we are going to have to rely on them more as we move toward the future state described in these pages. I've written a chapter at the end that talks directly about COVID-19, how all of these issues play out in the context of a pandemic, and what the world can, should, and will look moving forward—but the rest of this book is no less relevant than it was a year ago, and the pandemic mostly serves to point out how critical all of this thinking really is. We can dramatically improve the future by embracing the patient equation-powered world described in the pages that follow.

As we refine the mathematical models for a long list of diseases, it will truly be transformational. We'll be able to make better predictions about what will happen to patients, and engage in smarter interventions, create smarter drugs, and build smarter devices, the ultimate goal being not just that our customers live longer but that they live longer with a higher quality of life, avoiding as many bad health outcomes as they can, and making sure the right people get the right therapies faster and more cost-effectively.

There are huge business advantages to being ahead of the curve, to being faster and more accurate about iterating and delivering new treatments, and to being able to effectively apply technology while still upholding the principles of traditional therapeutic medicine. Finding and applying the next great digital technologies in health care is the biggest business challenge facing us all.

Right now, we're merely scratching the surface. No less an authority than the *New England Journal of Medicine* wrote recently that "[t]here is little doubt that algorithms will transform the thinking underlying medicine" and that "[t]he integration of data science and medicine is not as far away as it may seem."[2] The article I'm quoting, titled "Lost in Thought: The Limits of the Human Mind and the Future of Medicine," argues that the health care system is ill-prepared to meet the needs of the new technologies, and that medical education is "absurdly outdated," doing "little to train doctors in the data science, statistics, or behavioral science required to develop, evaluate, and apply algorithms in clinical practice." This book is an attempt to remedy these failings, bring everyone in the industry up to speed, and reveal the truly critical steps we must take to ensure the best possible future for all of us.

Notes

1. Peter Andrey Smith, "One Inventor's Race to Manage His Parkinson's Disease With an App," Medium (*OneZero*, May 22, 2019), https://onezero.medium.com/one-inventors-race-to-treat-parkinson-s-with-an-app-f2bf197ee70.
2. Ziad Obermeyer and Thomas H. Lee, "Lost in Thought—The Limits of the Human Mind and the Future of Medicine," *New England Journal of Medicine* 377, no. 13 (September 28, 2017): 1209–1211, https://doi.org/10.1056/nejmp1705348.

SECTION

1

From Hippocrates to Epocrates

1 | Before We Cured Scurvy

What do we know about a person? If you asked Hippocrates, he might not have that much to say. Hot or cold. Big or small. Dead or alive. Ask a physician today, and the answer is much more complex. There are thousands of medical tests we can run on a person, inside and out. Blood chemistry, urinalysis, X-rays, Dopplers, and more. We can track these results over time, in various systems, or research information online, with powerful programs like Epocrates, a medical reference app, and others. We can sequence the genome. Or we can count how many steps someone takes in a day.

Categorizing all of these observations about a person is important as we think about them as inputs to patient equations. Whether ancient or modern, these observations come with different levels of reliability and resolution. For example, movement and mood have been observed by physicians for centuries, but we can now check them digitally, reliably, and automatically—without the biases or endurance limitations of a human observer. Hippocrates could certainly count steps—but nowhere near the way a fitness tracker can.

A useful first step in our categorization comes from what most people learned in high school biology: the difference between genotype and phenotype. Before Gregor Mendel's experiments with the physical attributes of peas in the 1800s, we had little knowledge about inheritance from a medical perspective. And until James Watson and Francis Crick's famous work with DNA less than a hundred years ago, we had no notion of the mechanisms by which our genetic makeup was stored and transmitted to subsequent generations. Our genome is incredibly important in determining our health—but it is merely a starting point.

Phenotype, on the other hand, includes every observable aspect of ourselves that is not encoded in our DNA. Everything about us and how we exist in the world is phenotype: our hair color, eye color, height, weight, and so much more. The observation of phenotypes begins well before the days of Hippocrates. Imagine an ancient doctor simply using a hand to determine if a person had a fever. Or, not even a doctor—we should instead use the term "healer" in that example, since people were likely checking for fevers long before any notion of the structured discipline of medicine.

Of course, this technique continues today. Imagine a parent touching a child to check for the same. These kinds of observations certainly go under the heading of phenotype. But even what goes on in our heads—our cognition—and how those thoughts manifest in what we do every day—our behavior: it's all phenotype.

Over time, the precision with which phenotypes can be measured has continued to evolve. The hand, to start, was replaced by a thermometer to check for a fever. A modern mercury or alcohol-based thermometer can be read to a tenth of a degree of precision. 37.0° Celsius is the widely accepted average "normal" value of a healthy person's temperature. On a modern analog thermometer, that is distinguishable from 37.1° or 36.9°. A digital thermometer might be even more precise, perhaps to the level of hundredths or even thousandths of a degree.

These digital readings show a greater resolution—which is another useful dimension that we can use to categorize phenotypes. An inexperienced hand might be able to distinguish between two states: fever and no fever. For those familiar with the language of computers, we can represent this in binary as a zero or a one. Perhaps a more experienced nurse, physician, or mom can distinguish between a low fever and a high fever. Add hypothermia (the body becoming too cold for normal functioning) and we've got four possible outcomes of the measurement. The computer-literate will realize that this is now not one binary bit, but two digits, each a zero or one. If we want to know if a patient is recovering from a fever (or hypothermia), we probably need to grab that liquid thermometer and measure the temperature more precisely, so that we can see the value change over time.

As we look at more complex problems in disease diagnosis, or, for instance, predicting fertility, we may indeed need the digital version. As we take these more-and-more-precise measurements (and need more and more computer bits to store them), you can start to see how the convergence of biology and digital technologies is inextricably linked to the resolution at which we measure phenotype.

Nanometers to Megameters

Beyond resolution or precision, we can think of the available knowledge about a person in terms of scale. Starting small: individual atoms combine to form molecules that define the tiniest end of our scale, at least when it comes to our current knowledge about how to observe our state of health. (A keen futurist—or a particle physicist—might predict that future editions of this book will reflect not-yet-uncovered findings about subatomic interactions being relevant to predicting or managing our health. But, for now, the atom is as small as it gets.)

Let's begin with our DNA, at a couple of nanometers in size, as the starting point. When our genes are turned on—activated as a first step in a cascade of observable phenotypes—they are transcribed to RNA. We're still talking nanometers. Ultimately, those genes produce proteins, protein complexes, organelles (just as our body has organs, so do the cells that make it up), and we reach the next milestone of scale: a cell, at tens

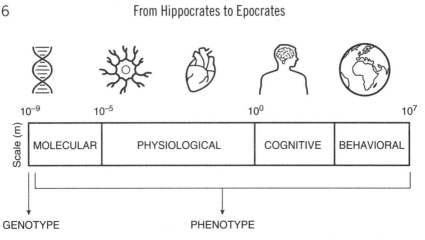

Figure 1.1   A multiscale view of health

of micrometers in size. Figure 1.1 illustrates this continuing progression of phenotypic scale.

Our organs, in centimeters, are next. And if we look at the ways phenotype has been measured over time, the organs were the smallest level at which we could observe for many, many generations. The Greek anatomist Herophilus, around the year 300 BC, is said to be the first to systematically dissect and start to understand the human body.[1] He described the cardiovascular system, the digestive system, the reproductive system, and more.

Perhaps embarrassingly, more than 2,000 years later, Herophilus's work still dictates much of how we divide up medical specialties. Doctors are trained in and specialize in the brain, the heart, the liver, and more—disciplines in medicine are largely still organ-based. But as we look at how impactful observations as well as medical interventions are now happening at smaller and smaller scales, the inevitable need for specialization at these smaller dimensions will become obvious. It's not that one scale is more important than others. Of course the brain and all of its complexities merits its own field of study. But as we look at cancers, and how interactions at nanometer and micrometer scales determine what kinds of treatments will be most beneficial for different patients, specialization in molecules, in pathways, and in fields that allow us to recognize that cancer isn't one disease but many will all be critical.

Professor Paul Herrling, who among several distinguished positions in academia and industry was the head of research at Novartis Pharma AG as well as a scientific advisor to Medidata, once told me that evolution was the ally of the drug discoverer. He was referring to the fact that once the molecular mechanisms that function in our bodies emerge through evolutionary processes, they are reused, sometimes over and over again.[2] They will perform the same—as well as sometimes different—functions in different types of cells, and in different organs. This is a fact that life scientists ought to keep in mind. A drug that is useful for one particular purpose in treating a specific disease probably has other uses, in other diseases.

Imagine having no tools and deciding you need to tighten a particular bolt on a specific model of refrigerator (a somewhat ludicrous analogy, but I think also a useful one). You end up designing something to perform that function—much like creating a drug to treat a particular kind of cancer in a particular organ. Depending on the size of the bolt, the tool you create may well end up being able to tighten (and loosen) lots of other bolts as well, on lots of different models of refrigerators—not to mention on lots of other things too. Similarly, if that cancer treatment works in one specific instance, it may have the potential to be used in other cancers, as well as for noncancerous conditions.

As we move up the scale to our bodies, in meters, we realize that much of what we can see now has been detectable since the beginning of mankind—our moods are often quite obvious, our knowledge can be tested, our movements tracked—but not truly measurable in the way it is today. Going even bigger—if we start to not just count our steps but observe how our cognition drives the behavior of where we go and what we do in the world—we reach the scale of kilometers. Sometimes by the hundreds or thousands. Scaling up, sometimes what we think about or what we do can affect entire societies, entire countries, or the whole world.

We need to be open to these different levels of observation, these different scales. We need to look smaller and larger than the organ-based classifications modern medicine has often settled at. Joel

Dudley, executive vice president for precision health for the Mount Sinai Health System as well as director of the Institute for Next Generation Healthcare and associate professor of genetics and genomic sciences at the Icahn School of Medicine at Mount Sinai, spoke about this at a recent Medidata event, explaining that humans are complex adaptive systems and we simply can't understand the entire person by looking at the individual parts.[3]

Organizing our study by symptoms and anatomy, he said, is like learning about the world from shadows. It is critical that we redefine our understanding of human disease with data—seeing clearly the overlaps between, say, brain disease and skin disease. Our assumptions about the relationships between systems in our body, and therefore the relationships between diseases, are outdated and incorrect, Dudley insists. We haven't even begun to define what health actually is, he says. Today, health is crudely defined as the absence of our flawed concepts of disease. But the remainder of what it truly means to be healthy is still to be fully figured out.

If we think about our journey since Herophilus, it is indeed only a few hundred years ago that we started to be able to look at things at a cellular level at all, with the invention of the microscope and the discovery of these tiny building blocks inside of us. And about halfway along the road between Anton van Leeuwenhoek viewing the first live cells in the late 1600s and the development of modern cell theory in 1839 (and the realization that everything in our body is made of cells), the world of clinical trials began.[4] It is there that we could truly start building objective knowledge about how our bodies work.

Scurvy

James Lind, a surgeon in the British Navy in 1747, saw seaman after seaman dying of scurvy (on one voyage in the year 1740, almost three-quarters of the 1,900 sailors succumbed), and decided to test six potential remedies for the condition.[5] He gave a different concoction to each of six pairs of sick seamen—vinegar, cider, mustard and garlic, seawater, sulfuric acid, and, to the final pair, two oranges and a lemon.[6] The citrus eaters were the only ones to recover.[7] Lind wrote up his findings, and they have stood the test of time as the first reported controlled clinical trial. (Although, interestingly, Lind misinterpreted his own results, believing there was no one cure for scurvy, and that the problem was a combination of environment and diet. It would take another 50 years before citrus was routinely given to sailors and the problem of scurvy on the high seas was eradicated, at least when the right fruits were available.)

The relevance here is that just as we have been learning more about the human body throughout history, we have also been learning more about how to test our hypotheses about the human body, how to develop treatments that work, and how to do good science. James Lind began with the null hypothesis: the assumption that none of what he was giving to the seamen was going to change their course of disease. And his experiment proved the null hypothesis wrong.

This is the most fundamental principle when designing a good scientific experiment. It is what we need to do today with patient equations. The null hypothesis tells us to start off with the assumption that there is no statistical significance to what we are testing. It asks us to assume that taking multiple observations, inclusive of genotype and varied resolutions of phenotype, and combining them to predict the onset of disease, the effective treatment, or any useful preventive courses simply won't give us any meaningful information. Then, like Lind, we need to prove that null hypothesis wrong. In doing so, we can prove the utility of our patient equations, and establish their worthiness in the future state of medicine.

In this chapter and the ones that follow, I'll talk about all kinds of possible new data sources, all kinds of bits and pieces that we've been ignoring—not on purpose, but largely because there has simply been no way to measure them, at least not consistently or rigorously enough to involve them in the good science we've been trying to do. Then, starting with the null hypothesis, the game is figuring out what is in fact additive in value. We need to determine what newly-measurable phenotypes, and in what combinations with traditional measurements of phenotype and genotype, will be truly useful to our understanding of disease and show themselves to matter.

Our understanding of the human body has grown so much since the time of James Lind—but I should note that our clinical trials largely haven't. We haven't had the infrastructure, the connectivity, or the information to enable us to think differently about the way we do research. Now we do. Now we can learn so much more about a person, across so many more dimensions. The magic is figuring out which of those dimensions matter, and how. But back to history . . .

The False Promise of Genotype

Okay, that's a deliberately misleading section title. In 1953, Watson and Crick discovered the structure of DNA and launched the modern era of genetics. It was a monumental discovery, and it will continue to propel our ability to predict and treat an incredible number of conditions and diseases. But I think we often err on the side of thinking that genotype is the most important piece of knowledge we can have about a person. Twenty years ago, when sequencing the human genome started to look like something that could plausibly be done at a mass scale, it was far too easy to imagine that we'd understand the nature of and be able to cure virtually every disease. It would all be there in those nucleobases of our DNA—the adenines, cytosines, guanines and thymines, the As, Gs, Ts, and Cs you might remember from high school. The only thing we thought we needed to do was decode it, and a future of longevity and robust health would be upon us.

The 1997 film *Gattaca* put onscreen the kind of genetic-determinist thinking that was emerging in society.[8] In the movie, there are "valids," who have been genetically engineered to perfection, and "in-valids," whose genetic makeup has been left to chance. Valids were the privileged class and in-valids were left behind, denied opportunities, locked out of the best schools and jobs, and assumed to be inferior in just about every way. As the movie concludes, as one might expect from a Hollywood ending, the in-valid proves to be the better man . . . but it's not just a Hollywood ending, it's a very real illustration that genetics only gets you so far. The hero's drive—his cognition, and the behaviors it leads to—proves over the course of his life to be far more important than the makeup of his DNA at birth when it comes to his ability to become an astronaut.

To be explicitly clear, genotype is spectacularly important for the normal functioning of our bodies and for our overall health. It is quite literally the most important single source of information about us as organisms, and the main (albeit not the only) baseline from which virtually every other aspect of us—from molecular biology to behavior—emerges. Single variations in our DNA sequences can cause fatal inherited conditions like Tay-Sachs disease, and point mutations that occur during our lives can cause cancer. However, if we take a mathematical view of how much "genotype" versus "phenotype" knowledge we have, and how they change relatively over time (Figure 1.2), we can start to see how, and often why, phenotype trumps genotype.

As you can see from the graph, our genotype never grows, even as our phenotype becomes richer and richer, building more and more

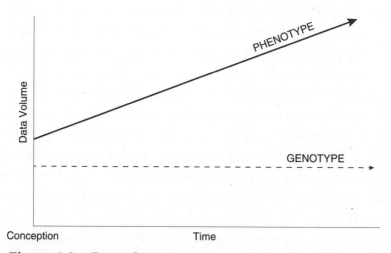

Figure 1.2   Data about you

information about us over time. Even from the very beginning of life, the environment in and around us is hugely important in turning that consistent genotype into the beings we are, orders and orders of magnitude more complex than a sequence of DNA. We start out as a one-celled zygote, which then splits into two cells. One of those two cells is destined to ultimately produce (and become part of) our head, and the other is destined to become our feet. The most important factor that creates that differentiation is the local chemical environment within that zygote.

Morphogens—signaling molecules present in cells at varying concentrations—are part of what makes cells differentiate. Different morphogen concentrations that are the result of gradients (relatively larger and smaller amounts of them) within that first zygote, and then their relative concentrations as cells continue to divide, are what define our axes of front-to-back, head-to-toe, and inside-to-outside. And the environment only gets more important from there, both inside and around our bodies.

It's perhaps extreme to make the case that I can't tell you anything more about your state of health from your DNA (your genotype) at any point in your life than I could have at conception—not literally true, as mutations occur in our genes over time, and the proliferation of those mutations as some of our cells naturally die off, while others divide and grow, can be the cause of devastating diseases—but if we look at our original DNA, what's referred to as our germline that we get from our parents, there are things that can be derived from the sequence, and we can make weighted guesses as to whether certain conditions might affect us at different times in our lives. Those derivations and guesses don't get more precise over time. The effect of phenotype, and how it evolves based on the changing environment in and around us (inclusive of all the genotypes and piled-on phenotypes in the organisms that live in and on us: our microbiomes), makes an overweighted contribution to our health.

Even in the areas where we think genetics gives us a deterministic ability to derive something important about ourselves—normal or related to disease—we're realizing more and more that it simply isn't so straightforward. Yes, we know that certain genes or combinations are involved in a wide range of different cancers, but the complex machinery, the activation and deactivation of different genes though multilayered feedback loops, intertwined pathways, intercellular communications, and additional complexity at every scale we can consider means that often a purely genetic view of health is a useless oversimplification. Even the idea that genes can be "on" or "off" is a gross simplification of a much more involved system, where anything from huge amounts of a protein being produced at any given moment to none of it being produced are all possible scenarios. As researchers at Stanford have written, traits, conditions, and diseases are "omnigenic."[9] Yes, the genes matter. But so many of them are contributing to a given condition that trying to trace it back to a particular set of genes is an exercise in futility.

In sum, genetic information can enrich our models of disease, without question—but a good model will need much more than that. We need to combine the genetic information with physiological data, with behavioral data, and with information about our activity, our sleep, and our mood—information that we simply weren't able to measure objectively, at scale, until the past decade, but that can and does enrich our models of people and what is going on inside their bodies.

Figuring out how to think about all of these factors—seeing them as inputs in a formula whose output is a simplified but useful statement about our health, and about what treatment we should or shouldn't get—is what patient equations are all about. We may all be on a path toward clinical dementia. But as we proceed into this world of patient equations, remember that genetics are not destiny. So many of the factors that may influence whether or not we get a particular disease or condition—or at least how quickly we are progressing toward that disease or condition becoming a problem worth treating—are, at least to some extent, observable (if we know how to look) and in some cases even under our control. This includes what we eat, or where we live, or any of the dozens, hundreds, practically infinite number of things that we can either measure now, will be measuring soon, or would be able to measure if we could only identify what exactly they are.

Your Very Own High-frequency Medical Device

I've said that now, for the first time in history, we can measure more than we've ever been able to measure, at scale, objectively. And I think it's just as much of a breakthrough as that of Herophilus, or van Leeuwenhoek, or Watson and Crick. We're measuring physiology, cognition, and behavior like never before, via sensors, in a world where sensors are literally everywhere. As I write this, I'm wearing a wristband and a chest patch—and, no, I know you probably aren't, at least not until you get to the end of this book and realize perhaps you ought to be, but I bet there's a smartphone either in your pocket, on your desk, or somewhere within reach. That smartphone, as I'll explain in just a moment, is a high-frequency medical device just as much as the patch that's tracking my heart rate, body temperature, and livestream ECG, and uploading it to the cloud in real time.

Devices like these are adding layers and layers of information onto what we can already know about people, and what we can use to add to treatment decisions and our models of disease. Doctors used to diagnose based only on physiology—things like temperature, skin color, hot and clammy versus cold and dry. Add blood chemistry, and the treatment decision becomes more reliable, maybe a hundred times as good. Now add imaging—X-rays, CT scans, MRIs. We can now diagnose and stage cancer, look at organs, and more. Maybe our diagnoses are another hundred times as accurate. Now, add sensors, some of which can do what we've always done—only with greater ease, frequency, and without needing a trip to the doctor's office or hospital (real-time continuous temperature readings, blood pressure, glucose measurements)—and some of which can measure things we weren't measuring before, like the number of steps we take or the places we travel.

There are two sets of axes along which we can think about sensors and the devices they live in, or at least two sets of axes along which we've thought about them in the past. First, we've had medical-grade devices and consumer-grade devices. It used to be that thermometers were a foot long and took 20 minutes to deliver a reading. They were cumbersome and hard to transport, and you were only getting your temperature taken in a clinic setting, certainly not at home. Obviously, that has changed. Similarly, blood pressure, glucose monitoring, and pretty much everything else follows that same pathway. Doctors now send patients home with Holter monitors, we have devices that can analyze sleep outside of a sleep lab, and more.

Second, there are low-frequency devices and high-frequency ones, staccato measurements versus continuous feeds. My wristband is measuring my number of steps—a low-frequency piece of data. My chest patch is measuring my heart rhythm, which requires a lot more information.

These distinctions matter less and less these days. Pretty much every low-frequency device that exists today has a high-frequency device inside of it. The chip inside my wristband is more sophisticated than the accelerometer that was used in the 1960s to put men on the moon. The devices that used to be medical-grade are now sold to consumers, and the ones that aren't yet will be—soon. And anyone with a smartphone—yes, even those of you who scoff, for now, at the wristband and chest patch I'm wearing—is walking around instrumented with a high-frequency consumer device that is capable of measuring physiological, cognitive, and behavioral elements that we could never measure before.

So we can measure things more easily and more objectively than ever in history. But what should we be measuring, and why? And how do we even figure out where to begin taking all of these new streams of data and incorporating them into the models of disease and diagnosis that already exist? How, in other words, does the iPhone matter to the life sciences business? To answer that question, we need to begin to look at just what we mean by patient equations.

Notes

1. Noel Si-Yang Bay and Boon-Huat Bay, "Greek Anatomist Herophilus: The Father of Anatomy," *Anatomy & Cell Biology* 43, no. 4 (2010): 280, https://doi.org/10.5115/acb.2010.43.4.280.
2. Courtesy of Paul Herrling.
3. Joel Dudley, Conference Talk at Medidata NEXT Event (November 2016).
4. Paul Falkowski, "Leeuwenhoek's Lucky Break: How a Dutch Fabric-Maker Became the Father of Microbiology.," *Discover* magazine, June 2015, http://discovermagazine.com/2015/june/21-leeuwenhoeks-lucky-break.
5. Milton Packer MD, "First Clinical Trial in Medicine Changed World History," Medpagetoday.com, August 15, 2018, https://www.medpagetoday.com/blogs/revolutionandrevelation/74568.
6. Jeremy H. Baron, "Sailors' Scurvy Before and After James Lind— A Reassessment," *Nutrition Reviews* 67, no. 6 (2009): 315–332.
7. Michael Bartholomew, "James Lind's Treatise of the Scurvy (1753)," *Postgraduate Medical Journal* 78, no. 925 (November 1, 2002): 695–696, https://doi.org/10.1136/pmj.78.925.695.
8. David A. Kirby, "The New Eugenics in Cinema: Genetic Determinism and Gene Therapy in GATTACA," *Science Fiction Studies* #81, Volume 27, Part 2, 2000, https://www.depauw.edu/sfs/essays/gattaca.htm.
9. Evan A. Boyle, Yang I. Li, and Jonathan K. Pritchard, "An Expanded View of Complex Traits: From Polygenic to Omnigenic," *Cell* 169, no. 7 (June 2017): 1177–86, https://doi.org/10.1016/j.cell.2017.05.038.

2 | Inside the Equations

To think effectively about these new types of data and the value they can add to our disease models, we need to start by talking about "biomarkers" and "biospecimens." As with so many things in science and medicine, they're just fancy words for relatively simple things. We usually think about biomarkers and biospecimens in the context of traditional medical measurements, our genes, and physical tissue samples.

A biomarker, according to the International Programme on Chemical Safety, led by the World Health Organization, is "any substance, structure, or process that can be measured in the body or its products and influence or predict the incidence of outcome or disease."[1] In slightly simpler terms, it's something we can measure that tells us something about a person's disease. If someone has cancer, for example, we can go in and take a sample of their tumor—a biopsy. The tissue sample from that biopsy—a biospecimen—will be used by pathologists and evaluated in laboratories. Microscopes and assays are used to examine the physical and biochemical properties of that tumor, looking for useful biomarkers. We can search for specific sequences of DNA, such as a particular mutation that allows us to predict how aggressive the cancer might be. Or we can examine the shape of the cells or the presence of estrogen or progesterone receptors. All of this measuring and evaluating is typically done in real time, in the best cases helping to decide on the right course of therapy or determining whether a patient is responding to a therapy that he or she is currently on.

But we can also take that biopsy and preserve it for future use—often by freezing it. Now, we have a biospecimen that researchers can thaw at some later point in time to look for biomarkers that may have been missed or misunderstood.

We shouldn't associate this idea of biomarkers and biospecimens only with a chunk of tissue. Biomarkers can be found in liquids just as easily. My first research project out of college happened to do precisely that kind of searching. Most men over 40 are (or at least they were, until recent changes to the standard guidelines) tested for PSA, or prostate-specific antigen. The presence of this protein—how much of it is produced by the body, and then how much of it leaks out of a patient's prostate and into their bloodstream—is easy to measure, and can be useful in diagnosing and determining the progression of prostate cancer or other more benign prostate disorders. All it takes is a tube of blood, and the presence of the PSA protein—a biomarker—can be measured in a lab.

In the mid-1990s, I was fortunate to get to work on another dimension of what we could measure in the blood of prostate cancer patients.[2] Every cell in our body has largely the same DNA sequence (the exceptions being in cases of disease where DNA is mutated, and in red blood cells, which don't carry copies of our DNA at all). But as our tissues differentiate, and in the course of normal physiological function, various genes get turned on or off. In the case of a theoretical prostate cancer patient, if we only looked at the DNA of the cells in their blood, there wouldn't be much more useful information that we could find about their cancer. However, the prostate cells that are actually making PSA—and only those cells—should have the gene that encodes it "on," and that, we found in my research, could tell us something interesting.

We looked for PSA RNA in the body—the essential piece of the PSA production process that should have only been able to be found within cells inside the prostate. We had the ability not only to look for the PSA protein itself leaking out of the prostate, but we could also determine if there were prostate cells themselves that had escaped from the prostate and were swirling around the patient's body in their bloodstream. This is how cancer metastases occur. Cancer cells migrate from the original tumor and find places—in lymph nodes, bone, and other organs—to establish new tumors. The presence of RNA that was a precursor to the production of PSA was a biomarker associated with the potential for metastatic cancer. Like peeling back the layers of an onion, we were looking one level deeper into the molecular nature of cancer in a given patient, and using that data to help physiologically locate whether that cancer might be in their blood.

This research is an example of how we can find new biomarkers, and also illustrates how and why biospecimens are preserved. Imagine if there was blood stored from prostate cancer patients around the world. We could go back and look at whether there were prostate cells present, and then we could compare that biomarker with what we retrospectively know happened in the course of their treatment. Was the presence of circulating prostate cells associated with more aggressive cancers? What interventions—surgical or pharmaceutical—were associated with the best outcomes for patients where we could detect those cells?

Instead of proactively having to find patients for that research (which kept a lab researcher—namely, me—frantically running around the Columbia Presbyterian Medical Center 25 years ago), we could thaw those biospecimens and investigate them.

Of course, PSA RNA is just one possible biomarker. Since I worked on that particular research project, the ability to sequence single-cell DNA to look for specific mutations in cancer has evolved spectacularly. More and more layers of useful measurements in determining the course of a condition can be checked, as long as we have those specimens preserved, our patients' permission to use them for research, and the ability to connect those specimens with the eventual outcomes related to the therapeutic courses given.

We now know that biomarkers can be found in our genes themselves, such as mutations in p53 that are associated with increased susceptibility to certain types of cancer, and that they can come from any of the phenotypic manifestations of what defines "us"—what genes are on or off, what proteins are present, where certain cells can be found in the body, and more. Looking particularly at the presence and function of proteins—proteomics—will tell us far more than we know today about what's going on inside our bodies. Researchers are discovering biomarkers with the potential to diagnose cancers, Alzheimer's disease, and more, well before we see symptoms.[3] "Proteins can confirm an illness is underway, and they often appear in our blood long before we feel sick—months or years before symptoms, when many diseases are still curable," wrote Michael Behar for the *New York Times* in 2018, explaining the potential of proteomic analysis to change the way we diagnose nearly everything. And I certainly agree.

However, it's important to look beyond just the physical biomarkers. The same way as we can look at cognition and behavior as measurements of health, they are also potentially useful as biomarkers in the way we think about a PSA level. In the patient equation, all "inputs" are really biomarkers. Perhaps the number of steps taken or the average daily territory a patient covers are useful predictors of cancer progression. Perhaps alone they're not, but instead they tell us something useful when combined with other inputs—in a multivariate patient equation. Keep this in the back of your mind as we continue this discussion.

Along the same lines, as I've said already, biospecimens don't just have to be physical samples of tissue or blood. We can log someone's step count today and go back a year from now to take another look. We can log everyone's step count today, and then, for the people who develop cancer in the future, go back and see if there were any hidden indicators. Perhaps it doesn't matter if someone is taking 12,000 steps a day or 10,000 steps—but maybe the rate of change in their pattern of movement is useful. If someone took 10,000 steps every day last year, but just 5,000 this year, perhaps that indicates that something is going on in their body—and perhaps it could indicate it even before a CT scan picks up evidence of a tumor. Perhaps that alone isn't enough, but if we combined it with their PSA, could we detect a pattern that is associated with prostate cancer? The more data we have—the more biospecimens—the more we can replay the past and test the patient equations of the future.

There is the potential for, say, Alzheimer's disease research to approach problems this very same way. We have traditional data about how patients are progressing with the disease, and we also have activity data, these digital biospecimens about their daily behavior, and their quality of life. We can look, perhaps, at how many times someone checks the calendar on their smartphone, and map that against traditional measures of disease progression. If I normally check my calendar three times a day, and then suddenly I'm checking it 8, 10, 12 times—does that mean my memory is getting worse? And does that data add to our understanding of my disease progression, or is it simply noise?

Like Lions of the Serengeti

There is potential for this type of data to be useful in diagnosis, prognosis, and even as a way to measure the value of therapies. Can we catch something earlier with cognitive or behavioral data than we can with traditional measures? Can we quantitatively and objectively detect changes in behavior that might give additional insight into what is happening at the molecular or cellular level in a patient—like, is their tumor burden growing or shrinking? Can we use a measurement—again, an objective and quantitative one that is free from the biases of a patient's self-assessment or the limitation that a health care professional can't observe patients 24/7—as a proxy for quality of life or socioeconomic engagement?

The definitive answers to these questions are being researched right now, but two examples across behavior and cognition can frame the idea.

And I am certainly hopeful that at least one of them, if not both, will prove to be worthy of inclusion in our patient equations.

Imagine a patient diagnosed with cancer. Assume for this exercise that there are two drugs available on the market—both indicated for the patient's condition, with no contraindications on their respective drug labels—that can extend life for what amounts to equal durations, based on all available research with previous patients. Let's say this extension of life is two years. Assume as well that the drugs have similar safety profiles—similar side effects and chances of, say, cardiotoxicity that could weaken the patient's heart.

So which drug does the patient take? Drug A or Drug B? Since there is no difference in predicted outcomes, there's no good way to choose. The patient and physician might as well flip a coin.

Now, consider the same choice if the patient and physician knew that previous patients taking Drug A spent three-quarters of their survival period—a year and a half of the two years—bedridden, whether in the hospital or their home. But patients on Drug B were mobile and able to travel, work, and spend time with their families and friends for the vast majority of those two years. The choice becomes easy. You take Drug B.

Let's assume that a government is paying for the drug. If the patient takes Drug B, they will be buying plane and bus tickets, consuming food in restaurants, and producing products or intellectual property at work—they will be socioeconomically engaged, producing and consuming more outside of their health care than someone on Drug A. So the payer wants them to take (and would rather pay for) Drug B as well.

But how could we possibly know this information about Drug A and Drug B? That's where the idea of "patient territory" comes in.[4] If we can measure how much a patient moves around, not necessarily with steps, but in terms of their home range—just like we would observe a pride of lions to see how far they roam—that should be a good proxy for socioeconomic engagement.

The patients on Drug A will be living in 100-square-meter areas on an average day—in a bed, perhaps moving to a bathroom or occasionally to a clinic or another part of a hospital. But the patients on Drug B, depending on how far their travels take them, may be roaming around thousands or tens of thousands of square meters in that same typical day.

We don't need to track people or rely on self-reporting to get this measurement of territory. Virtually all of us—trending toward absolutely all of us, on a global scale—keep our mobile phones within a meter of us all day, every day. We keep them charged the whole time so we are ready for texts, emails, and social media. (And before you start to worry that the idea of patient territory is based on some Big Brother–esque tracking of our precise locations, there are other algorithms that can be used to compute territory based on anonymous positioning data.)

By taking location data at multiple timepoints throughout the day—kept within a phone, never shared on the cloud or with another party—we can assemble a series of vectors. Each vector has a direction and a magnitude. Two meters to the north, two meters to the east, two meters to the south . . . and you can see how a four-square-meter area is circumscribed. We don't need to know where. We just need to know the total.

If we had collected anonymous territory data from those patients previously taking Drugs A and B, the clear choice of Drug B could be made—with hard, numerical data. Playing with this thought experiment across different dimensions is another interesting exercise. Perhaps Drug A, although resulting in patients being largely bedridden, has an average of two years' additional survival, but Drug B only 12 months. If the patient is more interested in living to see, for instance, a family member's graduation 18 months from now than they are in travel, Drug A is the obvious choice. The point is not to create rules based on the territory data, but to make that data available in an equation (illustrating the trade-offs between longevity and quality of life, in this example) that patients, physicians, and even payers can use to ensure that desired outcomes are achieved as much as possible.

If you look at the territory example as a behavioral marker that can be a proxy for socioeconomic engagement and quality of life, you can look at a similar example, but in the digital world, for cognition—say, a simple measurement of bandwidth usage. Everyone with an online existence, whether through texts, emails, and social media or the generation or downloading of large-format audio or video files, uses bits and bytes of bandwidth. Again, the idea isn't to peer into what those bits and bytes are—download the media that you like, it's not anyone else's business—but if we were to merely look at the total amount of bandwidth you are using every day, is it a reasonable hypothesis that it will trend down with neurodegeneration and up with socioeconomic engagement? I think the answer is clearly that it will.

The Layer Cake

Imagine all of these different measurements—these biomarkers—stacked up on top of one another. There's temperature, weight, blood chemistry, scan results, genes, proteins, step count, territory, mood, what we're eating, how much sleep we're getting, and, say, the amount of pollution in the environment around us. Every time we discover something new that we can measure—or a way to measure it with a higher resolution—layers get added. We can measure more of these layers now than we could just a few years ago, and a few years from now we'll be measuring even more.

What we need to determine is which layers are helpful, and which layers add information that we can use to improve diagnosis, treatment, or quality of life. We need to figure out which layers indicate shared characteristics that lead to similar outcomes for certain conditions, and the same treatments working effectively. We need to see which layers glow most brightly in terms of helping us predict successful outcomes before we treat, or, once we do treat, showing us as quickly as possible whether or not the treatment is working. We need to figure out which layers can be useful inputs that indicate who we are and how best to treat us, which layers can be outputs that tell us whether and how much a treatment is working, and which layers can serve as both. And we need to figure out how different layers might combine and interact to produce surprising and useful answers about how to improve treatments, products, and lives.

I've already mentioned some of my favorite layers of the cake. I believe the rate of change in our step counts will turn out to have value, as we collect and analyze more and more of that data. I believe territory covered in an average day is a useful way to measure quality of life. I believe resting heart rate, as a continuous stream, can tell us something useful about our bodies—which is why I'm wearing the patch on my chest. I believe that the patterns of our posts on social media—the word clouds of what we're thinking about, and what we're sharing—can tell us something about our mood, our happiness, and our overall health. I believe that what we now call "junk DNA"—the introns that we now discard because they don't encode proteins—might actually contain useful information. I believe our sweat matters—whether we can use it to sound an alarm when we're becoming dehydrated, or when we need the next dose of a particular medication, or whether there's even more information we can gather from it. I believe our socioeconomic production and consumption can serve as a proxy for how we feel—how much we are able to contribute or consume in a given day, with an active, healthy person able to engage far more in the world than one who is suffering.

But it doesn't matter what I believe. We have the computing capability and the potential data to determine whether I'm right or wrong about the usefulness of these measures, and to figure out in what ways they can help us.

Patients Like You, Patients Like Me

Anecdotally, people have been talking about the layers of their layer cake for a long time. We don't need sensors to know that some days we feel good, and some days we don't. Some treatments seem to affect us one way, and some treatments affect us quite differently. Sensors can make the measurements more objective, bring scientific rigor to our anecdotal evidence, and uncover patterns our brains haven't been able to recognize—but underneath it all, the information itself has been there forever.

PatientsLikeMe, purchased in 2019 by UnitedHealth, is an online network of over half a million members tracking their diseases and conditions, sharing treatments that work for them, and connecting with others on similar health journeys. The site has collected a huge amount of self-reported data from patients dealing with virtually every illness or condition there is. The company's research team has published over a hundred studies, attempting to identify better treatments for patients, particularly in cases where rigorous clinical trials have not yet yielded useful answers. The company's co-founder, Jamie Heywood, believes that the greatest impact of these new data-collecting sensors will be to enable us to finally examine variables that have previously been ignored by the medical community—including hormones, social factors, air quality, metals and toxins in the environment, stress, metabolism, sleep, nutrition, activity and exercise, and more.[5] If you want to know what layers of the layer cake we should consider looking at—and how we should look at them—Jamie is a great place to start.

What's interesting is that PatientsLikeMe launched in part because of Jamie's sense that the great leaps forward in treatment—for lots of conditions—weren't going to happen without examining the kinds of individual, personal experiences that were being ignored by traditional clinical trials because they lacked the objective and mathematical rigor that trials required. The thought was that by harnessing enough of that information, with big enough sample sizes, the scientific flaws would work themselves out. And while that reasoning made sense in 2004, when PatientsLikeMe launched, we're now in the position to have the best of both worlds. We can still analyze these rich personal accounts—these individual experiences and feelings—but sensors have made it possible to bring enough rigor to the measurements that we can in fact incorporate them into clinical trials without compromising on the scientific standards.

Heywood's frustration is that the layers we've always looked at—and assumed to be sufficient for developing drugs and treating disease—just aren't enough. If we want to optimize health—and not just spot-treat specific illnesses—he believes we need to look much more at things like our circadian rhythm, parasites, inflammation, and the biome of flora and fauna in our environment, just as examples. His list goes on from there: our social relationships, the virome, the anxiety and mental health issues that come with chronic disease. And if we could gather all of these layers of information from everyone on the planet—which, more and more, we can—and track them against health outcomes, we would see connections that we've missed for thousands of years.

There are obviously implementation issues, even if you accept that this is a worthy direction to explore, and I'll talk more later in the book about harmonizing data sets and integrating real-world experiences into the clinical trial framework. ("We can't make health data meaningful until it's digital, and right now it's not digital," Jamie says.) At its core, PatientsLikeMe is seeking to find those same inputs for patient equations that we're looking for, but instead of coming at it from the point of view that many of us in life sciences have—"what can we do inside of clinical trials?"—they're looking at what we can do outside of a research environment.

Talking to Jamie hammers home what is one of the most important points about patient equations: useful models for diseases are multivariate. There are so many influences, so many interacting elements that we have never considered before in the treatment calculation, not necessarily because we didn't think they might be important—though possibly that—but also because we couldn't measure them. Now we can, and we can measure them with even more rigor than Jamie Heywood imagined we could when he started PatientsLikeMe hoping to aggregate people's lived experiences in order to help patients make more informed decisions about how to approach their conditions, and how to optimize health and wellness.

Where PatientsLikeMe has had a great deal of success is in helping patients manage disease in pockets that research hasn't touched and where doctor intuition isn't necessarily accurate or robust. For instance, compared with a study interviewing 20 neurologists, the PatientsLikeMe recommendations for how to manage excess saliva for ALS patients were better. Comparing different ventilators, comparing the effects of different mental health treatments, or figuring out whether a multiple sclerosis patient can maximize quality of life by starting on medication, by changing diet, or by installing an air conditioner to better manage heat in the summer are all things that have always been theoretically measurable, but impossible to actually, rigorously measure. PatientsLikeMe set out to get around the measurement problem by collecting anecdotes. With the right technology, patient equations can do even better, and translate those anecdotes into real data.

"So many things are so much better than drugs," Heywood says. "Things we are not even running studies on." And the studies we *are* running, he says, are too narrowly focused on one dimension of illness, on the pathology of the disease state rather than on more broadly-defined wellness. He is skeptical right now of the sensors and wearables we have—and, the truth is, despite my chest patch and my wristband, so am I. We're measuring a set of isolated variables right now, but the algorithms in the background are still at the level of needing more information to even know what we ought to be measuring, let alone how to act on those measurements, and how to combine them in useful ways and get real information out of them. "There's lots of signal, but not a lot of meaning yet," Jamie says. Indeed, we still have a long way to go. But there are some big conceptual ideas in the rest of this chapter that we can think about as we look ahead, as we start to imagine a world driven by more accurate, more comprehensive, more predictive patient equations.

Incidentally, that potentially meaningful territory measurement I've talked about emerged from a patient anecdote—not on PatientsLikeMe, but from a conversation at Medidata. Barbara Elashoff (a former FDA statistical reviewer, and founder of a startup whose company was acquired along the way by Medidata) was a weekend-warrior athlete.[6] Her step counts would have been through the roof—until she broke her leg, ironically while jumping over a trench in a tough mudder-style event. We were discussing how, if you had been measuring only her step counts, you would have seen them go to almost zero, almost instantly. However, alone, that wouldn't have told us much about her health. It could have meant she was hospitalized for some reason not related to a musculoskeletal injury, or just that she started a new job or a project that forced her to spend her days and weekends behind a desk.

But combined with other information—lifestyle questions, her blood chemistry, and cardiac markers—we were thinking about how we could use proxy data to determine that it was, in fact, an injury from exercise. And about how we could use that same data to plot her recovery. Again, one measurement alone won't do it, but a stream of data, over time, could tell us something important about her life. During that conversation, the idea of patient territory was born, when someone pointed out that steps may not be the right measurement of activity (since taking the bus should count for something). Apps were built, and algorithms for calculating and summing area from vectors were designed that could run in the privacy of a patient's own phone (with Barbara's husband and her company's co-founder Mike furiously reading academic papers on monitoring wildlife and writing code to turn techniques from ethology into useful tools for human medicine). The future clinical utility of patient territory is yet to be proven—but the pursuit of it and ideas like it is continuing.

Changing the Frequency

Traditional medicine—and the traditional medical biomarkers that go along with it—typically involves discrete measurements taken at relatively distant timepoints. A physician sees a patient, measures certain things, prescribes a course of therapy, and then days, weeks, months, or maybe even years later takes the measurements again to see what the effect was on the patient. But the fact that these measurements are taken at single moments in time gives us very little understanding of how they might be changing, particularly when timepoints are so far apart that we may miss entire cycles of the value being elevated, continuing to go up, then coming back down, and eventually returning back to normal, just as an example. The measurement itself may be perfectly precise, but it's actually a very imprecise way to measure the range of values the patient lives with, or the rate of change of those values.

This isn't meant to condemn the physician. It is based on the very real limitation that we typically have only been able to measure things reliably about patients when they were physically present with a health care professional. We measure blood pressure and heart rate, or take blood samples, at selected moments in time—usually in a clinic setting. We potentially take action based on a perceived trend in those numbers, but there's inevitably an element of guesswork. Are we catching the patient only at moments when their heart happens to be in sinus rhythm, when in fact they're having significant episodes of atrial fibrillation when they aren't hooked up to an ECG machine? Is the patient experiencing "white coat hypertension," with higher blood pressure readings in their doctor's office than they would have at home? Are we only flossing right before we go to the dentist, and is that changing his or her read on the condition of our dental hygiene? Is whatever measurement we're looking at a straight line between two timepoints, or a punctuated equilibrium, with periods of stability and then sudden spikes that we might miss?

Sensors allow us to move from the staccato rhythm of traditional medical care to a continuous stream, from a low-frequency data environment to a high-frequency one, and one where real-time access to that data allows us to act instantly. Ideally, we can now see right when alarming trends begin rather than hoping we'll catch them before it's too late. Plus, with a well-instrumented patient, we can be measuring the things we don't yet know we need to measure in order to find evidence that we're not yet even looking for. Taking the atrial fibrillation situation as an example, normally it wouldn't be diagnosed until a stroke or some other potentially-damaging event, because we aren't typically on heart monitors without a previous episode. But if we can catch those patients most susceptible and start them on blood thinners before that first stroke, we can save lives. (As one example, a 13-year-old boy's Apple Watch detected a heartbeat of 150 bpm, the boy was rushed to the hospital, doctors found that he was in atrial fibrillation, and were able to intervene before there was a problem.[7])

When it comes to white coat hypertension, a study reported in the *New England Journal of Medicine* in 2018 found that 24-hour blood pressure monitoring was more predictive of mortality than if it was merely measured in the clinic.[8] This begs the question of what might change, with regard to how we treat hypertension, and how we measure how effective those prescriptions are, if we could measure all of our blood pressures 24 hours a day.

These high-frequency data streams also allow us to break the need to have the patient physically present with a health care professional to reliably measure things about them. The doctor is just as much a beneficiary as the patient here, as we try to understand the nature of diseases. Patients can be monitored continuously, not just at those discrete moments every six months when they have an appointment, with data alerting physicians if something requires their attention, a change in a critical measurement, or a progressing trend that could be missed. Of course you can't do a full-body PET scan every day. But a passive device working in the background can collect data 24/7. And on a patient's end, high-frequency feedback can help optimize medication dosing and manage conditions as effectively as possible, alerting them when something is just beginning to go off course, rather than when damage has already occurred.

Patient equations in this high-frequency world move us from the stock pages in the business section of the next morning's newspaper to the constant scroll on the Bloomberg terminal. The newspaper is for amateurs. The Bloomberg terminal is for professionals. We don't have to wait until the next day. We can see the patient's condition in real time, the terms of the equation changing as the patient moves through the world.

Reverse-engineering the Critical Layers

Right now, the equations we use in diagnosis and treatment are often univariate—one variable, simple if-then formulas: if cholesterol is greater than 180, then prescribe a statin. This is not because we truly believe 180 is a magical cutoff between safety and danger. It's not even because we believe cholesterol is the perfect solo measure of whether someone needs a statin. It's because it's the best we can easily do. It's a useful abstraction of a problem, allowing us to treat people at a societal scale. However, that's the kind of model that I'm hoping this book can help move us beyond. Technology now gives us the ability to add new terms to the equation not just because they're easy to measure but because adding them makes the equation work better, giving us the ability to diagnose and treat more effectively.

The way we'll get there is by instrumenting patients, storing those digital biospecimens, and replaying the past. (And it's cheap—we can store digital streams at a far lower cost than keeping tumor specimens on ice.) It may be, as Jamie Heywood might argue, that the micronutrients in our diet have serious implications that we simply don't realize right now. We need certain metals at trace amounts in our bodies, but we're not monitoring that intake. Would it make a difference for some of us if we did? At the same time, what about those of us eating too much? Is, say, mercury toxicity affecting our health in subtle ways we're not picking up on? We can measure these things and then, in a few years, look at outcomes across a population. We may uncover a real connection. We may not, but then we'll have that added piece of knowledge. Do this across a range of variables—sleep, resting heart rate, performance on brain-training games, anything else we can imagine and track—and we will start to be able to reverse-engineer the best-fit, most accurate patient equations out there.

Too often, discoveries are therapeutic accidents. Former Senator John McCain's deadly glioblastoma was found incidentally during surgery on a blood clot. It's not an atypical story. Therapeutic accidents aren't a good strategy for increasing health in a population. They're a lesson that there's something we should be finding in a different way. We tell patients that a drug works for, say, 80% of the people to whom it's prescribed. But how do we know who is going to be in that 20% of nonresponders, in a perfect world even before we write the prescription? Right now, we probably don't. That doesn't mean the data isn't out there somewhere, waiting to be discovered.

There is, undoubtedly, a point of decreasing returns. There are infinite things we can measure, but perhaps only a few that will make significant differences in most cases. We're not there yet. We don't yet know the five terms or the 500 terms that will make the biggest difference in most of these equations. We'll get there, and then we can start simplifying—then we can say, "well, if we're worried about long-term outcomes, we just need to look at hemoglobin A1c, total cholesterol, blood pressure, and a self-assessment of diet and exercise, because even a thousand other variables won't add more than 1% accuracy to our overall score." We know that if you manage your cholesterol and blood pressure, then there's a much lower chance of having a stroke or heart attack. But are there things we can supplement those tests with to get us to an even better prediction? How much benefit is there to adding the resting heart rate, the calcium score, or the continuous ECG feed? Are there other multidimensional ways to look at cardiac health that will have greater mathematical impact on our long-term livelihood?

We know that if we keep anyone on a Holter monitor for long enough, we will find abnormal moments, unusual blips. But how do those compare to what we see on a problematic ECG? What is the spectrum of good to bad readings, and how much data do we need to plot someone's results accurately on that chart? Or does it depend on other variables? Do two readings that look the same mean very different things depending on other measurements that we perhaps haven't yet identified as being related? The better we can understand how to draw lines between readings, the better predictions we'll be able to make about disease, the better decisions we can make about optimal care.

We certainly won't be able to predict a heart attack based on step count alone, but maybe we can get closer. Maybe we can't. Some of the cleverness of the new technologies (some of which we'll examine in Section 2) is in figuring out what not to measure, and separating which measures are useful and which aren't. We are just beginning the journey from univariate to multivariate approaches to modeling disease. Right now, to most of these questions we're asking, the answer is that we just don't know. One day, we will.

The Cognitive Dimension

I think it's almost impossible to overstate how much we are missing from our disease models right now when it comes to cognitive measurements. We may think of the body and the brain as separate spheres, that your state of health and your state of mind are independent actors. But there is so much underappreciated connection between the two—optimism and pessimism related to hormone release, changes in metabolic rates, and so much more.

The connections between brain and behavior are obvious and easily observed. We decide to walk from point A to point B. We consciously or subconsciously fidget. Our sympathetic and parasympathetic nervous systems make us run (or hide), yawn, and sleep. Without getting into any metaphysical discussion of the mind or the soul, it's the inarguable truth that inputs from our sensory organs stimulate the voluntary and involuntary movements of our muscles, and our autonomous physiological functions work with the same types of feedback loops.

There is mounting evidence of how large a role behavior and cognition play—in ways I find unsurprising—in the progression of disease. A landmark study in 2018 suggests that prescribing a Fitbit can affect cancer survival.[9] Is this the result of patients moving more, and thus keeping their metabolic rates up? Maybe. There are well-known connections between the immune system and our metabolic rates, the reasoning at the very least circling around the idea that there is energy required to produce an immune response, and so our ability to supply that energy has an impact on the immune system. There are also links between our immune system and cancer, so it is not a stretch to hypothesize that more active patients might have better outcomes.

However, in this study, the incorporation of the Fitbit device itself—which measures our activity and feeds it back to us, numerically—adds a fascinating cognitive dimension to consider. Can stimulating patient motivation to exercise through a wearable device reliably produce a cognitive effect that cascades down to cause a significant change in the survival probability given an otherwise-fatal diagnosis?

There is significant work to be done, but there is reason to think the logic may hold up.

An entirely different kind of mind-body connection emerges when we look at the placebo effect. In the world of research, we need to control for this very carefully. It isn't just that people believe that they feel better when they receive a sugar pill instead of an active drug. They actually do feel better. This makes the placebo effect confounding to researchers. It isn't just an effect on someone's mental state; it is a true physiological effect. Endocrines are released, and motivations are introduced. Patient engagement and patient involvement in treatment can have both psychological and actual physiological consequences that we need to make sure research studies account for.

Given all of that, the placebo effect is often looked at as a problem right now in clinical trials, something that gets in the way. But maybe it can be harnessed for benefit instead. That's not to suggest by any means that we treat patients with ineffective treatments. However, we need to remember that it can be a means of manipulating our health as a force for good, not just a statistical complication. We need to figure out how to use that force in a positive way, to optimize improved outcomes.

In this respect—and, truly, in a lot of respects—we can learn from companies like Amazon. While they're not trying to optimize health outcomes, they *are* trying to optimize consumer habits, and they're doing so in a way that fits very much with the idea of patient equations. They're doing A/B testing, which is basically randomized research in the same mode as clinical trials. They're showing two different groups of people a different set of recommendations and figuring out which works better. The algorithm learns, and then it keeps refining to get the best outcome.

What's interesting—and may or may not turn out to be relevant here—is that Amazon and companies like it have figured out that their predictive engines suffer if they're too good. People don't want their recommendations to be perfect—they get put off, creeped out, and they buy less. Imagine a dial that can be set from 1 to 10 with regard to how good recommendations are, based on previous purchases and browsing history. They've collected data to show that 10 is too high, and maybe people are most comfortable at an 8 (in reality, I'm sure it's much more complicated and whatever "consumer equations" e-commerce companies have created are highly guarded trade secrets). Where this may have implications for us is that maybe it turns out that people's health care isn't fully optimized when we show them all the information we have about a disease or condition. Maybe people do better when they have slightly less information or worse recommendations—when they think things are more random than they actually are, perhaps, or when they believe they have more control.

The "why" doesn't necessarily matter, but if the data were to tell us that people have better outcomes when we show them 80% of the relevant information we have rather than 100%, then maybe that is what we ought to be doing. The FDA certainly seemed to think that there were potential negative consequences from the genetic diagnostics that the company 23andMe was making broadly available to consumers.[10] Too much information—particularly misinterpretable information—can lead to unnecessary overtreatment and negative effects on quality of life and medical outcomes.

There is a company called Mindstrong that is attempting to translate what we do on our smartphones to actual data about our health, tracking how quickly we scroll, how frequently we check our phones at night, what we post and who we call, and seeing how that data correlates with disease symptoms.[11] As Dr. Steve Steinhubl, director of digital medicine at the Scripps Translational Science Institute in San Diego, quoted in the *New York Times*, said, "if a sociable person suddenly stopped texting friends . . . it might indicate that he or she had become depressed . . . [or] it could mean that somebody's just going on a camping trip and has changed their normal behavior."

With this perspective, the world of cognitive data starts to resemble that of activity, whether we mean steps, territory, or a raw accelerometer stream digital biospecimen: we are collecting a rich, multilayered set of potential biomarkers, inputs to our patient equations. Within these biomarkers are useful measurements that, alone or more likely in combination, can predict, track, or act as proxies for disease progression.

Better Measurements at Virtually No Cost

I've already talked about the de minimis cost of storage for digital biospecimens. It's also increasingly the case that taking these measurements in the first place costs almost nothing. As I said in the Introduction, I often ask rooms full of people, "How many of you are wearing an activity tracker or medical device?" Inevitably not everyone in the room will raise their hand, but of course every smartphone in the room contains what is effectively a step counter, an altimeter, and a territory tracker all in one. Furthermore, with the proliferation of watches, rings, and a range of smart devices that we'll discuss, all around us every day, our phones can become an incredibly convenient hub for the acquisition of a huge range of behavioral, cognitive, and physiological data.

Contrast the cost, and, more importantly, the quality, of the same medical concept—your cardiac fitness, as the example here—measured three different ways. You have perhaps been asked by your doctor, "How many flights of stairs can you climb before you are out of breath?" It's a pretty easy question for a health care practitioner to ask, and pretty easy to answer. But if you think of the number of times each day that question is asked in the world, and the number of total minutes it takes to get written down in a medical chart or recorded by a patient in a diary as part of a research project, the cost is certainly non-zero. Moreover, our expectation of accuracy—based entirely on the biased recall of a party very much interested in presenting a certain picture to his or her doctor—should be low.

At the other extreme, if we want higher accuracy, we can use a cardiac stress test and actually put patients, wired to the combination of an incline treadmill and an ECG, in a position that will give us an objective, quantitative measurement. However, this option comes at tremendous cost, thinking about time for the patient, the provider, and the cost of the device itself. It is also measuring just one moment in time. That measurement could change based on the amount and quality of sleep the patient got the night before, for instance. The result can also change over time—for example, with a dramatic shift in diet and exercise right after a clinic visit. This makes the single measure of limited use, and suggests the need for continued, expensive measurements made over time.

As a third option, we can use the smartphones that are already, in the background of our patients' lives, doing the measuring we need. Already, most phones have an altimeter in addition to an accelerometer. More and more people are wearing a supplemental device checking heart rate. Instead of asking the question (or spending time and money on the stress test), we can get objective, quantitative measurements of how many flights of stairs we actually climbed and exactly how out of breath (or not) we were while climbing them. All day, every day.

Consider another example: the 6-minute walk test. Patients are timed as they walk back and forth down a hallway of a known length. The distance they travel over six minutes is their score, and it is used as an endpoint in clinical trials to demonstrate the therapeutic response for conditions that impede mobility, such as muscular dystrophy. The measurement works, in many cases. Patient response to treatments correlates with the test results. However, the measurement is also flawed, in some ways deeply.

In the case of Duchenne muscular dystrophy, the 6-minute walk test is often used as an endpoint for submission to the FDA. But there are some patients who cannot walk at all.[12] Clearly the test in these cases is meaningless, and in cases where the patient is simply having a "bad day"—and often these are children, given the life expectancy for the disease—the test may result in patients being excluded from a study simply because they weren't able to set an acceptable baseline against which progress could be shown later.

This is an unfortunate consequence of the test being used for a single critical decision—whether a child will be allowed access to an experimental therapy, in this instance—as well as a proof point regarding the statistical weakness of point-in-time observations in conditions associated with intermittent symptoms. Consider a series of "good days" and "bad days." The average score can be very different from the score at one point in time. Yet, right now, tests like the 6-minute walk are used in a range of conditions, and the data is critical to get new drugs approved. With digital devices, measuring continuous activity in the background, we can do far better than the 6-minute walk test and truly establish meaningful baselines for all patients, through good days and bad.

Imagine a patient with a condition that flares up. There are days they get, for example, a migraine, and days they don't. In the calendar month depicted in Figure 2.1, days that are shaded are days when flares occurred. The patient was seen by a physician and interviewed on the last day of the month, marked by the double-ringed circle. The days the patient can clearly remember (the previous week) are circled with one ring. Either at a glance, or by computing the frequency of problem days versus the total days measured, you can see that there are inconsistencies between the direct observation of the health care professional, the patient's recall, and the actual nature of the condition.

Ten years from now, there won't be a clinical trial that isn't measuring potential biomarkers continuously rather than at discrete points in time, whenever they can. This can be with a biochemical or physical replacement for something done in clinic, or with the integration of

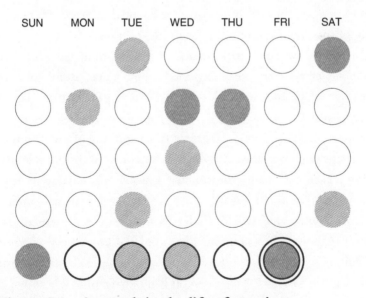

Figure 2.1   A month in the life of a patient

digital biomarkers that cause no additional cost or pain—to the patient or anyone involved—using phones, watches, or other sensing infrastructure that is already there. This isn't simply a nice-to-have new set of tools. It's a paradigm change from needing physical interaction with a patient at a particular moment in time to being able to conduct trials remotely at a fraction of the cost with more reliable results. We are breaking the need for labor-intensive, time-intensive physical access to the body and allowing measurements at scale, irrespective of "good days" and "bad days," instantly transmitted to the cloud and analyzed by a powerful algorithm.

From Hypothesis Confirmation to Hypothesis Generation

Today, the world of medical data is about hypothesis confirmation—we suspect something, and we send off a test to see if we're right. In the future, these tools can move us toward hypothesis generation instead. The data tells us something first—and then we go off to investigate. Decide based on a moment versus predict based on stream—it's a huge difference, powered by digital data. We already know that not every moment in a patient's life is the same, and a prediction based on a larger sample of that life is going to be far more accurate.

Once we have the entire stream of information, we need to take all of that data and translate it into medical evidence, useful conclusions about how we should proceed—in the doctor's office, in the lab, or in the marketplace.

I mentioned Alzheimer's disease at the beginning of this chapter, and that perhaps knowing how many times someone checks the calendar on his phone each day is an indicator that a problem is starting to emerge. That may not be the measure. But the data may lead us somewhere useful. And what that will do is let us make smarter predictions and narrow the range of possibilities. Instead of not knowing if you're on a trend line toward needing intervention sometime in the future, maybe we can say there's a 75% chance you'll hit that point where we need to treat. Maybe we'll be able to tell 30% of the population that they're likely to die of something else long before dementia is an issue. Maybe these improved models of disease allow doctors to point their concern toward the right patients, payers to stop treating the wrong people for diseases they're never going to get, pharmaceutical companies to create better-tailored drugs, and, ultimately, patients to have better outcomes.

The smartest biotech entrepreneurs are thinking about these things right now—narrowing the cone of possibilities, improving our decisions about who to treat, for what, when, and how. And, of course, there are other entrepreneurs simply looking to capitalize on trends, employ catchy buzzwords, and release products out into the world that don't actually deliver on the promise of truly transformative patient equations. In the next chapter, we'll look across the landscape of products—technologies, drugs, devices, wearables—out in the marketplace today, and develop a toolkit for separating the hype from the worthwhile, learning from the failures, and, as we think about translating these ideas into practical business reality, figuring out what's most important to consider.

Notes

1. Kyle Strimbu and Jorge A. Tavel, "What Are Biomarkers?," *Current Opinion in HIV and AIDS* 5, no. 6 (November 2010): 463–66, https://doi.org/10.1097/coh.0b013e32833ed177.
2. Carl A. Olsson, Glen M. de Vries, Ralph Buttyan, and Aaron E. Katz, "Reverse Transcriptase-Polymerase Chain Reaction Assays for Prostate Cancer," *Urologic Clinics of North America* 24, no. 2 (May 1997): 367–78, https://doi.org/10.1016/s0094-0143(05)70383-9.
3. Michael Behar, "Proteomics Might Have Saved My Mother's Life. And It May Yet Save Mine.," *New York Times*, November 15, 2018, https://www.nytimes.com/interactive/2018/11/15/magazine/tech-design-proteomics.html.
4. Glen de Vries and Barbara Elashoff, Mobile health device and method for determining patient territory as a digital biomarker while preserving patient privacy. United States Patent 9,439,584, issued September 13, 2016.
5. Jamie Heywood, interview for *The Patient Equation*, interview by Glen de Vries and Jeremy Blachman, February 27, 2017.

6. Courtesy of Barbara Elashoff.

7. Uzair Amir, "7 Times Apple Watch Saved Lives," HackRead, April 27, 2019, https://www.hackread.com/7-times-apple-watch-saved-lives/.

8. José R. Banegas et al., "Relationship between Clinic and Ambulatory Blood-Pressure Measurements and Mortality," *New England Journal of Medicine* 378, no. 16 (April 19, 2018): 1509–20, https://doi.org/10.1056/nejmoa1712231.

9. Gillian Gresham et al., "Wearable Activity Monitors to Assess Performance Status and Predict Clinical Outcomes in Advanced Cancer Patients," *npj Digital Medicine* 1, no. 1 (July 5, 2018), https://doi.org/10.1038/s41746-018-0032-6.

10. "In Warning Letter, FDA Orders 23andMe to Stop Selling Saliva Kit," *GEN: Genetic Engineering and Biotechnology News*, November 25, 2013, https://www.genengnews.com/news/in-warning-letter-fda-orders-23andme-to-stop-selling-saliva-kit/.

11. Natasha Singer, "How Companies Scour Our Digital Lives for Clues to Our Health," *New York Times*, February 25, 2018, https://www.nytimes.com/2018/02/25/technology/smartphones-mental-health.html.

12. Craig M. McDonald et al., "The 6-Minute Walk Test and Other Endpoints in Duchenne Muscular Dystrophy: Longitudinal Natural History Observations over 48 Weeks from a Multicenter Study," *Muscle & Nerve* 48, no. 3 (2013): 343–56, https://doi.org/10.1002/mus.23902.

3

Fitbits, Smart Toilets, and a Bluetooth-enabled Self-driving ECG

We looked in the previous chapter at the medical and life sciences implications of digital data. And yet, when we examine the world right now, it seems like there's a lot of hype about what we might call the non-clinical applications of sensor technology—or, perhaps even more to the point, the aspiring-to-be-clinically-useful-but-not-quite-there-yet applications. Full of promise and potential—and clever marketing—but, at the end of the day, as surgeon and writer Dr. Atul Gawande told economist and author Tyler Cowen in an interview, "it's a dump of a ton of data that a clinician is supposed to use and know how to integrate into practice, [but the information] hasn't been able to be used in such a way [that it's] actually demonstrating major improvements in people's outcomes."[1]

We're at this in-between stage in the technology. The wearables market is undeniably huge—forecasted by one advisory firm to be over $34 billion by the time this book is in print[2]—and yet . . . we're still very much at the beginning of fulfilling the promise of multivariate patient equations changing the way we diagnose and treat most conditions.

43

In addition, there have been high-profile mistakes (Theranos, IBM's Watson, and Verily's glucose-sensing contact lens, to name three that we'll talk about more in just a bit) that make it far too easy to write off the entire category of highly-hyped "digital breakthroughs" in medicine. In this chapter, I want to explore what's out there, but I want to do it with a particular point of view hovering in the background: that is, looking at wearables for their own sake seriously misses the forest for the trees. No matter what the companies behind these devices say, the truth is that it takes much more than a wristband to power meaningful change.

The true difference-making is going to come from inside the life sciences industry rather than from the world of tech, when those wristbands become inputs to patient equations and part of feedback loops to continually hone them. The biggest impacts are going to involve using these new technologies not on their own but in concert with the kinds of things the life sciences industry is already doing and already understands—namely, rigorously scientific drug and device development and a legitimate understanding of medicine. The real work to make these technologies meaningful is expensive, and it's going to be pharmaceutical companies, medical device companies, and patient advocacy groups that have both the money to invest in building these equations and the long-term business interest in taking advantage of the information that emerges. The smartest and most lasting business success in health care and life sciences will be when systems incorporate these technologies in meaningful and measurable ways with our foundational biology, physiology, cognition, and behavior.

That said, I don't want to undersell the exciting devices and initiatives out there—from "smart" everything to ingestibles and implantables purporting to change our lives and our futures. It is not hard to get excited about the digital world we're living in—and even more excited about the promise of the digital world to come. As sure as I am that these technologies alone won't power the future of health, they will be a part—an essential part—of it.

Are Apps the New Snake Oil?

An app called Cardiogram, available on the Apple Watch and other devices, sends heart rate and step count data to a machine learning algorithm they call DeepHeart, which aims to predict sleep apnea, high blood pressure, early signs of diabetes, and more.[3] Its atrial fibrillation screening has been shown to be 97% accurate, and it has been able to stratify patients into risk groups for cardiovascular issues.[4]

Babylon, based in the UK, has claimed to be able to improve on WebMD, and in fact uses artificial intelligence within its app to diagnose patients even better than a doctor can. "I don't think it is going to be as good as a doctor," Ali Parsa, Babylon's founder, told the *Financial Times*.[5] "I think it is going to be 10 times more precise than a doctor. No human brain is ever going to be capable of doing anything of the sort." (Unsurprisingly, that claim has been disputed in a study published in *The Lancet*: "Babylon's study does not offer convincing evidence that its Babylon Diagnostic and Triage System can perform better than doctors in any realistic situation, and there is a possibility that it might perform significantly worse."[6])

Another app, Healthymize, listens to a user's voice and breathing patterns while talking on a smartphone in order to detect signs of chronic obstructive pulmonary disease and alert users and caregivers.[7]

One more app, Migraine Alert, is designed to predict migraines before they happen, collecting a set of potential triggers (weather, activity, sleep, stress, and more) and using machine learning to create personalized predictions—with 85% accuracy after logging 15 episodes for a particular migraine sufferer.[8]

These apps, and countless others like them, may or may not prove to have clinical value over time. It's one thing to be able to predict a migraine three days in advance with 85% accuracy[9]—it's quite another to be able to help patients actually do something to prevent the migraine, guide them toward treatment, or change something about their behavior or environment in order to make fewer migraines happen for them over time. Machines generating information can sometimes seem like enough to impress—but unless that information is useful or actionable, it's hard, once you get past the initial "wow" factor, to see the point.

Skepticism also requires asking the question of how often the subjects in the study had a migraine. If they get them six days a week on average, and we guess they get one every day, we will be right 85% of the time. The point isn't to poke snarky holes in research like this. The point instead is that we need to be scientifically responsible and make sure we are creating useful predictions, paired with—or at least leading to—useful preventions and interventions. We need systems that are able to connect the dots between the data and the larger understanding of disease progression, creating beneficial outcomes for patients. We need more than just the raw data. And we certainly need more than product marketing.

Wearables for Panicked Dogs

It's not just apps out there. A recent annual Consumer Electronics Show (CES) featured over 250 exhibitors displaying new products across the wearables category—from tech-enabled rings and sneakers to pajamas and pet collars.[10] One company has developed what they claim is an emotion-sensing wristband that can tell you whether you're happy, sad, or stressed.[11] Another claims to have created a sensor that can detect panic attacks—which is coupled with an app that can help guide you through them.[12] Combine the emotion sensor with the pet collar, and an entirely new market might emerge, tracking the inner lives of our pets.

Not long ago Apple made news by filing a patent application for a new wearable device—a piece of jewelry capable of performing an electrocardiogram beyond what an Apple Watch can do, generating accurate readings regardless of where it is worn on the body.[13] At Northwestern University, researchers have developed a sweat-analyzing skin patch that can monitor glucose levels and other indicators of health.[14]

And Google's life sciences company, Verily, has expressed a desire to make bodies produce streams of telemetry like race cars—by instrumenting people with glucose-sensing contact lenses, handing them tremor-canceling silverware, and more.[15]

It is not impossible to imagine a future world where the devices truly make a meaningful difference, where people have 3D medication printers at home producing custom supplements for them every morning, built off data generated by the waste collected in their smart toilets, optimizing what they need for the day. It is not impossible to imagine implanted or ingested devices measuring temperature, heart rate, and blood chemistry, operating quietly in the background of our lives, not requiring any particular attention from us, sending data into the cloud that will send back prompts and recommendations.

But we're not there yet as far as clinically-validated usefulness, not even close. And the line between fashion and medicine, between glitz and medical value, is fuzzy, to say the least—and getting fuzzier all the time. It is easy to dismiss all of this as a fad, or at least as a set of products that exists in an entirely different business space than the traditional field of life sciences. We all know about the failures of companies like Theranos, which raised more than $700 million promising breakthrough technology in blood testing that turned out to be built on a platform made of quicksand.[16] IBM's Watson supercomputer was supposed to be able to use data to cure cancer, but ended up recommending unsafe treatment plans.[17] And that glucose-sensing contact lens that Google was developing? After much hype, the project was summarily cancelled.[18]

In reality, even the best wearables have issues. One is that people just don't use them. According to one study, a third of people who buy "smart clothing" stop wearing it.[19] Significant numbers of people wearing fitness bands, smart watches, and smart glasses simply find them uncomfortable, unstylish, or inconvenient to charge or sync with their smartphones. (That's a problem we can perhaps overcome as more actionable health information emerges from these devices. It's one thing to stop wearing a tracker because you stop caring about your step count.

It's a different issue if instead of step count, it's telling you whether or not your chemotherapy is working.)

Battery technology is probably the biggest barrier to compliance with wearing devices consistently and getting good data from them. But this issue is being worked on by industries beyond just wearable devices. Whether we're talking about our cars, or homes, or our wearables, batteries are getting better at holding larger charges and for longer periods of time. The electronics they power—from motors to microchips—are getting more efficient at using that power. Wireless charging continues to grow, and there are promising technologies for making it work at greater distances. So at least with regard to the wearables that connect to our patient equations, it's probably just a matter of time until the issues of charging are solved. The material science and electrical engineering is being taken care of. But we also need to look at other issues.

A report in *PLOS Medicine*, titled "The Rise of Consumer Health Wearables: Promises and Barriers," explains that despite the hype, there is no evidence that wearables impact behavior, let alone improve health.[20] "Many wearables suffer from being a 'solution in search of a problem,'" write the researchers. The people drawn to using them are already healthy, they don't stick with the wearables long enough, and the data produced hasn't been proven to mean much in the first place.

Finally, another issue is the problem of data misinterpretation. One study in Sweden has shown a correlation between low resting heart rate and a propensity for violence.[21] But causation isn't the same as correlation, and if that information were to be used to profile individuals or potentially even convict someone of a crime, then it would seem that we would certainly be taking a huge and unjustified leap from the data. An article in the online magazine *Slate* wonders about the implications of data being used in the workplace: just taking sleep data, for instance, and the idea that a well-rested employee will produce better work, "imagine if your manager began making decisions about which projects to assign you based on whether you were well-rested."[22]

I spend lots of my time on the road, talking to people on all sides of the life sciences industry, and they all tell me versions of the same story. People have been talking about precision medicine for years now, and where has it led us? Down a lot of blind alleys, chasing magical cures that turn out, upon real analysis, to be largely mirages. Clinical trials have been running the way they do for generations—and there's a reason for it.

My response? Yes, not every prediction of technology-powered industry transformation has come true, sure. But that doesn't mean we haven't made incredible progress, and that we're not on the cusp of true transformation. Even with the unanswered questions and doubts, we shouldn't make the mistake of throwing the baby out with the bathwater. It's fair to be a skeptic—indeed, it's smart to be a skeptic, until science proves otherwise. But if you're not seeing the potential behind the headlines, you're at risk of missing out on the undeniable future. I am as much of a skeptic as anyone—and this book will talk later about how wearables and smartphone apps ought to be subjected to the same regulatory approval as prescription drugs before they're deployed to the public—but I also wear my chest patch and wristband. It's not that they're changing my life—yet. But there's a real error to be made in assuming that the underlying potential isn't there, and that achieving that potential isn't closer than it might first seem.

It's the Equations, Not the Devices

What the glitz and the headlines allow us to forget is that it's not about the devices themselves. It's not about the apps, and it's usually not about the front-end technology at all. It's about the systems behind the scenes—and that's where the attention needs to be. Even the fanciest, most futuristic-sounding new devices are largely built on sensor technology that has been around for years—decades, even. The accelerometers in our phones and smart watches use the same piezoelectric technology—the ability of certain materials to generate an electric charge in response to applied mechanical stress[23]—that helped put people on the moon. Step counting, sleep tracking, measuring your pulse by shining a light onto your skin—these may be new applications, but the underlying technologies date back to the Eisenhower administration.

There are absolutely exciting new sensor technologies—measuring tiny metabolic changes in cancerous tumors or continuously monitoring blood chemistry via a patch on the skin, just to name two—but the most exciting sensors for extending and improving life right now are available on Amazon and have been (albeit for a long time in much larger physical packages) on the market for years. The game-changer isn't the wearables themselves, but the algorithms behind the scenes, armed with sufficient data and computing power to do the real work needed to draw powerful connections.

As we proceed into the rest of the book, we have to think not just about the current state of the science, but about the promise of the future. It is entirely realistic to expect that these algorithms may one day soon be able to take the data from the devices I'm wearing—combined with genetic data or other inputs in those multivariate equations we've already talked about—and tell me if I'm on a course toward depression, Alzheimer's disease, cancer, or more. They may catch virtually imperceptible movements in my hands, setting off a virtual alarm that harkens the possible onset of Parkinson's disease. Other devices might help detect pollutants in one's home and guide their doctor to order blood work, or use sleep patterns to tune the dosage of heart medications. These devices might not just measure a user's resting heart rate, but also notify them when it's optimal to exercise and how much exercise to do—based on metabolism, medical history, and environmental conditions—and whether or not a cheeseburger was eaten earlier that day.

With millions of people around the world carrying smartphones in their pockets or wearing them on their wrists, collecting data at mass scale, it's shortsighted to deny the potential. The smartphone is a game-changer for medical research in much the same way that reliable Internet was a game-changer for the entire technology industry. When we started Medidata more than 20 years ago, our premise—that clinical trial data could and should live in the cloud, accessible to everyone on all participants in the process—was questioned by many. What if a doctor didn't have a computer? What if the Internet line wasn't working? Our key insight was realizing that an inflection point was coming so very quickly. Doctors were going to have computers. And if the Internet wasn't working, they were going to get it fixed as soon as they could, because they weren't just going to be using it to upload data from their clinical trial—they were going to be using it for medical records and billing and to tell their family when they'd be home for dinner. In the span of less than a decade, we went from Internet connectivity being something we had to seek out to the Internet being ubiquitous in our lives.

It's been the same thing with smartphones. The proliferation of connectivity proximal to everyone's body is what has created an inflection point in the world of sensor data. Accelerometers have been around for decades. They've been in medical devices, pedometers, and toys. But all of a sudden, they became part of the infrastructure in our pockets, and we can measure people's data continuously.

Although I certainly wasn't privy to any early design conversations about the iPhone, all the available information points to the incorporation of accelerometers into the device in an attempt to conserve battery life. Once again, the battery—and its limitations—rears its head, this time not as a limiter to how compliant a patient might be with a wearable, but as a catalyst for innovation. Just as Steve Jobs demonstrated, the earliest iPhones would turn their screens off whenever they weren't needed, for instance, when the phone was against the user's face for a call, or placed on a tabletop.

Was it the case that the incorporation of the battery-conserving accelerometer was part of a grand scheme to revolutionize the world of medical devices? That's possible, of course, but the simplest—and more plausible—explanation is that it was only after the technology was already in the phone that people realized the medical implications, for example, of counting steps with the accelerometer. Honestly, we haven't even figured out all the potential measurements we can gather, just based on the sensors we have. Withings—formerly Nokia Health—uses an electrical sensor measuring resistance as an indicator of cardiac health. This application wasn't even on anyone's radar screen a couple of decades ago.

Of course, measuring how many steps we take each day is not an interesting fact on its own—until and unless we are able to discover that the number of steps someone takes in a day is somehow correlated with a medical outcome we're interested in, like the tumor burden in a growing cancer. At that point, depending on how closely those numbers track, it may become hugely valuable to throw a Fitbit on a cancer patient, especially if it gives us the possibility of seeing that increasing tumor burden more quickly than we could otherwise measure it in any realistic way. This is where these devices enter the patient equation.

Similarly, a smart toilet analyzing what comes out of our body may sound like satire, until and unless we're able to discover that there's some biomarker we're able to measure that tells us whether or not someone is going to be a good responder to some new probiotic, or if there is predictive power in the relative abundance of species in our microbiome. Beyond the glitz of these wearables and smart devices is the real promise of helping us to better understand disease—but the way we're going to find that out is through disciplined research, including clinical trials. There is no shortcut to this process. We need to do the hard (and often expensive) work of testing those connections and figuring out what really matters when we're looking for the inputs that are useful for measuring and predicting patient outcomes.

This is where the life sciences industry can come in. It may be that step counts tell us a lot when we're looking at tumor burden but nothing at all when we're looking at who's on a road toward Alzheimer's disease. Or maybe it's the reverse. There's an industry that is spending the money and putting the effort into measuring and understanding the progression of cancers and neurodegenerative diseases. Drug and medical device companies are already running research projects with a rigorous scientific and regulatory framework, and given the minimal incremental costs of these digital measurements, there is a tremendous opportunity to incorporate them into existing research projects and to begin to answer these questions. These answers are the holy grail—not the devices, not the apps, not the newest press release about smart glasses.

What's happening in the world of sensors is exciting, but what is most exciting is the science of using that sensor data to define, measure, and create mathematical models of disease that can lead to better outcomes—and huge benefits for everyone in health care and life sciences. Doctors are going to have more successful outcomes with patients, pharma is going to have more targeted and more successful drugs, and payers are going to have more success in managing huge numbers of people. Patient equations are going to help us uncover breakthrough new drug approaches, epidemiological discoveries that are going to change health across populations, and new ways to engineer clinical trials that will bring us into the twenty-first century.

Let's Start with the Thermostat

In the next section of the book, we'll start to look at some examples of applications that are doing things right, using these new technologies to better understand disease, to generate actionable information, and to make a difference in people's health and wellness. But we can start here with a really simple example from outside the world of medicine.

The Nest Learning Thermostat—now owned by Google—was the first "smart" thermostat to enter the market at scale. The user starts by putting data in—what temperature they want their house to be, what time they leave the house, what time they return—and, after a few weeks, the thermostat starts to be able to make predictions, to learn when users are home and when they aren't, and to switch the system into energy-saving mode when the house is empty.[24] It builds its schedule around you and learns from you. With limited inputs, and with continuous learning, your energy usage and comfort are optimized. This is the climate control version of a patient equation. Inputs, algorithms, outputs, and benefits—for your home, as opposed to for your health. (Or, at least, not yet for your health. Perhaps our smart mattresses will provide inputs one day that, combined with our smart air conditioners, will work to optimize sleep patterns by controlling the temperature of the bedroom. But one step at a time.)

The world of home heating and cooling seems to have been permanently altered by Nest. A quick search on Google or Amazon shows a huge range of companies that have since entered the marketplace, including the old-line manufacturers of traditional (a nicer way to say "dumb") thermostats. Most of these advertise their ability to integrate with Apple HomeKit, Amazon Alexa, or Google Home. If the thermostats are a stand-in for the sensors and systems that power patient equations for specific diseases or conditions, the analogy can be extended into the theoretical platforms we will discuss later that gather and apply all of these inputs and algorithms to more holistically manage our health.

With thermostats, it's about the right temperature in the right room at the right time. With the patient equation, it's about giving the right patient the right treatment at the right time. We aspire to use traditional medical measures, digital instrumentation, and math, all combining to figure out who to treat (and how to treat them), and who not to treat. We have trouble predicting the weather when it's more than a week away. But we are starting to have the tools to predict disease, to predict drug success, to predict our medical futures. We are starting to have the tools to expand patient value, extend the years of quality life. We can harness data to deliver more precise therapies that turn death sentences into chronic diseases, and chronic diseases into curable issues. In the next section, we will look at areas where this is already being done well, and which can serve as models for the rest of human health.

Notes

1. Mercatus Center, "Atul Gawande on Priorities, Big and Small (Ep. 26)," Medium (*Conversations with Tyler*, July 19, 2017), https://medium.com/conversations-with-tyler/atul-gawande-checklist-books-tyler-cowen-d8268b8dfe53.
2. "Wearables Momentum Continues," *CCS Insight*, February 2016, https://www.ccsinsight.com/press/company-news/2516-wearables-momentum-continues/.

3. Caroline Haskins, "If Your Apple Watch Knows You'll Get Diabetes, Who Can It Tell?," *The Outline*, February 21, 2018, https://theoutline.com/post/3467/everyone-can-hear-your-heart-beat?zd=1&zi=ixcc7c67.

4. "Cardiogram—What's Your Heart Telling You?," Cardiogram.com, 2018, https://cardiogram.com/research/.

5. Madhumita Murgia, "How Smartphones Are Transforming Healthcare," *Financial Times*, January 12, 2017, https://www.ft.com/content/1efb95ba-d852-11e6-944b-e7eb37a6aa8e.

6. Hamish Fraser, Enrico Coiera, and David Wong, "Safety of Patient-Facing Digital Symptom Checkers," *The Lancet* 392, no. 10161 (November 2018): 2263–2264, https://doi.org/10.1016/s0140-6736(18)32819-8.

7. Eric Wicklund, "MHealth Startup Uses a Smartphone App to Detect Sickness in Speech," *mHealthIntelligence*, November 13, 2017, https://mhealthintelligence.com/news/mhealth-startup-uses-a-smartphone-app-to-detect-sickness-in-speech.

8. Dave Muoio, "Machine Learning App Migraine Alert Warns Patients of Oncoming Episodes," *MobiHealthNews*, October 30, 2017, https://www.mobihealthnews.com/content/machine-learning-app-migraine-alert-warns-patients-oncoming-episodes.

9. Second Opinion Health, Inc., "Migraine Alert," App Store, August 2017, https://apps.apple.com/us/app/migraine-alert/id1115974731.

10. Victoria Song, "The Most Intriguing Wearable Devices at CES 2017," *PCMag*, January 9, 2017, http://www.pcmag.com/slideshow/story/350885/the-most-intriguing-wearable-devices-at-ces-2017.

11. Karthik Iyer, "Sence Wearable Band Accurately Tracks Emotional States & Productivity," *PhoneRadar*, November 26, 2016, http://phoneradar.com/sence-wearable-band-accurately-tracks-emotional-states-productivity/.

12. Andrew Williams, "Panic Button: How Wearable Tech and VR Are Tackling the Problem of Panic Attacks," *Wareable*, December 3, 2015, https://www.wareable.com/health-and-wellbeing/wearable-tech-vr-panic-attack-sufferers.

13. Ananya Bhattacharya, "Apple (AAPL) Filed a Patent Application for a New Kind of Heart-Monitoring Wearable," *Quartz*, August 11, 2016, https://qz.com/756156/apple-signaling-a-new-direction-filed-a-patent-application-for-a-new-kind-of-heart-monitoring-wearable/.

14. Brad Faber, "Skin Patch: New Device Collects Sweat To Monitor Health [Video]," *The Inquisitr*, November 26, 2016, http://www.inquisitr.com/3746360/skin-patch-new-device-collects-sweat-to-monitor-health-video/.

15. Jonah Comstock, "Verily's Goal: Make Our Bodies Produce as Much Data as Our Cars," *MobiHealthNews*, October 3, 2017, https://www.mobihealthnews.com/content/verilys-goal-make-our-bodies-produce-much-data-our-cars.

16. Polina Marinova, "How to Lose $700 Million, Theranos-Style," *Fortune*, May 4, 2018, https://fortune.com/2018/05/04/theranos-investment-lost/.

17. Felix Salmon, "What Went Wrong With IBM's Watson," *Slate*, August 18, 2018, https://slate.com/business/2018/08/ibms-watson-how-the-ai-project-to-improve-cancer-treatment-went-wrong.html.

18. Michela Tindera, "It's Lights Out For Novartis And Verily's Glucose Monitoring 'Smart Lens' Project," *Forbes*, November 16, 2018, https://www.forbes.com/sites/michelatindera/2018/11/16/its-lights-out-for-novartis-and-verilys-glucose-monitoring-smart-lens-project/#18933d4f51b2.

19. Eric Wicklund, "MHealth Engagement Issues Still Stand Between Wearables and Healthcare," mHealthIntelligence, May 13, 2016, https://mhealthintelligence.com/news/engagement-issues-still-stand-between-wearables-and-healthcare.

20. Lukasz Piwek, David A. Ellis, Sally Andrews, and Adam Joinson, "The Rise of Consumer Health Wearables: Promises and Barriers," *PLOS Medicine* 13, no. 2 (February 2, 2016): e1001953, https://doi.org/10.1371/journal.pmed.1001953.

21. Elizabeth Weingarten, "There's No Such Thing as Innocuous Personal Data," *Slate*, August 8, 2016, http://www.slate.com/articles/technology/future_tense/2016/08/there_s_no_such_thing_as_innocuous_personal_data.html.

22. Ibid.

23. "The Piezoelectric Effect—Piezoelectric Motors & Motion Systems," Nanomotion, August 28, 2018, https://www.nanomotion.com/piezo-ceramic-motor-technology/piezoelectric-effect/.

24. "Nest Learning Thermostat—Programs Itself Then Pays for Itself," Google Store, 2009, https://store.google.com/us/product/nest_learning_thermostat_3rd_gen?hl=en-US.

Applying Data to Disease

4

Ava—Tracking Fertility, on the Road Toward Understanding All of Women's Health

It seems like a simple problem. There are just five days in a typical monthly cycle that a woman is able to get pregnant. Identifying those days can be the holy grail for a couple trying to conceive, but, historically, the tools available to make an accurate prediction have been deeply flawed. There's the calendar method, where a woman uses past cycles to predict the length of her current one, with roughly 30% odds of identifying the right days—not much better than chance. There's the temperature method, which, for best results, involves taking a rectal temperature reading first thing in the morning and watching for a 0.4-degree increase—an increase that tends to come at the very end of the fertile window, often too late to act on. And there's the cervical mucus method, which requires a woman to interpret subtle changes (as at least one website puts it[1]) from tacky to cloudy to slippery.

No matter the approach, a complex, multivariate process is being reduced to just one set of measurements, just one source of data.

Add to that the inconvenience of collecting that data and the potential difficulties in interpretation, and we're left with a real lack of useful and accurate information. Use whichever method you want, you're still not able to be particularly confident that you're identifying the optimal days to try for conception.

From a patient equation perspective, ovulation—while informed by multiple inputs—is closer to the Nest Learning Thermostat than most of the issues we deal with in health care. It's a closed-ended system with one yes/no output: is an egg being released? And while it's a complex equation to get results more accurate than traditional univariate measures, it is far less complex than what we'll see in later chapters. Ovulation is a baby step (no pun intended) into the world of applied patient equations, but in taking that step, we can learn a lot about how a business can successfully put these new technologies into practice.

Enter Ava

Ava is an ovulation-tracking bracelet released to market in 2016, approved by the FDA in the United States (and sold in 35 other countries to date), and improving its predictions and insights month after month as it builds what is now the largest database of women's health measurements in the world. Ava noninvasively sits on a woman's wrist while she sleeps and, using temperature sensors, an accelerometer, and a photoplethysmograph (which detects changes in different layers of the skin), it collects information about pulse rate, breathing rate, heart-rate variability, sleep duration and phases, skin temperature, and perfusion (blood flow)—along with data inputted by the user through a smartphone app about her menstrual cycle and when she has intercourse. Ava uses this multivariate data to predict (as of last report, with 89% accuracy) the five fertile days in the user's cycle—with minimal demands of the user.

The algorithm behind the scenes is both diagnostic and prescriptive. It identifies the fertile days, and then tells a couple when to act in order to maximize the chances of conception (or when not to act if they're using it to help avoid an unwanted pregnancy, which is a use case the company is working on). Those two sides—the diagnosis, and then the actionable intervention—are what make for a useful application of the data technology. Telling someone that they're, for instance, on the road to Alzheimer's disease is of limited value if there's not also an action to take, an intervention that will alter the default outcome.

An article in the *New York Times* described one woman who "discovered she had been missing her fertility window by about a week because her cycles were longer than normal and regular period-tracking apps didn't pick that up."[2] Within a few months of wearing Ava, she was pregnant. There are countless other stories like that, for sure. In 2019, the company announced that 20,000 babies had been born to women using the Ava bracelet. But the bracelet is just the beginning—and the current algorithm is just the beginning as well. As the company collects and tracks more and more information from women around the world, its data scientists have two aims—(1) to continue to make the fertility predictions more accurate, and (2) to be able to make broader connections about women's health that no one has yet had the data to make it possible to consider.

As just a few examples: how a woman's cycle impacts mood swings, headaches, and overall health; how to understand and manage the hormonal swings of pregnancy and, later, menopause; how one might even be able to use this data to find early signs of heart disease, cancer, and more. The company has already launched a study tracking a group of women hospitalized with preterm premature rupture of membranes (PPROM), looking to identify data patterns that could detect infection before it presents through traditional methods.[3]

From Ava's initial goal of helping couples get pregnant, the plan all along has been to add functionality that can make Ava a value-add for women no matter their age or reproductive goals. In an interview, Pascal Koenig, Ava's co-founder and CEO, told me, "Our vision is to understand the influence of hormonal changes on women throughout their lives—from the very beginning, when menstruation starts, up until menopause, and maybe even after."[4]

Koenig continues: "It's about the entire reproductive journey, from issues on the conceiving side, with couples trying to get pregnant, and then also on the contraceptive side, with people who want to take hormones, and then during pregnancy itself. Finally, menopause, which is a completely underresearched area. Our goal is to come up with products and services that can impact people's lives at each of those points."

The data creates a feedback loop enabling continuous improvement —the more they collect, the more they can refine the algorithm, the more accurate the predictions can be, the more hypotheses that can be tested, the more insights that can ultimately be learned. With the opportunity, of course, to add more data sources should they prove to add incremental value in the algorithm, or should technology make them easier to capture.

Koenig explains: "We started at the beginning with a smaller data set, and then we went through the data to really try to understand it, and see what we could add to make the prediction even better. Now we're using more and more factors no one would have expected. Of course our data scientists are making sure the correlations are real and not just effects we should be filtering out . . . but we see a lot of connections that we wouldn't have expected."

Some of those connections have been easy to understand, Koenig told me, and some have been more difficult to explain. They have looked at the hormonal effects of traveling to different time zones, exercising at night, sleeping badly, and more—all in the spirit of trying to isolate the layers that make a difference, and where the device can add value to end users.

One of the studies the company cites on its website is from all the way back in 2000, a paper on blood pressure and heart rate and how they affect menstrual cycles[5]—but two decades ago, there was no practical technological way to measure that at home, to make Ava a reality. I wrote in the previous section about how we're at an inflection point in history: for the first time, we have the sensors to collect the data—and we have the computing power to turn that data into actionable information. In many areas, we had the sensors but we just didn't know what layers to look for. Here, we've known some relevant layers for a while—but we didn't have the necessary wearable technology until recently.

The Changing Role of the Patient

What something like Ava does is give the patient power that was never before possible with this level of accuracy. Instead of the fertility specialist holding all of the information in the patient-doctor relationship—being the one who tells the patient what is happening in her body, and when to act in order to maximize the chances of conception—the patient gets to be part of her own care and own her information stream. The patient becomes empowered to proactively make decisions and treat herself, instead of just making sure she gets herself to the doctor. It's a small example here—just a few bits of information being transferred from the clinic setting to becoming trackable at home—but the idea extends further when we look at other conditions. The patient no longer has to be just a passive recipient of information.

But there's another side to it. In exchange for owning that information, the patient is forced to take on more responsibility for his or her care. In a technologically-enabled health care world, it's not enough just to make the doctor appointment. The patient is expected to use Ava consistently, to check the results, and to act on the information. And the life sciences company, for its part, is expected to make the information accessible not just at a level that can be understood by an educated medical professional but also by a relatively unsophisticated (perhaps) end user. It's not that the doctor's role is eliminated—if someone gets pregnant using Ava, of course the first step is going to be to see the OB/GYN. But it is the case that the patient has more tools in her toolkit.

As an industry, we've never really had to think much about information presentation, or about the accessibility of our equipment and devices. It was okay to be hard to use, to some extent, because our products were going to be used by trained professionals. That isn't necessarily the case anymore. Testing one's cervical mucus or basal body temperature is invasive and time-consuming. You have to remember first thing in the morning. It interrupts your life. Ava is just a bracelet. It syncs to the phone automatically. It, to its creators' credit, has a spectacular engagement model to keep it charged—it syncs when you plug it in, creating a virtuous cycle of engagement and compliance. This doesn't matter in a clinic setting—no one worries that a blood test is too much of a bother when the patient is already at the doctor's office. But it matters a tremendous amount at home, without the supervision of a health care provider.

From a business perspective, it's possible to see a range of different models playing out. Ava's website addresses potential customers—but there's also a section aimed directly at health care professionals. If someone is having a fertility issue, it's not out of the realm of possibility that a doctor could pull this out of his or her toolkit and recommend that the patient try Ava before moving to further treatment. It's also not out of the realm of possibility, from a payer perspective, that an insurer might say that before they pay for IVF or another expensive intervention, a patient must try something like this, to make sure it's not simply an issue of incorrect timing.

The Motivation to Comply

Pascal Koenig worked for years in digital health before co-founding Ava, and has found that it has been much easier to get people to comply with wearing a device when the goal is something they're personally excited about—conception—and they're not just being told to do it by their doctor. "I had much more struggle with getting congestive heart failure patients to wear devices or fill out surveys," he explains. "But with women trying to conceive, they're very motivated to follow the protocol."

Even better is when the device makes it easy. Koenig admits that solely from a medical perspective it's not necessarily the case that the wrist is the absolute best place to put the wearable—but in testing, they found that it was the most successful because it was the least intrusive in the users' lives. In improving the device itself over time, the company has tried to remove pain points, making the wristband easier to close, less likely to accidentally open during the night, and easier to charge—it recharges when it syncs with the user's phone instead of requiring another step. "With fitness trackers, people complain about having to recharge on a daily basis . . . but with Ava," Koenig explains, "we wanted to make it an easy daily routine; you just charge and sync."

It's also the case that tradeoffs have been made to balance most-accurate data with creating a reasonable experience that users will enjoy and actually comply with. "Urine or saliva may improve the accuracy of the product . . . but it's even more critical for people to use it. If you talk to a hundred doctors around the world, they will all say you need to use blood results, vaginal temperature . . . but even if from a medical standpoint it's a little better, the challenge to get people to do it is a big one." Instead, the goal is good enough—and at 89% accuracy, it is already far beyond what single-variable measures can even hope to attain, so the balance, for now, has worked.

A Man Who Just Can't Ovulate

I actually bought an Ava bracelet before I met Koenig, because I really wanted to understand the device. I have a habit of wanting to try every latest-and-greatest activity-tracking gadget, but a fertility band for women was a fascinating leap beyond my usual interests. I wore it for a few weeks, and it's absolutely the case that some of the measurements recorded were interesting to see—its measurements of my resting heart rate, perfusion, and stress level—and as relevant to a man in some applications as they are to a woman trying to conceive. Fortunately, it did not tell me I was ovulating. And Koenig speaks to the need to keep focus on the problem you are actually trying to address and figuring out your target market instead of trying to reach all people with all conditions. "We saw a clear opportunity in women's health, and we want to be the best in the world there. We're not competing with Fitbit. We want to be the leaders for women, throughout their reproductive lives."

It's an important point to stress—a successful device for one audience is not necessarily going to look the same as a successful device for another. It's not just about the technology. It's about tailoring the device to the problem on the table, finding a question that users want answered and then building a system that is best equipped to answer it, through whatever inputs make sense, with whatever hardware ultimately fits the issue best.

Finding a Niche in a Crowded Field

Ava is not the only data-driven technology player in the fertility space. But it is the case that a number of different companies have found success aiming their products at slightly different places on the patient journey. Bloomlife is a rental device that records contractions for women in the final stages of their pregnancy . . . though, like Ava, they plan to build beyond their initial entry point into the marketplace.[6] The company's CEO told the website *MobiHealthNews*, "[Our] sensor tracks a lot more than [contractions]. We can monitor fetal movement, fetal heart rate, various aspects of maternal health, all through the same sensors, essentially upgrading software and algorithms."[7] They're starting with contractions, but clearly the goal is data support for the entire pregnancy, and perhaps beyond.

There are also players on the men's side, including YO's at-home semen analysis by smartphone,[8] and Trak, a similar at-home testing kit with accompanying app.[9] These are entry points for potential patients, empowering them to do something on their own before seeing a doctor, and giving them the tools to gather their own personal medical information.

With conditions like infertility, the outputs enabled by thoughtful, clinically-validated patient equations are fairly straightforward.

People want information, and, in the case of well-designed products like Ava, actionable information that can change their lives. Things get more complicated when we look at chronic diseases—where the stakes are potentially higher, and the need for help is ongoing rather than limited to a defined point in time in the user's life. In the next chapter, we'll look at two issues where technology has started to make real differences in the lives of patients: asthma and diabetes. The challenge is greater in many ways than it is for a relatively simple system like Ava's, but the potential rewards are bigger as well.

Notes

1. "What's the Cervical Mucus Method of FAMs?," Planned Parenthood, 2019, https://www.plannedparenthood.org/learn/birth-control/fertility-awareness/whats-cervical-mucus-method-fams.
2. Janet Morrissey, "Women Struggling to Get Pregnant Turn to Fertility Apps," *New York Times*, August 27, 2018, https://www.nytimes.com/2018/08/27/business/women-fertility-apps-pregnancy.html.
3. Dave Muoio, "Ava Announces New Feature for Cycle-Tracking Bracelet, Clinical Study," *MobiHealthNews*, January 31, 2018, https://www.mobihealthnews.com/content/ava-announces-new-feature-cycle-tracking-bracelet-clinical-study.
4. Pascal Koenig, interview for *The Patient Equation*, interview by Glen de Vries and Jeremy Blachman, February 23, 2017.
5. "Ava's Research—Science-Backed Technology | Ava," Ava, 2015, https://www.avawomen.com/how-ava-works/healthcare/research/.
6. "Bloomlife," https://www.facebook.com/Bloomlife, Bloomlife, 2019, https://bloomlife.com.
7. Jonah Comstock, "Bloomlife Gets $4M for Wearable Pregnancy Tracker," *MobiHealthNews*, August 15, 2016, http://mobihealthnews.com/content/bloomlife-gets-4m-wearable-pregnancy-tracker.
8. "YO Sperm Test | A Male Fertility Test You Can Use At Home," YoSperm Test, 2017, https://www.yospermtest.com/.
9. "How the Trak Male Fertility Test Works," Trak Fertility, 2018, https://trakfertility.com/how-trak-works/.

5 | One Breath, One Drop—Asthma and Diabetes, Chronic Conditions Being Conquered with Technology

On the face of it, asthma and diabetes don't look like they have much in common. And the deeper you dig, the more you realize—they don't. Which is why talking about both of them here offers a lesson: patient equations aren't just about solving one kind of health care problem, or about one template we can apply over and over again. The game is really different when we compare asthma to diabetes. In one (asthma) we're trying to keep people out of a dangerous situation. Our inputs are all about the combination of internal and external variables. There's how the patient is breathing—and then there's also the environment outside and what triggers may be present. In the other (diabetes) it's all a single internal process we need to try to keep in balance—the regulation of sugar level and insulin.

What they both do have in common is the need for real-time intervention and adjustment. This isn't like cancer, where we're looking for signifiers about a larger process, indicators that might be able to tell us sooner than traditional measures. This isn't something where we can wait to sync with our phones, check an app, study the data. This is now, in that moment—we need to leave for a better air quality environment (asthma), or we need to dose insulin right away (diabetes). There is no margin for error if patients are going to trust these devices or the algorithms behind them. There is no time for human analysis. The equations have to be right, every time. They have to work.

Out of the Danger Zone

Dr. Veena Misra is a Distinguished Professor of Electrical and Computer Engineering at North Carolina State University, and the director of the university's ASSIST program—the Nanosystems Engineering Research Center for Advanced Self-Powered Systems of Integrated Sensors and Technologies—whose work centers around building health-monitoring wearables and the sensors that power them.

Dr. Misra's special interest—and one of the key differentiators as ASSIST works to bring its products to market—is in developing devices with ultra-low battery needs. The goal, she explained in an interview with me, is to make devices that can run entirely off of the exceedingly small electrical charge generated by our own bodies.[1] This means never having to remove the device in order to charge it, and never having to think about it once it's been placed on or in the body. Charging one's device is a huge roadblock right now in subject adherence—as evidenced by Ava's thinking in combining charging and syncing—and Dr. Misra and her team hope to make this problem a worry of the past. "We have picked our goal, which is ultra-low power," she told NC State's engineering magazine in an interview in 2017, "and in that space ASSIST stands out uniquely."[2]

Among the platforms that Dr. Misra's team has developed is an asthma wearable aimed at eliminating attacks. Through a wearable wristband and patch, and an integrated spirometer into which patients breathe several times a day, the system can combine user data and environmental information—heart rate, the amount of oxygen in the blood, hydration levels, air quality, ozone, carbon monoxide, nitrogen dioxide, humidity, temperature, and other factors—and create predictions as to whether an asthma attack is on its way. If so, it can warn the subject to head elsewhere and take steps to hopefully prevent the attack from occurring.

Preliminary test results, presented in May of 2019, showed that this kind of monitoring can detect physiological changes in lung function and is useful for preventing asthma exacerbations.[3] Dr. Misra's team ultimately hopes to partner with companies that can produce the wearables for widespread use and collect data along the way to provide new insights about the disease.[4] Her team is also working on applications for cardiac health, pre-diabetes, and wound care, using a range of different low-power sensors.

Lowering Barriers to Zero

Ava is trying to make charging its device an easy part of a daily routine, but Dr. Misra wants to see charging go away entirely. She explains that her goal is to see fully-connected patients, without any logistical hurdles to get them there—"just like you put on your clothing, you put on these devices and they become your companion, warning you about your health or the environment, and enabling you to live a better life," she says. She envisions healthy people choosing to wear devices like hers—to catch warning signs across a range of conditions, whether it's environmental exposures in the workplace, or heart arrhythmias, or glycemic index management to avoid diabetes. We can collect clues that over time can lead to better and better predictions about when we should go to the doctor and get something worked up by a physician.

"We don't want you to have to go to the doctor for a periodic measure of what's in your sweat, what your sugar level is, and more," Dr. Misra explains. "These technologies can allow people to keep an eye on what is going on with their health, what changes if they change their diet, what is affecting their respiration. . . . And as we get more data, we can see what aspects are correlated, and what is most useful in predicting the future."

In a TEDx Talk in Raleigh, North Carolina in 2016, titled "Powering Your Own Wellness," Dr. Misra painted a picture of a future of self-powered wearables—engaging us, alerting us, empowering us all, rich and poor, healthy and sick—without maintenance of any kind. We are the batteries that power our sensors, and, in addition to the four times a year the average person sees a doctor, we can be monitored for the 8,700-plus hours a year we are currently unwatched.[5]

Maybe it's too much. Maybe we don't all want to be watched all the time, especially if we're healthy (or we think we are). Maybe we don't always want to know that we're putting ourselves in danger when we get off the plane in a smog-filled city on vacation, or if we eat that second, third, or fourth doughnut. But if we have a chronic condition, like asthma, that can become life-threatening at a moment's notice, then we probably do. And there's perhaps no common condition that requires more constant, vigilant monitoring than diabetes—which is why it has become an area of huge excitement and activity in terms of wearables.

A Perfectly Artificial Pancreas

Diabetes is the ultimate biological incarnation of the smart thermostat I talked about earlier in the book, a true closed-loop system: you measure your blood sugar, you dose your insulin, repeat as needed. Which is why "solving" diabetes with an artificial pancreas-type solution has seemed attainable ever since wearable technology began to emerge. It has been a race to bring to market the perfect machine to make active management of one's diabetes a thing of the past. Kady Helme, a type 1 diabetic, had the opportunity back in 2014 to test within a clinical trial a device that combined a continuous glucose monitor with an insulin pump, and an algorithm that learned her body's rhythms. She gave a talk at a Forbes Healthcare Summit that summarized her experience:

"I could do everything right, and my sugar levels are still a total roller coaster. [But] this artificial pancreas trial basically took my management right off the table.... [The] pump would read [my glucose level] every five minutes, and decide what to do . . . like a normal person's pancreas would."[6]

Helme talked about how she was able to eat "crazy things" that she would have previously felt guilty about: pasta, alcohol, dessert. "I really gave it a test run," she said, "and I had to put my trust in that system." She didn't realize until the trial was over that she'd really fallen in love with the device, and the quality of life it allowed her to have.

This is the dream for diabetics. The reality, however, has been more complex. The FDA has approved only one commercial artificial pancreas-style system in the United States (for children above age 7 and adults with type 1 diabetes), the Medtronic Minimed 670G, although many other companies have been developing their own versions, for years at this point.[7] The problem—and it's certainly not unique to the Medtronic device—is that these machines are not perfect. One recent study found that nearly 40% of users of the Medtronic device stopped using it over the 15-month study period.[8] The device alarmed too often, had trouble adhering to the skin, misread sensor input, and often switched out of automatic mode into manual delivery, making it no better from the patient's perspective than a traditional glucose monitor.

The problem, explains writer Clara Rodriguez Fernandez in Labiotech.eu, a digital media site covering the European biotech industry, is that "the system can only make predictions when the person is not eating or exercising, and if the sugar levels go too high or too low, it will switch back to manual mode."[9] The device isn't fully automated: it's not a closed loop. Fernandez calls it a "hybrid loop" instead.

The challenges to a more perfect system, Fernandez goes on to explain, are that, first, current forms of insulin need to be faster-acting when facing big changes in blood sugar; second, insulin alone is not sufficient to regulate blood sugar as well as the body can in nondiabetics; and, third, the algorithms need to be smarter, and better customized to how each patient's body reacts to the insulin dose.

Indeed, when it comes to the second of these challenges, a recent report in *Science Translational Medicine* backs up the need for a multi-hormone closed loop system instead of just relying on insulin.[10] Dual-hormone systems have been able to achieve more glucose control and keep patients out of a hypoglycemic state with more success. But the innovations needed—more stable forms of other useful hormones, faster-acting insulin, and smarter algorithms behind the scenes—are still part of the future rather than the present.

Hacking One's Own Device

There has been a movement—the Open Artificial Pancreas System project (#OpenAPS)—to take the building of artificial pancreas systems out of the life sciences industry and put it into the hands of type 1 diabetics themselves.[11] It is estimated that between one and two thousand people have attempted to build their own artificial pancreas devices out of available parts—combining a glucose monitor, an insulin pump, and a computer to communicate between the two. Predictably, this has not been an unmitigated success. In May 2019, the FDA issued a warning after learning that one diabetic had accidentally overdosed using one of these hacked systems.[12]

This is a serious problem, of course, but it speaks to the desperate desire of patients to have these new data-powered tools to manage their chronic illnesses. It doesn't take much interpretation to hear Kady Helme's account of her time with her artificial pancreas and realize how significantly something like this can change a patient's life. Diabetes is a uniquely interesting area of development because patients are already using devices to manage their condition—the new generation of machines just makes it easier for them, and optimizes a situation that they have had to manually manage for their entire lives. The real-time actionability of the information makes the condition feel conquerable in a way that cancer and other conditions don't. There is good work being done in this area by lots of companies, and the game now is improving these devices enough to say that we have mastered diabetes.

One Drop at a Time

Jeffrey Dachis is the founder, chairman, and CEO of OneDrop, a diabetes management approach that isn't quite tackling the artificial pancreas problem, but trying to use patient data (and its own hardware and software platforms) to get as close as it can—without actually dispensing the insulin automatically. On its face, OneDrop is simply a better version of what already exists across the industry—a fancier glucose testing device, with a well-designed app, a direct-to-consumer subscription plan for testing strips, and a community element for patients to connect with each other online.

But there's more—in 2018, OneDrop unveiled its Automated Decision Support system, which leans on data from its users to predict future blood glucose values—helping users decide how much insulin they need.[13] The algorithm working behind the scenes uses personal data along with information about "similar" users, ending up with 91% of predictions falling within a plus-minus range of 50 mg/dL of glucose and 75% within 27 mg/dL. It's not quite an artificial pancreas, but it does add value beyond traditional blood glucose meters, which merely report the numbers.

The company was started after Dachis, a co-founder of the media agency Razorfish, was diagnosed with diabetes at age 47. According to a profile in the online site New Atlas, Dachis had suddenly lost 20 pounds in less than eight weeks and was constantly thirsty.[14] He ended up diagnosed with latent autoimmune diabetes of adulthood (LADA), a rare form of type 1 diabetes often misdiagnosed because it appears after age 30.[15]

Dachis was surprised to be given almost no guidance upon diagnosis—"six minutes with a nurse practitioner, who gave him an insulin pen and a prescription"[16]—and so he decided to take matters into his own hands, interviewing hundreds of diabetics to figure out how he could best address their needs with technology. "This is really a user experience problem, not a medical problem," he told New Atlas in 2017. "There's all this complex, psychosocial stuff going on with this diabetes condition that has nothing to do with the medical industry."

The OneDrop system collects glucose readings, physical activity measures (synced through trackers like the Fitbit or Apple Watch), food intake, and medication tracking and presents the data through easy-to-read visualizations in its app. Plus, there is chat support with certified diabetes educators and community features so patients can learn from experts and from each other. Dachis told the online site Healthline, "When I was diagnosed I thought, there has to be somebody who's cracked this code already—there has to be the cool gear, the stuff that's going to combine Internet of Things, Quantified Self-ers, Mobile Computing, and Big Data."[17] He couldn't find it. And so Dachis created OneDrop.

Clinical studies have borne out the usefulness of the OneDrop system. The journal *Diabetes* reports on OneDrop's Automated Decision Support feature, finding that in one sample of 28,838 forecasts sent to 5,506 users, 92.4% were rated "useful" by those users.[18]

It's all about connecting the disparate buckets of data, Dachis told the industry site Diabetes in Control.[19] "[D]iabetes is such a data-driven disease and yet all the data that you need to manage the disease, sits in all these different places," he said. Between carbohydrate data, medication data, insulin data, physical activity, and blood glucose levels, everything was in disparate places without any coordination. "We automatically track your blood glucose if you're using one of the connected meters," Dachis said, as well as everything else, coordinating it to provide recommendations and advice to patients, and let them make more informed choices.

As opposed to the Medtronic artificial pancreas, and the others in development, OneDrop isn't just for type 1 diabetics, who make up just 5% of the diabetic population. The decision support specifically is meant for type 2 diabetics, the more than 400 million people worldwide who have to think about this problem every day.[20] The app pops up notifications with actionable tips—take a 15-minute walk if your blood glucose is going up, for instance.[21]

"You can only learn so much by looking back at what already happened," said Dr. Dan Goldner, vice president of Data Science Operations at OneDrop, in a press release announcing the Automatic Decision Support feature. "We want to empower you to look ahead—to see what's coming and know what you can do about it. Like the collision-avoidance system in your car, glucose forecasts give you information in time for you to take action and shape the course of your diabetes."[22]

Goldner provides a great analogy—the collision-avoidance system in your car—that encapsulates what we can hope to be able to accomplish for chronic diseases beyond just diabetes. These systems can be more than just trackers, but real tools to get patients to behave in optimal ways and avoid problems that would otherwise arise. For too long, we have been forced by the available technology to be satisfied with "good enough"—as long as you weren't in crisis, you were doing okay. But now, we have the ability to be genuinely proactive in our approaches, to not just settle for good enough but to aim for optimal.

Of course, chronic diseases give us time to learn from an individual's data and patterns, and the ability to refine our predictions day after day, week after week, month after month. There is another set of problems out there that bring a different challenge—acute problems like the flu and sepsis—which are the next ones we can take a look at.

Notes

1. Veena Misra, interview for *The Patient Equation*, interview by Glen de Vries and Jeremy Blachman, August 11, 2016.
2. Engineering Communications, "NSF Engineering Research Centers: ASSIST and FREEDM," *College of Engineering News*, @NCStateEngr, October 9, 2017, https://www.engr.ncsu.edu/news/2017/10/09/nsf-engineering-research-centers-assist-and-freedm/.
3. Veena Misra, "Smart Health at the Cyber-Physical-Human Interface," NAE Regional Meeting at the University of Virginia, May 1, 2019, https://engineering.virginia.edu/sites/default/files/common/offices/marketing-and-communications/Veena%20Misra%20NAE%20Talk%20Final.pdf.
4. Engineering Communications, "NSF Engineering Research Centers: ASSIST and FREEDM."
5. Veena Misra, "Wearable Devices: Powering Your Own Wellness | Veena Misra | TEDxRaleigh," YouTube Video, June 14, 2016, https://www.youtube.com/watch?v=noiKR_yWniU.
6. Kady Helme, "Why I Miss My Artificial Pancreas," *Forbes*, December 22, 2014, https://www.forbes.com/video/3930264846001/#7eff48c61e78.
7. Amy Tenderich, "Artificial Pancreas: What You Should Know," Healthline Media, April 2019, https://www.healthline.com/diabetesmine/artificial-pancreas-what-you-should-know#1.
8. Craig Idlebrook, "38 Percent of Medtronic 670G Users Discontinued Use, Small Observational Study Finds," Glu, March 25, 2019, https://myglu.org/articles/38-percent-of-medtronic-670g-users-discontinued-use-small-observational-study-finds.
9. Clara Rodríguez Fernández, "The Three Steps Needed to Fully Automate the Artificial Pancreas," Labiotech UG, March 11, 2019), https://labiotech.eu/features/artificial-pancreas-diabetes/.
10. Charlotte K. Boughton and Roman Hovorka, "Advances in Artificial Pancreas Systems," *Science Translational Medicine* 11, no. 484 (March 20, 2019): eaaw4949, https://doi.org/10.1126/scitranslmed.aaw4949.
11. "What Is #OpenAPS?," Openaps.org, 2018, https://openaps.org/what-is-openaps/.

12. Craig Idlebrook, "FDA Warns Against Use of DIY Artificial Pancreas Systems," Glu, May 17, 2019, https://myglu.org/articles/fda-warns-against-use-of-diy-artificial-pancreas-systems.

13. One Drop, "Predictive Insights | Automated Decision Support," One Drop, 2019, https://onedrop.today/blogs/support/predictive-insights.

14. Michael Irving, "One Drop: The Data-Driven Approach to Managing Diabetes," New Atlas, August 14, 2017, https://newatlas.com/one-drop-diabetes-interview/50885/.

15. "What Is LADA?," Beyond Type 1, 2015, https://beyondtype1.org/what-is-lada-diabetes/.

16. Michael Irving, "One Drop: The Data-Driven Approach to Managing Diabetes."

17. Amy Tenderich, "OneDrop: A Newly Diagnosed Digital Guru's Big Diabetes Vision," Healthline, March 19, 2015, https://www.healthline.com/diabetesmine/onedrop-newly-diagnosed-digital-guru-s-big-diabetes-vision.

18. Daniel R. Goldner et al., "49-LB: Reported Utility of Automated Blood Glucose Forecasts," *Diabetes* 68, Supplement 1 (June 2019): 49-LB, https://doi.org/10.2337/db19-49-lb.

19. Steve Freed, "Transcript: Jeffrey Dachis, Founder and CEO of One Drop," Diabetes In Control. A free weekly diabetes newsletter for Medical Professionals., November 19, 2016, http://www.diabetesincontrol.com/transcript-jeffrey-dachis-founder-and-ceo-of-one-drop-diabetes-app/.

20. Adrienne Santos-Longhurst, "Type 2 Diabetes Statistics and Facts," Healthline, 2014, https://www.healthline.com/health/type-2-diabetes/statistics.

21. One Drop, "Predictive Insights | Automated Decision Support."

22. One Drop, "One Drop Launches 8-Hour Blood Glucose Forecasts for People with Type 2 Diabetes on Insulin," *PR Newswire*, June 8, 2019, https://www.prnewswire.com/news-releases/one-drop-launches-8-hour-blood-glucose-forecasts-for-people-with-type-2-diabetes-on-insulin-300864192.html.

6

Flumoji and Sepsis Watch—Two Approaches to Predicting and Preventing Acute, Life-threatening Conditions Through Smarter Data

It's almost a governing principle in health care: the earlier you detect a problem, the less painful (and the more cost-effective) the treatment will be. If you can identify problems early, you're stacking the deck in your favor, on all sorts of metrics—predictability of the course of treatment, odds of success, and reduced risk for an additional cascade of potentially costly and harmful problems down the line, as just a few examples. With the flu, catch it early and you can minimize the severity (and lower the overall productivity loss, if you're looking at things from a societal level) by giving patients an antiviral like Tamiflu. With sepsis, catch it early and you're absolutely saving lives. Or, to flip the statement around, catch it late and people will die.

Looking at the big picture, early (and accurate) detection—of every condition, every response, every reaction—is the ultimate reason to put energy into finding and deploying sophisticated patient equations. Whether we're looking for cancer, Alzheimer's disease, or, as in the previous two chapters, diabetes, asthma exacerbations, or if someone is about to ovulate—or whether we're looking for how a patient is responding to a treatment, or whether they're responding at all—the earlier we know, the more options we have, the more room to maneuver and find the optimal solution going forward. It's important, whether it's going to be a long-fought war (like cancer) or a quick battle. Nowhere does this play out more critically than with fast-acting issues like the flu or sepsis, where mere days or even hours can absolutely mean the difference between life and death.

Catching Sepsis Earlier

Sepsis—a patient's inflammatory response to an infection, leading to rapid organ failure and 50% mortality if it progresses to septic shock[1]—causes 6% of all deaths in the United States and $23 billion in annual medical costs,[2] with over 1.5 million cases every year and more than 250,000 deaths.[3] And yet early identification, as the researchers and clinicians behind Duke University Hospital's Sepsis Watch system put it, "remains elusive even for experienced clinicians."[4]

The national average as far as catching sepsis "is about 50 percent," Duke's Dr. Mark Sendak told *Inside Signal Processing* newsletter.[5] "A lot of places struggle with this problem." At Duke, an average of seven to nine patients develop sepsis every day, with a nearly 10% mortality rate.[6] The problem is that there is no one test, no one symptom, no one sure sign of sepsis. So finding it—and fighting it—has for too long been an idiosyncratic process, with doctors and nurses trying to get lucky and notice it before it's too late. Data, researchers at Duke realized, can help us.

In November of 2018, Sepsis Watch was launched at Duke after months of testing. It is a data-powered artificial intelligence system designed to identify sepsis cases earlier than ever before, and to stop them before it's too late. The system incorporates dozens of variables— 86 in all—including patient demographics, comorbidities, lab values, vital signs, medications, and more—pulling information from medical records every five minutes to try to identify patients with signs of sepsis before a doctor could possibly notice, and then alerting the hospital's rapid response team, prompting them to evaluate and potentially intervene.[7] Once patients at risk are identified, their progress is tracked through four stages—triage, screened, monitoring, and treatment—ensuring that they are not ignored once they've been flagged by the system.

Before launch, Duke tested the model on retrospective patient data, finding that it could identify sepsis as much as five hours earlier than was typically happening—a huge advantage when it comes to treatment.[8] In an interview with *American Healthcare Leader*, Eric Poon, Duke's chief health information officer, said, "All of us as clinicians have had experiences where we know the patient isn't quite looking right, but with so many things happening, it's hard to pick out those faint signals from the noise."[9] Now, they can react more quickly and potentially make a real difference in patient outcomes.

Partnering with Doctors, Not Replacing Them

The Sepsis Watch system is not an artificial pancreas for sepsis. It does not deliver medication, or even recommend treatment. It puts up a warning sign—and makes sure that doctors and nurses step in to evaluate. It's an example of data working to empower doctors and hospitals to deliver better care, not replace them. The AI can't do it all, Dr. Sendak told *IEEE Spectrum*.[10] It's the doctors who are ultimately making the decisions.

But even this level of intervention can be difficult to introduce into hospitals and become a trusted part of the workflow, even when the data shows that it should. As the Duke team's submitted manuscript to the *Journal of Medical Internet Research* begins, "Successful integrations of machine learning into routine clinical care are exceedingly rare."[11]

Madeleine Clare Elish of the Data & Society Research Institute writes about the difficulties of establishing trust in an artificial intelligence-based system—and about Duke's Sepsis Watch system specifically—in a paper titled "The Stakes of Uncertainty: Developing and Integrating Machine Learning in Clinical Care."[12] She discusses how as something typically diagnosed by gut instinct, sepsis is a perfect candidate for machine learning, but that implementation of Sepsis Watch still had to be approached carefully to ensure that doctors wouldn't resent the perceived interference with their clinical judgment. Elish writes, "Healthcare, and in particular hospitals, have historically been slow to adopt new technologies . . . [even when they can] improve patient outcomes. . . . 'It's a low hanging fruit, but the fruit has a thick stem. You can't really hit it.'"[13]

With lessons that can apply to anyone trying to bring change to a health care organization, Elish goes on to explain that it was important to incorporate end users—doctors and nurses—from the very beginning, ensuring that stakeholders felt engaged in the process and invested in the project's success. She also describes how the Sepsis Watch system was deliberately limited in capability—designed just to predict the first appearance of sepsis in a patient and flag it for the team, and not to dictate anything beyond that, so as to ensure that the system was perceived as supplementing the doctor's role, not replacing it.

She talks in addition about "alarm fatigue," and the risk that alerts would be experienced as "more annoying than helpful." It was important in developing the system—as it is in all similar types of systems—that the right balance is struck between alarming too often (meaning doctors will end up ignoring the warnings) and not alarming often enough (meaning septic patients will be missed, and no one will end up trusting the system to catch the patients it purports to). Physicians needed proof that the system worked better than their judgment alone (which is why Duke ran its retrospective analysis to show that the system identified septic patients an average of five hours faster than baseline). At the same time, doctors also wanted to be sure that their autonomy was not threatened.

These social factors are critical—not just here with Sepsis Watch but with any new technological implementation. Another point Elish makes that is worth noting: she found in talking to stakeholders at Duke that people preferred to call Sepsis Watch a "tool" rather than anything else, and that the term "predictive analytics" was preferred to "machine learning" or "artificial intelligence," which both had more intrusive and threatening implications. A tool is simply there to help, not replace.

Eric Poon and his team are currently evaluating the initial results of Sepsis Watch at Duke.[14] "We're not afraid to put something in," Poon told *American Healthcare Leader*, "but we want to evaluate rigorously whether it makes an impact in patient care. . . . We want to innovate but make sure we are doing it smartly."[15] Indeed, smart hospitals need to be developing and deploying exactly these kinds of valuable tools in order to compete in the new data-driven world. Catching sepsis sooner than before can make a huge difference to a hospital's overall patient outcome statistics, giving it a competitive edge and helping the organization in a whole host of ways.

Looking Beyond Sepsis

Duke's Sepsis Watch is not the only hospital-based system looking to incorporate data intelligence into practice. El Camino Hospital in California is using machine learning around a set of risk factors in order to predict the likelihood of patients falling.[16] In the first six months of their program, they saw a 39% reduction in falls.[17]

Tested at Kaiser Permanente of the Northwest in Oregon and Washington State, ColonFlag is a machine learning algorithm that produces risk scores from patient data to determine who ought to be referred for colon cancer screening. The system was shown in one study to be 34% better than looking at low hemoglobin alone.[18]

Mount Sinai Hospital deployed an artificial intelligence model to look into a database of patient records and see what it could discover from the data. The result was an ability to predict patients who would be most likely to develop hypertension, diabetes, and schizophrenia.[19] There are other initiatives in place across hospitals and departments worldwide. The ultimate question is how useful they will end up being—how reliable the results will be over time, and how trusted the systems will turn out to be by the doctors on the front lines.

Using Crowdsourcing to Track the Flu

The systems so far discussed in this chapter center around individual patient records and lab data being mined to find patterns that human beings simply can't detect, at least not with the same speed and reliability. Beyond the individual level, we can also look at broader populations in order to track infectious diseases like the flu. If we can harness environmental data—whether the people around you are sick or not—in an effective way, we can potentially detect your illness earlier (thus leading to better, cheaper, easier treatment) or help you avoid getting sick in the first place by keeping you from the epicenters of disease. We can stack the deck in our favor using population-level information.

GlaxoSmithKline collaborated with MIT Connection Science in 2017 to launch Flumoji, a real-time crowdsourced tracking engine that the website FiercePharma called "Waze for the flu."[20] The app attempted to use changes in users' activity and social interaction patterns—combined with flu-tracking data from the Centers for Disease Control and Prevention (CDC)—to find outbreaks more quickly than traditional methods had been able to.

Flumoji was unique in using activity data as a proxy for wellness, but other crowdsourced engines have attempted to make similar predictions, including Flu Near You, which collaborated with Science Friday on NPR to track influenza outbreaks around the country.[21] The problem with legacy tools like the CDC's "Flu View" report is that CDC data has a gap of almost a week between diagnosis and when physician reports hit the system and are able to be analyzed.[22] Shortening that gap would save lives—allowing hospitals and doctors' offices to order sufficient supplies when a new wave of cases is expected, and giving people warnings to keep kids or the elderly home, or to make sure to get the flu shot.

For a number of years, Google tried to track the flu by using Google search activity data. But the company failed in 2015 to predict the flu season's peak.[23] The Weather Channel used social media activity to create a map of flu activity—but this was designed to be illustrative, not predictive.[24] The issue with all of these tools is whether they can prove reliable enough to move from merely interesting to actually useful in a way that changes behavior, treatment, and outcomes. We are likely not there yet.

A study in *BMC Infectious Diseases* looked at a range of crowdsourced flu-tracking systems, including Flu Near You, and found that while these systems can add some information at a broad geographic level (national or regional), once you drill down close enough the correlation between systems decreased and the value was questionable.[25] But it's at the neighborhood level where predictions can really make a difference in changing behavior and treatment . . . so it remains questionable whether these systems are truly adding value.

Stopping the Spread of Illness with Data Is Hard

I talked to Julian Jenkins, now at Incyte, but who spent seven years at GlaxoSmithKline and was working closely with MIT on the Flumoji project back when it launched in 2017.[26] The most exciting piece of it, Jenkins explained, was trying to find those new biomarkers that mattered, the new layers of the layer cake that would make a difference. With the app running, you could track whether bedtime changed the night before illness set in, if the pattern of what someone was looking at on Facebook or Twitter changed, or if something about the person's online presence signaled an illness even before there was a search for whether CVS was open. Could we learn someone had the flu even before they realized it themselves?

Jenkins believes there is much data out there that we're not yet effectively mining. Could our TV set, for instance, tell us something we don't know about ourselves, from our viewing patterns, from how much we're moving around while we're watching? Could the GPS on our phones indicate the kinds of restaurants we're visiting, or the kinds of stores we're shopping in—and could that add useful information to an understanding of our lives from a medical perspective?

This kind of thinking isn't limited to the flu. India Hook-Barnard, director of Research Strategy and associate director of Precision Medicine at the University of California, San Francisco, told *Mobi-HealthNews* that, on a population level, we can use activity data to better understand all kinds of conditions.[27] Are people in a certain neighborhood at greater risk of cancer, diabetes, or another illness? Is it because of their access to healthy foods? Is it because of the availability of medical care? Is it about the availability of effective messaging about health? About environmental factors we may not have previously considered? "Knowing that a given population is at a greater risk," Hook-Barnard told *MobiHealthNews*, "you can do earlier diagnostics and screenings for certain diseases and then be able to be more effective in your surveillance of those people."[28]

This keeps people healthier and allows for much earlier intervention. Yet, at the same time, Julian Jenkins believes that while technology can help us understand and predict disease in so many ways, there are many significant barriers still in place, not the least of which is broad participation right now in efforts like Flumoji and others. To get people to even download the Flumoji app was a challenge—and that challenge becomes even bigger when we're talking about data centered around clinical trials, where a very small percentage of patients will ever be involved. The lack of interoperability—for the Flumoji app, needing to develop a front-end app for multiple platforms (Apple, Android, etc.)—as well as the lack of data sources being able to communicate behind the scenes (a problem we'll talk much more about later in the book)—is a tremendous challenge we still need to overcome.

When it comes to the hospital-based projects we talked about earlier in this chapter—like Sepsis Watch and ColonFlag—a big part of the work is ensuring that the health records data is fully usable and can be reliably accessed in an efficient, streamlined way. It's a huge problem to try to integrate new technology with legacy data systems, and it's not a problem that's going to disappear anytime soon. The mere ability to have data entered automatically rather than requiring someone to manually do it—a process that takes significant amounts of time—is still something we are working on in a lot of situations, so real-time analysis isn't always possible, even if the algorithms are there.

When it comes to patient equations and precision medicine, if we're being realistic, the flu isn't the holy grail. It would be terrific to ease people's suffering—and, in the case of sepsis, it would be tremendous to save people's lives through better prediction—but where precision medicine is already making the most difference (and where hopes are highest) is in areas like cancer, where the stakes are so high, and the current landscape is so far from ideal. Death rates from cancer have declined by 27% since 1991,[29] but much of that progress has been from lifestyle changes like fewer people smoking. There is hope that precision medicine can lead to more than just incremental change, but rather to revolution in detection and treatment. It is a more complex problem than any we've looked at in this section of the book, but patient equations offer hope here that hasn't been seen in decades.

Notes

1. Yang Li, "What Should We Learn? Hospitals Fight Sepsis with AI," IEEE Signal Processing Society, November 5, 2018, https://signalprocessingsociety.org/newsletter/2018/11/what-should-we-learn-hospitals-fight-sepsis-ai.
2. Cara O'Brien, MD, and Mark Sendak, MD, "Implementation and Evaluations of Sepsis Watch – ICH GCP – Clinical Trials Registry," Good Clinical Practice Network, 2019, https://ichgcp.net/clinical-trials-registry/NCT03655626.

3. Laura Ertel, "Buying Time to Save Sepsis Patients," Duke University School of Medicine," June 4, 2019, https://medschool.duke.edu/about-us/news-and-communications/med-school-blog/buying-time-save-sepsis-patients.

4. Cara O'Brien, MD, and Mark Sendak, MD, "Implementation and Evaluations of Sepsis Watch – ICH GCP – Clinical Trials Registry."

5. Yang Li, "What Should We Learn? Hospitals Fight Sepsis with AI."

6. Mark Sendak et al., "Leveraging Deep Learning and Rapid Response Team Nurses to Improve Sepsis Management," 2018, https://static1.squarespace.com/static/59d5ac1780bd5ef9c396eda6/t/5b737a1903ce645e7ad3d9a2/1534294563869/Sendak_M.pdf.

7. Ibid.

8. Laura Ertel, "Buying Time to Save Sepsis Patients."

9. Will Grant, "Eric Poon's Boundary-Pushing Use of Technology at Duke Health," *American Healthcare Leader*, February 4, 2019, https://americanhealthcareleader.com/2019/poon-tech-patient-care/.

10. Eliza Strickland, "Hospitals Roll Out AI Systems to Keep Patients From Dying of Sepsis," IEEE Spectrum: Technology, Engineering, and Science News, October 19, 2018, https://spectrum.ieee.org/biomedical/diagnostics/hospitals-roll-out-ai-systems-to-keep-patients-from-dying-of-sepsis.

11. Mark P. Sendak et al., "Sepsis Watch: A Real-World Integration of Deep Learning into Routine Clinical Care," *Journal of Medical Internet Research*, June 26, 2019, https://www.jmir.org/preprint/15182.

12. M. C. Elish, "The Stakes of Uncertainty: Developing and Integrating Machine Learning in Clinical Care," *2018 EPIC Proceedings*, October 11, 2018, https://papers.ssrn.com/sol3/papers.cfm?abstract_id=3324571.

13. Ibid.

14. Cara O'Brien, MD, and Mark Sendak, MD, "Implementation and Evaluations of Sepsis Watch – ICH GCP – Clinical Trials Registry."

15. Will Grant, "Eric Poon's Boundary-Pushing Use of Technology at Duke Health."

16. "3 Considerations for Adopting AI Solutions," American Hospital Association, 2019, https://www.aha.org/aha-center-health-innovation-market-scan/2019-01-08-3-considerations-adopting-ai-solutions.

17. Bill Siwicki, "Hospital Cuts Costly Falls by 39% Due to Predictive Analytics," *Healthcare IT News*, April 12, 2017, https://www.healthcareitnews.com/news/hospital-cuts-costly-falls-39-due-predictive-analytics.

18. Paul Cerrato and John Halamka, "Replacing Old-School Algorithms with New-School AI in Medicine," *Healthcare Analytic News*, April 5, 2019, https://www.idigitalhealth.com/news/replacing-oldschool-algorithms-with-newschool-ai-in-medicine.

19. Thomas Davis, "Artificial Intelligence: The Future Is Now," ProCRNA, April 21, 2019, https://www.procrna.com/artificial-intelligence-the-future-is-now/.

20. Beth Snyder Bulik, "GSK and MIT Flumoji App Tracks Influenza Outbreaks with Crowdsourcing," FiercePharma, January 28, 2017, https://www.fiercepharma.com/marketing/gsk-and-mit-flumoji-app-tracks-influenza-outbreaks-crowdsourcing.

21. "Tracking The Flu, In Sickness And In Health," Science Friday, 2018, https://www.sciencefriday.com/segments/tracking-the-flu-in-sickness-and-in-health/.

22. Laura Bliss, "The Imperfect Science of Mapping the Flu," CityLab, January 30, 2018, https://www.citylab.com/design/2018/01/the-imperfect-science-of-mapping-the-flu/551387/.

23. Ibid.

24. Ibid.

25. Kristin Baltrusaitis et al., "Comparison of Crowd-Sourced, Electronic Health Records Based, and Traditional Health-Care Based Influenza-Tracking Systems at Multiple Spatial Resolutions in the United States of America," *BMC Infectious Diseases* 18, no. 1 (August 15, 2018), https://doi.org/10.1186/s12879-018-3322-3.

26. Julian Jenkins, interview for *The Patient Equation*, interview by Glen de Vries and Jeremy Blachman, March 24, 2017.

27. Bill Siwicki, "What Precision Medicine and Netflix Have in Common," *MobiHealthNews*, May 22, 2017, http://www.mobihealthnews.com/content/what-precision-medicine-and-netflix-have-common.

28. Ibid.

29. Stacy Simon, "Facts & Figures 2019: US Cancer Death Rate Has Dropped 27% in 25 Years," American Cancer Society, January 8, 2019, https://www.canccr.org/latest-news/facts-and-figures-2019.html.

7 | Cancer and Phage Therapy—Crafting Custom Treatments Just for You

In 1971, U.S. President Richard Nixon announced a war on cancer, and yet almost 50 years later, there has been relatively little progress made compared to expectations. The biggest challenge is the complexity of the disease—or, as we ought to say, diseases. Cancer isn't one disease, it's many—and, in fact, in some ways, it's a different disease for just about every patient, with a number of individual factors contributing to every tumor, and every case. It is often hard to find evidence of cancer before it is too late to cure, treatments that work for one person's illness often don't work for another's, and the cancer itself can change over time to become resistant to a treatment that's working and require an entirely new strategy. When we talk about personalized medicine, it doesn't get much more personalized than cancer treatment—and when we talk about the need for precision, the stakes are rarely as high as they are here.

Later in this chapter, we'll talk about another very personalized approach to a complex, individual problem: phage therapy, or using custom bacteriophages to treat serious bacterial infections. But we'll start our exploration of personalized patient equations with cancer. On the diagnosis end, there are certainly intriguing developments—just as one example, a startup, Cyrcadia Health, developed a patch for women to wear under their bra in order to track breast tissue temperature, alerting wearers to see their doctor for further examination if there is a change in pattern.[1] As another example, researchers are looking at detecting cancer via breath test, under the theory that cancers change the pattern of molecules in the breaths we exhale—and that in fact there may be molecular fingerprints within the data that can detect not just cancer in general but particular cancers, more quickly than traditional tests.[2]

But perhaps the most interesting breakthroughs concern treating cancers that have proven resistant to traditional treatments, and where the combination of genetic information with proteomics—the proteins in a patient's tumor sample—have opened the door to new approaches. Former U.S. Vice President Joe Biden is quoted by Dr. Jerry Lee of the University of Southern California (who you'll hear a lot more from in Chapter 9) in a piece about the global Cancer Moonshot effort as saying, "it's like the genes are the full roster of a basketball team but the winning strategy comes from finding out who their starting lineup is. The proteins are the starters you're going to play against—the five you are going to have to defend against."[3]

With information about those proteins combined with genomic information, we've been able to move from talking about breast cancer, for example, not as one disease, but one with subcategories, like triple-negative (meaning the tumor is absent the three most common receptors for cancer growth: estrogen, progesterone, and the HER2/neu gene), allowing us to customize treatments and get the kinds of results we've been dreaming about since Nixon's declaration of war.

Changing the Way We Look at Cancer

In the old way of looking at things, cancer is simply a disease of uncontrolled growth and uncontrolled cell division. But over time, we've learned that it's more than that. A successful cancer needs to build its own infrastructure. It needs to stimulate the growth of new blood vessels. It needs to invade. If we can cut off its ability to build what it needs to keep growing, we can stop it in its tracks. I like to think of this as a cybersecurity problem. What we need to solve it is an air-gapped computer—meaning it's not able to connect to the outside, no attached network peripherals, no USB drive, no access to the Internet. We need the cancer to become an isolated system.

Even in the computer realm, this is harder than it seems. Data can enter and leave even through a power cord. And if you're connected to a wireless network, then you're pretty much dead. Cancer has even more vulnerabilities it can exploit, lots of ways it can get what it needs and ultimately destroy its host. Traditional therapies have been like carpet-bombing, with all of the associated collateral damage that chemotherapy can cause. But if we can target angiogenesis, for example, we can limit the cancer's ability to grow. If we can successfully stop its progression without destroying healthy cells in the process, it's a huge victory.

Newsweek announced in 2008 that "We fought cancer . . . and cancer won."[4] Indeed, there is so much left to figure out. With undiagnosed disease, data can get us only part of the way there. With genetic sequencing we are able to diagnose about 40% of patients, and for only about 40% of those are we able to find a treatment that might work. It is sobering to realize that we can't (yet) cure cancer with math. Cancers are excellent at inventing ways to get around whatever particular pathway we are trying to block. Even with targeted therapies, we eventually lose. So we need not just a targeted first-line therapy but a second-line and third-line therapy as well. We need to be ready before the cancer forces a change. We need to track the cancer closely enough to beat it—and transform the disease from something deadly to perhaps something chronic, where we won't necessarily ever utter the word "cure" but where we can keep finding new ways to press the pause button.

In that spirit, the more we can measure, and the more intelligence we have about not just the right treatment but about whether or not the current treatment is still working, the better shape we are in. Judging whether a treatment is still effective is not always easy, and certainly not on a real-time basis. Traditionally, we need to cut and poke, or at least perform a time-intensive scan—but now, more and more, sensors can give us that continuous multivariate view we need, if not to measure exactly what we're looking for, then at least to measure potential proxies for it.

A wristband activity tracker can tell us your daily movements. This may show us if the tumor burden is growing or shrinking—is your activity level going up or down? Can we find ways to either see or see by proxy information about the blood vessels penetrating the tumor, about how many new ones are surviving and growing? Can we view biomarkers like this a hundred times a second instead of once every six weeks? We will never be able to predict everything about someone's course of treatment—some patients might get hit by a bus, after all—but over time we can get a higher and higher resolution view at a closer-and-closer-to-continuous time frame so that we can truly know everything possible about someone's individual cancer, in time to act on it and stay ahead of the disease.

p53-ologists of the Future

p53 is a tumor suppressor protein, encoded by a gene known as *TP53*. Mutations of p53 have been found in more than 50% of tumors, giving it a strong linkage to cancer.[5] Normally, a cell will proliferate and die on a certain schedule. Cancerous cells don't die—they have uncontrolled growth, along with the desire to distribute themselves to the rest of the body and spread. p53 is supposed to stop the uncontrolled growth; if it isn't working, the growth continues, and the cancer wins. This is new knowledge, from over the past couple of decades, and that knowledge is limited right now. But what we do know is that if someone has a p53 mutation, lots of cancers can be predicted, across all different organ systems—prostate, kidney, brain, more. And yet we don't yet have p53-ologists, people who have a single-minded focus on understanding from a molecular basis what can go wrong if you have a p53 mutation as part of your tumor, regardless of what organ we're talking about—and, with that single-minded focus, can start to experiment with what other layers of our layer cake we need to understand in order to begin to use our knowledge of p53 to eradicate disease. Instead of treating cancer organ by organ, for people with p53 mutations, it may be more useful to have someone who understands the protein and not necessarily the organ.

PP2A is another protein, a cell regulator involved not just in cancer cell growth but in all kinds of metabolic pathways, some of which are related to cancer and some which are related to other cellular functions. It is also a tumor suppressor, and, when activated, it can help stop cancer growth. What's interesting about PP2A—and I'll tie this into our larger patient equation story in a moment—is that its anticancer properties were discovered somewhat by accident. *Vector*, the blog of Boston Children's Hospital, wrote about a set of researchers' efforts to find new treatments for T-cell acute lymphoblastic leukemia (T-ALL) by examining a library of nearly 5,000 drugs, compounds, and other natural products.[6] What they discovered was that perphenazine, an antipsychotic medication, seemed to have a side effect: lower cancer rates. Its mechanism? Activating PP2A. "In reactivating PP2A," *Vector* writes, "the drug was reactivating a protein that the tumor cells had turned off, triggering the cells to die."[7]

This is sparking research into whether PP2A activation is limited to helping in cases of T-ALL, or if there are wider implications for other cancers. Between p53 and PP2A, scientists are starting to realize that if we can gain a better understanding of how to manipulate proteins that are critical to cellular functions, we can think about treating cancer patients based not on symptoms but on the very core of the disease. The thing is, these are just two of the 10,000 or 100,000 possible pathways toward solving cancer—and we are just at the beginning. It is data—well-collected, smartly-analyzed patient data—that will tell us more, and that will wake us up to molecular targets that are in the biosamples right now but haven't been identified yet. This is how patient equations will play out to their best effect in cancer: finding patterns we have never before been able to see.

Or Perhaps Car-t-ographers of the Present

In 2017, the FDA approved Keytruda as a cancer treatment "based on the genetic profile of a tumor, rather than the tissue or tumor type," writes *PharmaVOICE*.[8] It targets one particular genetic sequence found in a small (but significant) number of tumors—but more and more treatments like this are on the way. Joy Carson, senior director of oncology strategy for Novella Clinical, told *PharmaVOICE*, "We are just beginning to build a meta-database of cancer targets—many of which do not yet have approved treatments. . . . It is a data engine that will drive drug development, but it will take many years to reap the benefits of this knowledge with effective targeted therapies."[9]

Keytruda isn't about cancer based on location in the body, it's about one particular genetic abnormality—with success in one study on tumors of the pancreas, prostate, uterus, and bone.[10] According to the *New York Times*, "[o]ne woman had a cancer so rare there were no tested treatments."[11]

Fewer than 5% of patients benefited from these kinds of therapies in 2018—but that's still 60,000 potential patients for Keytruda alone.[12] And, according to one analysis, fewer than 1 in 5 biopsied tumors were able to be matched to any targeted therapy drug (of which there are now 30).[13] But this is the wave of the future. And the present.

Novartis developed Kymriah, a customized treatment for relapsed or refractory B-cell acute lymphoblastic leukemia, using the patient's own T cells to fight the cancer. Treatments cost nearly half a million dollars. But Novartis does not charge people whose cancers do not respond. The latest reported trial showed a remission rate of 82% within three months and overall survival of 49% after 18 months, compared to survival rates between 15% and 27% for these types of recurrent cases in the past.[14] Customized immunotherapy treatments are the purest form of personalized medicine—they are literally personalized for each patient, hence the hefty price tag. But they also serve to limit the damage to surrounding cells, acting as a surgical strike against the cancer specifically. "This is just the beginning," said Miriam Merad, director of the

Precision Immunology Institute at Mount Sinai School of Medicine, on a panel at Aspen Ideas: Health. Between Keytruda and Kymriah, "[t]here are two molecules on the market, but there are hundreds of them we can exploit."[15]

Personalized Immunotherapy Beyond Cancer

These same approaches that are showing such promise in cancer aren't limited to that disease. One startup, Alector, is developing drugs to target the brain's immune system in the hope that it can enable patients to fight off Alzheimer's disease.[16] "If the immune system in the brain is not operating normally, the nerve cells cannot function normally," Arnon Rosenthal, the co-founder and CEO of Alector told *OneZero*, a technology and science publication hosted by Medium. "Eventually they degenerate and die. This is what leads to the disease."[17]

There is also another immunotherapy-type approach that has recently made headlines for saving the life of a 15-year-old lung transplant recipient with cystic fibrosis—and a bacterial infection that wasn't responding to antibiotics.[18] The answer? Phage therapy, a form of immunotherapy for bacteria, looking for the perfect virus to target the precise bacteria colonizing the patient.

Phage therapy actually dates back to Russia, more than a hundred years ago. The government didn't want to pay for antibiotics, so instead, they looked for viruses that could kill bacteria. The therapy was mostly abandoned for years, but with the rise of antibiotic-resistant infections, new approaches have been needed—and phage therapy has been unearthed from the dirt, along with the viruses hanging onto it.

Graham Hatfull, a professor of biotechnology at the University of Pittsburgh, has been studying bacteriophages (viruses that prey on bacteria) for years—and collecting them, 15,000 of them, in storage at a deep freeze (−80° Celsius).[19] I spoke to Hatfull, who says he wasn't necessarily looking to find a therapeutic use for phages, but had an unexpected opportunity to intervene with a particular patient, and it has taken his lab research in a surprising new direction.[20]

At their core, bacteriophages can help us understand fundamental questions of diversity and genetics. Hatfull leads a program where 5,500 students each year, from 140 institutions, isolate new phages, categorize and examine them, and use them to better understand biology and evolution. But in October of 2017, according to an account in *Wired* magazine, Hatfull received a desperate email from a microbiologist in London hoping for a miracle. Two teenagers with cystic fibrosis had received lung transplants—but their bodies were fighting infections post-transplant that antibiotics simply couldn't resolve.[21] There was nothing left in the hospital's toolkit—so Hatfull's colleague imagined that phages might be the teenagers' last best hope. One of the teenagers died before Hatfull and his team could identify the right phage to fight their infection—but the other got lucky, and the team found a group of three phages able to effectively attack the bacteria that were making her sick. She has since recovered and is doing well.

The problem, Hatfull tells me, is that this is personalized medicine at its most personal—the specificity of the phages mean that they will work for one bacterial strain and one strain only. They'll work for one patient but no others, and each potential case requires a new search, a new cocktail, a new procedure. These are not (yet) off-the-shelf solutions, and if there is an off-the-shelf solution to be found, it is way down the road.

Because of the work done to catalog and categorize his phages, Hatfull and his team were able to bootstrap their way into success in this one case—but success is not always replicable. Hatfull in fact wondered if they had gotten lucky with this patient, and if her infection would have cleared on its own, with or without the phages. So he has done further testing, trying to figure out whether and how he could effectively move forward with therapeutic intervention in more cases. He has had some failures, where the right phage could not be identified in time to save the patient, and a few minor signs of success, including another lung transplant patient with a raging infection for whom the right phage was found in just 10 days—a remarkably short turnaround time, Hatfull told me, and was showing real progress until the patient died from complications four weeks later.

Over the next year, Hatfull hopes to take on more and more individual cases, hoping to put some process behind these one-off interventions and figure out if there is a path forward to intervene at scale. In the old model of life sciences, no personalized therapies could possibly be scalable. But now we might have the data to start to deliver even the most custom treatments like this. As Hatfull's team has collected different bacterial strains to search for effective phages, he has found that for around one-third of *Mycobacterium abscessus* strains, he can't find any good phages—but for the others, he finds at least one, and sometimes more than one. For his team, that presents two challenges: how to expand the set of known phages to get broader penetration, and how to speed up the screening process to find the ones that can be found more quickly and easily. The question still remains whether it will be economically viable to expand the program.

In the future—keeping in mind this is not a near-term likelihood—Hatfull imagines that we could figure out what makes the phages work and synthetically build them in the lab, tune our phages to be ideal attackers for whatever bacteria are presenting themselves, and make the phage treatment into a pharmaceutical solution. But, he says, we're not even close, and we don't yet understand why some phages infect some bacterial hosts and strains and not others. For millions of years, phages have been co-evolving with bacteria, and it's a very complex dance that we're only beginning to comprehend. Hatfull says that the Bill & Melinda Gates Foundation has called for proposals for the use of phages to engineer the infant gut microbiome—to turn unhealthy gut microbiomes into healthy ones—but it's still very early. Hatfull is working with others to improve the data sets and better understand phages and their potential applications. He sees a possible future in combination therapy for tuberculosis—to shorten antibiotic therapy from months to weeks by using targeted phages in addition to antibiotics, and to use the phages to make the treatments we already have more robust and lasting.

Immunotherapies for cancer and phage therapies for bacterial infections offer tremendous hope to patients for whom standard treatments have proven ineffective. But at least in these areas there have been traditional therapies to start from, and bodies of knowledge and research that have been in development for decades. In the next chapter, we'll look at Castleman disease—a rare condition that not much has been known about . . . until very recently. Castleman disease stands as an example of patient equations bringing us from near-zero to a much fuller understanding of disease, and of treatment, driven largely by the work and passion of one man, Dr. David Fajgenbaum, trying to save his own life as well as thousands of others with the disease.

Notes

1. Mike Montgomery, "In Cancer Fight, Artificial Intelligence Is A Smart Move For Everyone," *Forbes*, December 22, 2016, http://www.forbes.com/sites/mikemontgomery/2016/12/22/in-cancer-fight-artificial-intelligence-is-a-smart-move-for-everyone/.
2. *The Economist*, "Understanding Cancer's Unruly Origins Helps Early Diagnosis," Medium (*The Economist*), December 12, 2017, https://medium.economist.com/understanding-cancers-unruly-origins-helps-early-diagnosis-eb449e3ff466?gi=6a5cf570ac1.
3. Jerry S. H. Lee and Danielle Carnival, "A Global Effort to End Cancer as We Know It," Medium (*The Cancer Moonshot*), September 23, 2016, https://medium.com/cancer-moonshot/a-global-effort-to-end-cancer-as-we-know-it-42a9905327e8.
4. Sharon Begley, "We Fought Cancer . . . and Cancer Won," *Newsweek* 152, no. 11 (2008): 42–44, 46, 57–58 passim, https://www.ncbi.nlm.nih.gov/pubmed/18800570.
5. Francesco Perri, Salvatore Pisconti, and Giuseppina Della Vittoria Scarpati, "P53 Mutations and Cancer: A Tight Linkage," *Annals of Translational Medicine* 4, no. 24 (December 2016): 522—522, https://doi.org/10.21037/atm.2016.12.40.
6. Tom Ulrich, "When Is an Antipsychotic Not an Antipsychotic? When It's an Antileukemic," *Vector*, January 21, 2014, https://vector.childrenshospital.org/2014/01/when-is-an-antipsychotic-not-an-antipsychotic-when-its-an-antileukemic/.
7. Ibid.

8. Denise Myshko, "Trend: Advanced Diagnostics and Precision Medicine," *PharmaVOICE*, November 2018, https://www.pharmavoice.com/article/2018-11-diagnostics/.

9. Ibid.

10. Gina Kolata, "Cancer Drug Proves to Be Effective Against Multiple Tumors," *New York Times*, June 8, 2017, https://www.nytimes.com/2017/06/08/health/cancer-drug-keytruda-tumors.html.

11. Ibid.

12. Ibid.

13. Denise Myshko, "Trend: Advanced Diagnostics and Precision Medicine."

14. Matthew H. Forsberg, Amritava Das, Krishanu Saha, and Christian M. Capitini, "The Potential of CAR T Therapy for Relapsed or Refractory Pediatric and Young Adult B-Cell ALL," *Therapeutics and Clinical Risk Management* 14 (September 2018): 1573–84, https://doi.org/10.2147/tcrm.s146309.

15. Amanda Mull, "The Two Technologies Changing the Future of Cancer Treatment," *The Atlantic*, June 25, 2019, https://www.theatlantic.com/health/archive/2019/06/immunotherapies-make-cancer-treatment-less-brutal/592378/.

16. Ron Winslow, "The Future of Alzheimer's Treatment May Be Enlisting the Immune System," Medium (*OneZero*), June 4, 2019, https://onezero.medium.com/the-future-of-alzheimers-treatment-may-be-enlisting-the-immune-system-d4de95ac1cff.

17. Ibid.

18. Sigal Samuel, "Phage Therapy: Curing Infections in the Era of Antibiotic Resistance," *Vox*, May 14, 2019, https://www.vox.com/future-perfect/2019/5/14/18618618/phage-therapy-antibiotic-resistance.

19. Megan Molteni, "Genetically Tweaked Viruses Just Saved a Very Sick Teen," *Wired*, May 8, 2019, https://www.wired.com/story/genetically-tweaked-viruses-just-saved-a-very-sick-teen/.

20. Graham Hatfull, interview for *The Patient Equation*, interview by Glen de Vries and Jeremy Blachman, July 2, 2019.

21. Megan Molteni, "Genetically Tweaked Viruses Just Saved a Very Sick Teen."

8 | Castleman Disease— Not One Rare Disease with No Treatments, But Three Rare Diseases . . . with Hope, Thanks to Data

Let's talk about the typical model of drug development. Life sciences companies are normally looking for the blockbuster, a treatment for the masses that can cover as many patients as possible. Of course effectiveness is important, but we only need to be more effective than the current treatment in order to go to market, and if we can potentially meet the needs of millions, even if not absolutely everyone who tries the drug will wind up benefitting . . . well, that's just the reality of drug development.

Precision medicine turns that paradigm on its head. As we're able to get more precise with treatments, the number of patients for whom those treatments are relevant will necessarily decrease. This creates a huge shift in the kinds of business decisions a life sciences company will choose to make. It's a different goal, about taking all of the information we can generate and activating it to be something that really makes a difference for each and every patient.

We saw that in the previous chapter with immunotherapy for cancer and phage therapy for bacterial infections, and it's just as salient a point here, with Castleman disease. To go from treating a rare disease with one relatively low-effectiveness treatment to figuring out that the condition may actually be three distinct diseases, each of which may need a different treatment . . . we're talking about affecting lives deeply, but it's really just a few hundred or a few thousand lives at a time. This is a very different endeavor than searching for the next-generation cholesterol drug or antidepressant.

Finding Clusters in a Random World

Just a few thousand patients around the world are diagnosed with Castleman disease each year. It is a deadly condition that affects the lymph nodes and can cause the collapse of multiple organ systems throughout the body. Traditionally, the best treatment has been a drug that has been shown to be effective in just over a third of patients. The rest? There has been scarcely more than hope. It's true that we've had clinical data to analyze for a long time, and patient characteristics to look at, but now we can get biospecimens, genomic and proteomic profiles, more data than we used to be able to collect or comprehend—and things are changing.

Dr. David Fajgenbaum, an assistant professor of medicine at the University of Pennsylvania and the co-founder and executive director of the Castleman Disease Collaborative Network, is not just the most prominent researcher and advocate working on the condition. He's also a patient, who has survived five life-threatening hospitalizations with the deadliest form of the illness, idiopathic multicentric Castleman disease (iMCD), which kills more than a third of sufferers within five years of initial diagnosis.

One recent study found that incorporating additional patient data into a predictive model—powered by my colleagues at Medidata—was able to boost the percentage of cases in which the only traditional drug treatment for iMCD was effective. The study found six distinct sub-types of iMCD "that were completely novel to the medical community," said Medidata's chief data officer David Lee, talking to *Pharmaceutical Technology* magazine.[1] For one group, the traditional treatment had a 65% effectiveness rate, as opposed to 19% for the other groups—an obviously huge difference. But it means that instead of talking about a drug that works in one out of five patients—out of a population of tens of thousands—you have a drug that works for three out of five patients, but with a market size an order of magnitude smaller. It's a different ballgame if you're the life sciences company trying to develop a go-to-market strategy with a more targeted therapeutic.

As Lee said, the finding shows that data management is critical. "[I]f we didn't take the time to integrate the -omic data with the clinical trial data properly then we would never have been able to find these signals no matter what types of algorithms we had used."[2]

Dr. David Fajgenbaum's Quest for a Cure

That traditional treatment, a drug called siltuximab, the only FDA-approved treatment for Castleman disease, didn't work for Dr. Fajgenbaum in his own battle. Instead, he is leading a trial for another drug, sirolimus, after experimenting on himself and finding that it has been able to keep his iMCD at bay for more than five years.[3]

Fajgenbaum documented his journey in his memoir, *Chasing My Cure: A Doctor's Race to Turn Hope into Action*, published by Random House in 2019. He was in his third year of medical school in 2010, and suddenly he was tired, sweating at night, and losing weight. He eventually went to the emergency room at the University of Pennsylvania, after taking his OB–GYN exam at school.[4] Doctors told him his liver, kidneys, and bone marrow weren't working, and, after being hospitalized, a retinal hemorrhage caused him to temporarily go blind. He was there for seven weeks before recovering, and still didn't have a diagnosis. Over the next few years, he suffered four relapses, discovering along the way that it was Castleman disease, which is diagnosed in just 5,000 people in the United States each year (about the same number as ALS, also known as Lou Gehrig's disease). Instead of becoming an oncologist, Dr. Fajgenbaum went to business school after medical school and began diving headfirst into the study of Castleman disease.

As he waded through the research—and his own personal data—he decided to take it upon himself to find a treatment that would keep him out of the hospital, or at least buy him a little time. As he told me in an interview, he examined his blood samples in the months leading up to his most recent relapse of the condition and found markers of T cell activation and blood vessel growth, measured proteins during his flare-up, and ran the data through three different pathway analysis software systems to find that everything pointed toward the mTOR intracellular signaling pathway being involved in the disease.[5]

He performed an experiment in the lab that confirmed what the databases were proposing: mTOR was activated. He went to a database of FDA-approved drugs and found the mTOR inhibitor sirolimus, which was a drug approved 25 years ago for kidney transplants, and he tried it on himself. To his surprise, it has worked—in fact, he hasn't had a relapse since starting on the drug more than five years ago.

The question Dr. Fajgenbaum is trying to answer now is whether his finding is transferable to other patients—and he is currently running a trial to figure out just that, with 24 patients whose disease has been refractory to all other therapies. Anecdotally, he has seen some good response from previous nonresponders (although some patients still haven't responded), but the right step is a legitimate trial, as he hopes to figure out if there is a particular subgroup of iMCD sufferers who will benefit from sirolimus just like he has.

One of the biggest challenges in his research, Dr. Fajgenbaum told me, is a logistical one—the data he needs is simply all in different places. Patient medical records, proteomic data, clinical trial results, and more—answers may be out there, but you get so much more when you can see different layers of the layer cake. It's the fundamental patient equation story in a nutshell: for us to see the patterns that we may finally have the ability to see, we need all of the data to be accessible. It needs to be harmonized, sortable, accurate, and complete. Not just genes alone, not just proteomics alone, not just trials alone. How well do people do when they get one drug versus another? It's a question Dr. Fajgenbaum is trying to answer, but can't always answer it well.

We've done well with some of these questions in the cancer space, Dr. Fajgenbaum explains, but with rare diseases like Castleman disease, it's harder. There are simply fewer patients, fewer sources. Ninety-five percent of the 7,000 known rare diseases don't have a single FDA-approved drug, but there are 1,500 drugs out there—like sirolimus—that might have positive effects without our even knowing it. And the only way we're going to find them is through smart analysis of trial data, real-world data, as many layers of data as we can collect. "We need to think about creative ways to leverage data," he says, "and try new approaches out on patients with no options, look for promising hits, and see if we get real results."

Dr. Fajgenbaum talks about his frustration with serum samples being stored away—samples that would have been destroyed if he hadn't rescued them to analyze for the study he did that ended up finding a subtype of patients who had a superior response to siltuximab. The reality is that for a fast-moving disease like iMCD, any insight into whether someone will be a siltuximab responder can mean the difference between life and death. Patients like him don't have three weeks to wait to see if the drug works. If their profile says they might respond, they can give the drug three to five days before starting chemotherapy, just to see—but if they're likely not going to respond, now doctors can know to start chemotherapy right away, and avoid the increased risk that the patient tanks quickly.

Armed with the siltuximab study results, Dr. Fajgenbaum now plans to return to the samples and see if he can find other possible drugs that might work. Perhaps one group will show a benefit from siltuximab, one from sirolimus, and other drugs they haven't yet tried might show positive effects with other nonresponders. But without Dr. Fajgenbaum and his motivated work, Castleman disease would likely not be on the radar screen for many, since the population is just so small.

Rare Diseases, Common Problems

There are three big problems most rare disease researchers share, Dr. Fajgenbaum tells me: funding is hard to find, sample sizes are small, and the data just isn't as useful as it should be. Researchers may be interested and capable, but samples need to be well-curated—especially when there are so few, and data is hard to come by. If there's one action item Dr. Fajgenbaum wants life sciences industry readers to take from his work, it's to unlock their samples. If we can get samples out of freezers and into the hands of researchers who care about the diseases, we have the tools now to do so much more than we used to be able to. From large-scale proteomics analysis to RNA sequencing technologies, there is so much computing power we can exploit if the samples are there.

Further, Dr. Fajgenbaum believes clinical trials have to add some of these layers in order to maximize what we can do with the results. If proteomics and transcriptomics were part of the standard trial, and if more lab tests associated with proteomics and pathways were part of the standard trial, then we could find out so much more about these patients and how we might be able to subtype them. Researchers need the most fine-grained data they can have—in the spirit of eventually figuring out how little data we really need to make the best prediction. Hidden in the data may be simple answers—but we need rich data sets at the beginning in order to find them.

The work on Castleman disease suggests that there may be other diseases that sort themselves out in a similar way, with patterns revealing responders and nonresponders, and different drugs becoming the best treatments for various subgroups. Rheumatoid arthritis, lymphoma, and HIV are just three that come to mind as sharing some features that indicate the analysis may be transferable. We can only hope to find more and more data that supports this suggestion.

I've talked throughout this section about a range of conditions being looked at successfully through the patient equation lens, and how various doctors, researchers, and life sciences companies are approaching ovulation, asthma, diabetes, the flu, sepsis, cancer, bacterial infections, and rare conditions like Castleman disease. In the next section of the book, I want to shift focus just a bit, moving us from the work already being done to the important work we in the life sciences industry can and should be doing. I want to talk about how we can all start to build our own patient equations and apply the potential of these new data technologies to our businesses. We'll examine the importance of good data and data science, and about how we approach research and clinical trials. After that, we'll look at building disease management platforms that can actually turn data into actionable insights, to get treatments out into the world and to tell if they are working, to properly motivate and incent patients, and ultimately to put ourselves in the best position to achieve economic benefits from all of this critically important work.

Notes

1. Allie Nawrat, "Castleman Disease: Can Machine Learning Help Drug Development?," Pharmaceutical Technology, February 26, 2019, https://www.pharmaceutical-technology.com/features/castleman-disease-machine-learning-cdcn-medidata/.
2. Ibid.

3. John Kopp, "Penn Doctor Makes Research Strides into His Own Rare Disease," PhillyVoice, January 24, 2019, https://www .phillyvoice.com/penn-medicine-doctor-research-strides-own-rare-disease-castleman-disease-immune-system-disorder/.
4. David Fajgenbaum, *Chasing My Cure: A Doctor's Race to Turn Hope into Action.* (Random House Publishing Group, 2019).
5. David Fajgenbaum, interview for *The Patient Equation*, interview by Glen de Vries and Jeremy Blachman, June 26, 2019.

Building Your Own Patient Equations

9 | The Steam Table

It may not be since high school physics that you've seen a steam table (see Figure 9.1), a chart of the pressures and temperatures at which water turns from liquid into gas.

If you plot these numbers on a graph, you get a view of where you are in the world, based on these pressure and temperature variables, a point that tells you, with definitiveness, whether water will be water, ice, or vapor (see Figure 9.2). You know, because you have all the information you need for the equation.

Perhaps you see where this is going. In a mathematically-idealized world, we would build that "steam table" for every condition, every disease—so that you would know who to treat, who not to treat, and what we should be treating them with based on empirical results. Using the example of PSA, prostate cancer, and radical prostatectomy—the surgical removal of the prostate—the columns of our steam table could chart PSA results, the rows could chart the patient's age, and in each box we would look at the ratio of the number of people who didn't suffer from prostate cancer versus those who did, after their prostates were or were not removed.

	Temperature (°C)				
P (bar)	0	50	150	250	350
1	−0.09	0.46			
100	−0.05	0.46	0.99	1.85	
200	−0.01	0.46	0.96	1.70	6.92
300	0.02	0.45	0.93	1.59	4.28
400	0.05	0.45	0.90	1.49	3.32
500	0.08	0.45	0.88	1.42	2.79

Pressure (atm)

Figure 9.1　A steam table

Steam tables show the amount of a substance—typically water, hence the name—that is vapor versus liquid at a given set of combinations of temperature and pressure.

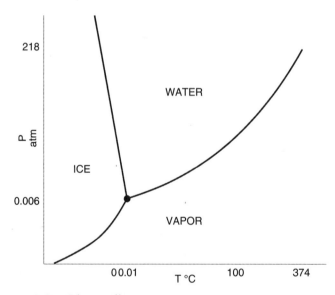

Figure 9.2　Phase diagram

Phase diagrams graphically illustrate the transition of matter from one phase to another (phase in this instance meaning liquid, solid, or gas). Illustrated here for H_2O.

This should start to sound both impractical and wildly unethical—but the concept is important. If we looked at that data, we'd find that at certain combinations of age and PSA (more advanced age, relatively low PSA numbers), treating the patient doesn't drive better outcomes than leaving them alone. That would define a set of patients we shouldn't treat. There would be another group of patients who, if we choose not to treat them (likely those with excessive PSA scores at relatively young ages), the data would show they will suffer, and perhaps die, from prostate cancer. That would start to form a shape defining the patients we should treat.

By adding a treatment alternative, say an experimental drug instead of surgery, we can add more data to the table, and start to look at the shapes forming in the diagram. Now we'll start to see shapes forming around which patients to treat with this new drug versus which patients to treat surgically (see Figure 9.3). However, the lines might not be that clear—not as crisp as those between water and steam. In fact, they probably won't be nearly as crisp in this example, because treating prostate cancer is vastly more complicated than boiling water. This is where we need to start to take these two simple ideas—the table of results (the steam table), and the graphical representation of that raw data (the phase diagram)—and open our minds and our analyses to more and more dimensions of data.

We could add the grade of the cancer based on a pathologist's examination of a tumor biopsy. Now we have a three-dimensional space, and yet another way to calculate the ratios for patients untreated or treated with different therapies. We could add a dimension for the RT-PCR for PSA assay that I worked on at Columbia in the 1990s. We could add a dimension for activity, or for patient territory. We could add even more treatment options—different kinds of surgery and drugs, experimental and not experimental.

It may sound overwhelming, but conceptually there is no change. When we move from two dimensions to three, the lines of transition become sheets. When we move to four and more dimensions, the shapes become harder to visualize—but they are still there. In the

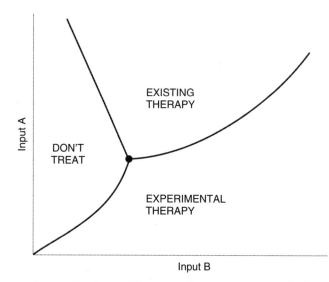

Figure 9.3   A phase diagram for treatment choices

Can the same principles visualized in a phase diagram be used to delineate the transitions between when or how a patient should be treated to receive what is computationally the best possible outcome based on existing data? This two-dimensional example is based on two biomarkers, instead of temperature and pressure from the purely chemical phase diagram in Figure 9.2. An actual phase diagram for a real disease and possible therapies would be much more complicated in structure, extending into many dimensions and likely with multiple existing and experimental therapies. But any given combination of biomarkers points to a region—or the transition between regions—corresponding to the patient equation output for the best treatment choice.

patient equation-driven future, we need to catalog our data so that we can fill in as much of the steam table as possible, and impute the rest. And we need to look for the transitions—the phase shifts—that define how to optimally treat patients.

It's more than just pressure and temperature that we need to know—and so that graph, in reality, is far more multidimensional than the one on the page. But for all of this talk about sensors and data collection, this graph is the goal. This graph is where we are headed. This graph is what we need to build in order to make more granular and accurate decisions than ever before about who to treat and how.

Our job in the life sciences industry is to make these graphs better and better, to figure out the layers that matter for every condition, the characteristics that need to be plotted, the codification of doctor's intuition, data-supported and scalable.

It's not about one good therapy—it's about putting a system in place to build all the good therapies, and then propagating them out into the real world, collecting more and more data to verify and sharpen our predictions, and ultimately generating consistent patient outcomes like we've never been able to generate before. It's an easy science experiment to see when water freezes or turns into gas—but for people it's far harder, with an uncountable number of variables, some of which matter some of the time, and some of which we don't even know exist yet.

Progressing Toward Alzheimer's Disease . . . or Maybe Not

Standing in front of a lecture hall at Columbia University not long ago, I found myself trying to establish for the audience of undergraduates and graduate students why the idea of patient equations would have such a huge impact for the future of health care. A visceral example, originally given to me by Paul Herrling of Novartis, popped into my head. It has proven to be incredibly effective—particularly with a room full of young people. It's a "good news, bad news" kind of scenario, applicable to every student in the room.

It's usually better to start with the bad news: the existence of beta-amyloid plaques—clumps of protein that are thought to clog our cognitive circuitry—has been widely debated as to its causal or coincident relationship with Alzheimer's disease.[1] However, even if their existence is merely something present in greater quantities as one progresses towards dementia, its utility as a biomarker for disease progression means that beta-amyloid plaques should be worrisome to all of us. That's the bad news for the students. There is evidence to show that even in the students' relatively young brains, the march toward dementia has begun.[2]

Were we to biochemically peer into their skulls, we'd see these beta-amyloid clumps beginning to accumulate, and, with multiple timepoints, start to be able to show that everyone in the room is already on a course that might one day result in a diagnosis of Alzheimer's disease. And at least at the time of this writing, there is no cure, nor any preventative measures. Bad news, indeed.

So what's the good news? Most of the class will die from cardio-vascular disease or cancer before that happens! (Restrained, uncomfort-able laughter is typically the result of delivering the punch line of that story, and, whether causal or coincident, the students' attention has been grabbed as far as why patient equations will be so important in the course of their own lives.)

The Alzheimer's example is one of many I can produce. As I dis-cussed in Chapter 2, before founding Medidata, I worked at Columbia, in a prostate cancer research lab. With prostate cancer, it can be the very same story. Many men over age 40 (and even by their 30s, according to some studies[3]) have detectable prostate cancer if you were to exam-ine a biopsy of their prostate glands under a microscope. They are on a path that inevitably leads to more advanced disease, ultimately toward metastatic cancer, and eventually death.

However, the studies showing this are done on men who have died of other causes. Just like in the Alzheimer's example, these cancers never progressed to the point that the individual's health or quality of life was affected. Even though—perhaps for decades—the disease was lurking inside of them.

But aside from being somewhat morbid examples to get the attention of a class, these ideas serve an important purpose as we think about how to treat patients, regardless of whether a disease is life-threatening or not. In the example of prostate cancer, with plenty of treatment options available (albeit with significant quality-of-life-impacting side effects), the studies were largely connected to concerns about overdiagnosis and overtreatment.

Almost every male over 40 reading this has probably had a PSA test. However, today, an elevated PSA alone is not enough to make treatment decisions. We need other data—other inputs to the patient equation—in order to decide how to diagnose prostate cancer. We need data to decide if the patient's prostate cancer should be treated at all.

So the fundamental question we have to answer isn't whether or not we can predict that someone is going to get these diseases. They are, and we know they are, on a long-enough time scale. The question is about the trajectory of the diseases' relative progression. We need to determine, as reliably as possible, if and when intervention—or even prevention—is worthwhile. Of course, we probably want to treat you if it turns out you're going to manifest symptoms in a year. And maybe it makes sense to treat you if you're going to manifest symptoms in 10 years. But perhaps not, if you're already 102 years old.

Some people have a genetic predisposition to get Alzheimer's disease at a young age. That's one more piece of data, one more input to the patient equation, that defines a population for which a more aggressive preventative or therapeutic course might be recommended. But for those without that predisposition, if we're probably going to manifest symptoms of Alzheimer's disease, the question is whether it's going to be when we're 72 or when we're 147.

Like many mathematical equations, it is helpful to visualize this. Figure 9.4 shows a theoretical progression of disease—Alzheimer's in this illustration, but the concept is applicable to virtually any condition. On the vertical axis is the progression toward dementia. On the horizontal axis is the progression of time. Each axis has an important cutoff point. If we cross the dotted line denoting clinically-relevant dementia before we cross the solid line denoting death, then treatment is going to be relevant for us. If we're going to die first (of something else), it's not.

The first two paths, looking left to right, belong to patients who will cross the line into dementia before they die, but the last one on the right (path B) will not—Alzheimer's won't impact that patient's life. But we don't know, right now, which path we as individuals are on. If we can figure out where on that graph we are, and what we can do, if anything, to either change that trajectory or at least get ahead of whatever treatments are out there, that would be huge progress.

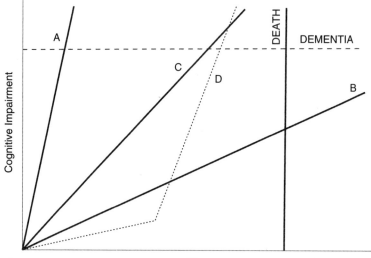

Figure 9.4   Theoretical paths for neurodegenerative disease

Looking at a plot of cognitive impairment over time, we must consider two important thresholds that a patient could cross. First, there is an impairment threshold for dementia. If the patient's impairment passes through that line, they have what is diagnosed—or at least diagnosable—as Alzheimer's disease, for example. Second, the threshold on the time axis is death, whether from the neurodegenerative condition being considered or any other cause. In this simplified illustration, a patient on path A needs therapy the most. If this were Alzheimer's, that path might be consistent with familial early-onset disease. Path B is associated with a patient who will never experience the disease in their lifetime, even though they are trending toward it. For them, treatment is not necessary, and may even be harmful in other ways. Patients on paths C and D also need therapy. The difference between the two illustrates that events along the course of our lives can change the slope of these paths. Patient D appeared for half of their life to never need therapy. Something changed (gene mutations, a cascade of phenotypic changes, their environment, or all of those) that shows why continuous monitoring is necessary if we are to best leverage patient equations.

Something all Alzheimer's researchers would agree with is that effective treatment, to truly improve lives, typically starts way too late. We need to start as early as possible—ideally, even before we're able to detect the disease clinically. We can't do that now. A preclinical diagnosis isn't something that makes any sense in the health care world today. That's where patient equations come in.

We need to be able to predict who is going to cross that line—before it happens. This is where the genetic and molecular data merges with the phenotype information we talked about in the first section of the book, the cognitive and behavioral data that may—no, almost surely will—be able to sharpen the prediction we would otherwise make about who is going to need treatment for Alzheimer's disease.

The graph in Figure 9.4 obviously simplifies things. First, I've drawn the paths as straight lines, when we don't actually know what they look like, at least not yet. Maybe they're curves, or some other shape. And we also don't know to what extent they're fixed or malleable. Maybe they change—in direction or slope, like the dotted line D, where a patient takes an unexpected and potentially explainable turn for the worse—based on exercise, based on doing crossword puzzles, based on certain medications, based on any of those layers we've already discussed. We just don't know. But the lines are a starting point. And then, in Figure 9.5, there's me. I'm headed in some direction—with some velocity—toward both of the thresholds (dementia and death), and we need to figure out which line I'm set to cross first.

With more and more data—from sensors, from traditional measures, from everything we've talked about so far in this book—we can narrow that cone of prediction, and we can plot patients with more and more accuracy. And then we can try to do something to help the patients we see headed on that path toward the dotted dementia line. The cost of treating dementia, worldwide, has been estimated by the World Health Organization at $818 billion in 2015 alone[4]—imagine the societal impact and the savings for health care systems around the world if we could catch this disease just a little earlier, a little more reliably, with a little more time to treat, across populations. Mathematical

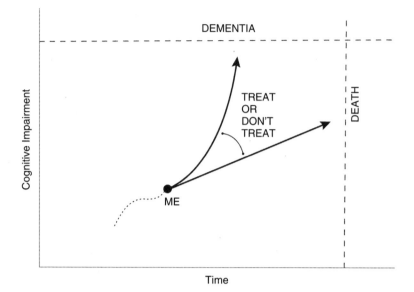

Figure 9.5   How I think about myself and cognitive impairment

The decision to treat or not to treat is illustrated here by a predictive range. Based on the path of my neurodegeneration—or likely biomarker proxies for it that we have access to now—my own patient equation will produce a range of possibilities. The better our patient equations are, with high-quality inputs for well-developed and validated predictive models, the tighter that range will be and the easier therapeutic choices will be to make. The correct placement of the dot representing the author on the *y* axis is an exercise left to the reader.

models can be powerful things. It's not like we're going to see the future. But the models, as we feed them better and better data, can give us a better chance of picking the right therapy and of making smarter decisions about care.

We'll talk more in Chapter 14 about how these kinds of patient equations can change the business models in life sciences and health care, but keep this thought in mind just for now: say I'm right there on the graph, as in Figure 9.5—no clinical symptoms of dementia. What if we could incentivize my doctors to try their best to keep me there? What if our reimbursement rules were framed by the idea that we reward doctors for patients whose diseases don't progress, and we penalize them, on a population basis, if their patients do? What if my insurer had to pay a penalty to my next insurer if I advanced at a faster rate than the data would expect? Incentives like these—once we understand these graphs better, once we have a firmer handle on the drivers of disease progression—could help shape behavior and treatment, push toward preventive care and rewards for lifestyle changes, and move the focus to keeping patients healthy instead of just treating disease once symptoms manifest themselves. Better information allows us to think far more creatively about how we structure reimbursement and the kinds of outcomes we want our health care system to drive patients toward.

Doctors are currently incentivized toward the short term, largely because the short term is all we can measure. But it's not all we'll be able to measure in the future, and that's where the power of patient equations can truly be realized.

When the Measurement and the Therapy Are One and the Same

I picked Alzheimer's disease as our example in this chapter not only because we all may be heading in that direction on the graph. The interesting thing about the lines on the graph is how malleable they may well end up being, especially if we start paying attention far sooner than we're currently able to. There are companies out there, such as Cambridge Cognition, trying to use smartphone apps to distinguish between Alzheimer's-like dementia and other memory issues that may merely be mimicking the symptoms due to depression or other mood disorders.[5] They may be able to find people on the graph who appear to be heading in one direction at a particular velocity and correct our assumptions—and then guide us toward treatment that can help resolve those particular memory issues that are being caused by something fixable.

There is also the often-maligned "science" of brain training. Lumosity, makers of a "brain training" memory game, was fined millions of dollars for claiming the game could stave off cognitive decline.[6] And yet, further research may in fact prove that there are some brain exercises we can do (perhaps not the same as those from Lumosity) that can slow the progress toward dementia, at the same time that these exercises may be able to help measure where on the curve we fall. Perhaps there is a future where doctors prescribe a set of exercises—partly to measure our state of decline, and partly to help us stop that decline in its tracks. We talked earlier in the book about using passive smartphone data—the number of times we check our schedule, for instance—to keep tabs on our cognition. It is also very possible to use active smartphone data—to require us to do something, click something, play something—to obtain cognitive biomarkers as well.

Lumosity may have shown itself unable to back up its claims, but at least one brain-training app has been shown, at least in one study, to lower the chances of developing dementia by 29% over the course of a decade.[7] BrainHQ was studied by researchers at the University of South Florida, who found that it made an impact. It is not hard to envision that, over time, we'll see more and more apps that can genuinely change the trajectory of our curves for a whole range of conditions.

Steam Tables for Cancer

Dr. Jerry Lee, a chemical engineer by training and associate professor at the University of Southern California, is the person who got me thinking about the steam table concept when it comes to patient equations and the graphing of disease. Dr. Lee deserves all of the credit here. I met him when he was working on the Cancer Moonshot, a project at the National Cancer Institute (NCI) aiming to improve our ability to prevent cancer, detect it at an early stage, and make more therapies available to more patients.[8] He was trying to obtain genomics, proteomics, and clinical phenotype information about tumor samples around the world in order to better understand—and find effective treatments for—cancers of all kinds. When he joined NCI in 2006, he told me, Dr. Lee knew that to better understand the molecular underpinnings of cancer, we needed to have more data.[9] That data, however, needed to be structured and reproducible, similar to steam tables and phase diagrams used by chemical engineers. To him, the steam table concept just made sense, to have as the ultimate goal a kind of reference table that could tell us what the drivers of cancer are, and what makes the cancer what it is. If we could create a cancer steam table, we could use it to derive phase diagrams and perhaps determine what conditions we could change in order to turn the cancer from dangerous to contained—from steam back to water, so to speak.

Dr. Lee and I talked about intensive versus extensive variables—the things that are unchanging characteristics of the cancer (intensive) versus the things that change depending on the system they're in (extensive). This is critically important, as phase diagrams require us to compare intensive properties. For example, if a liter of water at room temperature is split evenly into two cups, the resulting mass and volume is halved (extensive) but the temperature of the water remains constant (intensive). If we take a tissue sample, are we measuring something that is the same no matter whose body the cancer lives in, or are we measuring something unique to that ecosystem of cancer plus host?

This kind of thinking can lead us to better understanding what we may have some control over, from a life sciences perspective, and what is simply never going to be something we can change about that particular cancer. In cancer, few cases of truly intensive measurements exist—but some come close, including the presence of BCR-ABL fusion in chronic myeloid leukemia, or overall alterations in TP53, the gene in a patient's DNA that is responsible for causing the cancer. These changes can be found at the single cell, whole tumor, and population sample sizes. As we look at 10,000, or 100,000, or a million tissue samples, are the molecular signatures that we think mean something going to hold up as useful in finding a cure, or are they simply a function of the kinds of samples we are looking at?

By looking at these different properties, and thinking about what holds up as an intensive quality of cancer, we can start to figure out what the axes of our steam table for cancer might look like. It's not temperature and pressure that determine how we treat someone's cancer, but perhaps two of the n dimensions we might need to consider are, say, activity level and age. These are of course two good prognostic indicators of treatment outcome, but they are not the only things we need to know when trying to figure out treatment.

Primary untreated late-stage tumors are only beginning to be understood, Dr. Lee explained, and one thing he is doing is working with the Department of Defense and Department of Veterans Affairs to compare them to treatment-resistant disease over time.[10] Is there something to learn about the difference between late-stage tumors only first being discovered and late-stage tumors that have resisted prior treatment, or are these two kinds of disease always fundamentally the same? More study may reveal interesting insights that get us closer to understanding what that steam table for cancer might look like—but Dr. Lee isn't yet convinced we can get there soon. We are just starting to chip away at the multidimensionality of cancer, to find simple dimensions we can understand enough to take them off the table, and reduce the vast space that is still a black box.

The Data Problem

A huge problem in figuring out the contours of that black box—and we'll talk about this more in the next chapter—is the lack of usefulness of much of the clinical trial data we have, simply because it's not perfectly clean, or perfectly able to be integrated with the other data sources we have. Clinical trial data needs to be better leveraged, because it is our greatest hope right now for making breakthroughs and understanding the progression of disease. Dr. Lee talks about the difficulty of matching patients to each other—in trying to find similar patients who may have similar outcomes—when the data is inconsistent, or when some data comes from a real-world data set and other data emerges from a clinical trial.

There is a danger, he fears, that patients believe a clinical trial is always a better answer for them, when it's not always true that clinical trial therapy produces better outcomes than the standard of care. We forget that a good percentage of patients follow a trajectory that matches the expectations of the standard of care therapy. The big question is whether we can better identify the patients who won't follow that trajectory, the ones whose disease won't behave as we hope and expect and won't have the results with the standard of care therapy that we anticipate. Can we use data to find those patients prospectively instead of only realizing that they are outliers after the fact, when we look back on their courses of treatment and disease?

The answer for how to create our steam tables of the future, Dr. Lee emphasizes, is better data, more data, more and more of those layers of our layer cake, analyzed at a higher and higher frequency.

From Wellness to Illness—and Back Again

Another thing we can often forget as we think about steam tables and phase transitions is that it's not just the transition from wellness to illness—the initial treat-versus-don't-treat decision—that matters. It's also the transition—hopefully—back to wellness once the treatment is complete. And that is where we have a lot of work to do. How do we know when we can consider patients "cured" and back to a wellness state, especially with something like cancer? If a problem re-emerges years later, it is often very hard to figure out if it's a new-onset cancer or if it relates back in some way to the original. We don't have a good way right now of cataloging the data we need to make those judgments and build those steam tables. It's easy to think about, but not so easy to put into practice.

Similarly, we need to look at more and more patient data to understand the interaction of cancer with other diseases. What we do to treat a tumor may be different if a patient also has heart disease, or diabetes, or a neurodegenerative illness, and the lasting effects of treatment on those other conditions is also poorly understood right now. What it means to be sick with a certain condition, like cancer, may mean different things depending on what other comorbidities a patient faces—and all of this is a mystery right now, at least in terms of having some standard protocol and some standard set of expectations around what a patient's course will look like.

Dr. Lee compares the state of where we are right now to scientists in the sixteenth century thinking about the orbits of planets, based on discussions he's had in the past with Dr. Larry Norton of Memorial Sloan Kettering Cancer Center in New York City. As Dr. Norton has shared with Dr. Lee, there was documented data—all kinds of it—but it never really matched the motion of the planets perfectly until Johannes Kepler put it all together and realized that the orbits weren't spherical, they were elliptical—and then suddenly it all made sense. The data just needed to be looked at from a slightly different angle. That's where we are now. We are continuing to amass the data, but we haven't yet had the mindset shift that we need. And it won't come from an artificial intelligence system, but from humans looking at it differently, figuring out what they can see that no one else has seen, what we don't know yet that can explain things that we still have so much trouble explaining. The steam tables exist—we simply haven't figured them out yet.

So how do we figure out our patient equations? How do we start to move from this magic—this big black box of mysteries about disease and disease progression and the best treatments for the right patients at the right time—to a world that we can understand as easily as we can understand how to turn water into steam?

The answer, as Dr. Lee suggests, is data—but good data, matching data, useful data as the starting point for turning patient experiences into knowledge, for turning anecdotes and ideas into provable reality, into the spaces in our steam table that are just question marks right now. One thing Dr. Lee is doing is working with the Department of Defense and the Department of Veterans Affairs to create a learning health care framework that includes molecular, phenotypic, and real-world data in a longitudinal fashion.[11] Systems have to speak to each other. Data has to work. In a lot of ways, that's my story at Medidata, and it's what the next chapter is about.

Notes

1. Simon Makin, "The Amyloid Hypothesis on Trial," *Nature* 559, no. 7715 (July 2018): S4–S7, https://doi.org/10.1038/d41586-018-05719-4.
2. Alaina Baker-Nigh et al., "Neuronal Amyloid-β Accumulation within Cholinergic Basal Forebrain in Ageing and Alzheimer's Disease," *Brain* 138, no. 6 (March 1, 2015): 1722–37, https://doi.org/10.1093/brain/awv024.
3. Sahil Gupta et al., "Prostate Cancer: How Young Is Too Young?," *Current Urology* 9, no. 4 (2015): 212–215, https://doi.org/10.1159/000447143.
4. "Dementia," World Health Organization, December 12, 2017, https://www.who.int/news-room/fact-sheets/detail/dementia.
5. "Alzheimer's Disease," Cambridge Cognition, 2014, https://www.cambridgecognition.com/cantab/test-batteries/alzheimers-disease/.
6. Joanna Walters, "Lumosity Fined Millions for Making False Claims about Brain Health Benefits," *The Guardian*, January 6, 2016, https://www.theguardian.com/technology/2016/jan/06/lumosity-fined-false-claims-brain-training-online-games-mental-health.
7. Eric Wicklund, "Mobile Health App Helps Seniors Reduce Their Risk For Dementia," *mHealthIntelligence*, November 27, 2017, https://mhealthintelligence.com/news/mobile-health-app-helps-seniors-reduce-their-risk-for-dementia.
8. "CCR Cancer Moonshot Projects," Center for Cancer Research, February 14, 2018, https://ccr.cancer.gov/research/cancer-moonshot.
9. Jerry Lee, interview for *The Patient Equation*, interview by Glen de Vries and Jeremy Blachman, May 6, 2019.
10. Jerry S. H. Lee et al., "From Discovery to Practice and Survivorship: Building a National Real-World Data Learning Healthcare Framework for Military and Veteran Cancer Patients," *Clinical Pharmacology & Therapeutics* 106, no. 1 (April 29, 2019): 52–57, https://doi.org/10.1002/cpt.1425.
11. Ibid.

10 | Good Data

In building models that work, good data management and system infrastructure are the costs of entry; there is just no way around it. Machine learning and artificial intelligence are nice buzzwords, but you need humans to set the systems up, write the rules, figure out what kinds of data need to be collected in the first place, and work to get it all "fit for purpose" from an analytic point of view. Systems have to speak to each other—in a way that produces useful output and not merely garbage. There are so many examples of bad data out there, and lessons to learn—from the Mars Lander and from the failure of IBM Watson in the oncology area, to name two well-publicized disasters.

But even though those situations tell us what can go wrong, that knowledge doesn't, on its own, get us to something that will go right. I've been working in this area for my entire adult life, and I know data. I know what happens when it's not aggregated, standardized, and analyzed the way it needs to be to produce useful insights—and I know its power when the pieces are all properly in place.

The Failure of Watson

IBM's Watson supercomputer was supposed to revolutionize cancer treatment. A 2013 article in *Wired* announced, "IBM's Watson is better at diagnosing cancer than human doctors," that it had "a breadth of knowledge no human doctor can match," and that it had a "successful diagnosis rate for lung cancer [of] 90 percent, compared to 50 percent for human doctors."[1]

Five years later, the headlines were very different. Watson was recommending "unsafe and incorrect" cancer treatments, according to a report by *STAT*.[2] According to *Becker's Hospital Review*'s reporting on the *STAT* investigation, internal documents from IBM admitted that Watson was trained on "just a few hypothetical cancer cases instead of real patient data," was making recommendations that "conflicted with national treatment guidelines and that physicians did not find useful," and that the product was "very limited."[3]

A year after that report, IBM claims to be making "progress,"[4] but the system is more like a "librarian"[5] than a clinician, and simply hasn't shown the capacity for drawing novel conclusions that was promised initially. It is, as all artificial intelligence has thus far shown itself to be, only as good as the data originally entered into the system.

The Mars Climate Orbiter

On December 11, 1998, NASA launched the Mars Climate Orbiter, a $125 million robotic space probe intended to study the Martian atmosphere. Less than a year later, on September 23, 1999, communication with the orbiter was lost just as it made its way into Mars's atmosphere. It flew closer to the planet's surface than intended and was destroyed—an accident caused entirely by a mistake in the data.[6] One piece of software was calculating in English units—pounds of force—while another piece of software was analyzing that output assuming it was in metric units—newtons.[7] The result? The orbiter flew drastically off course and was torn apart by atmospheric friction. A "math error," announced the *Los Angeles Times* headline a week after the incident—but it wasn't exactly math, it was a $125 million example of what happens when two data sets aren't able to communicate with each other.[8]

At Medidata, we see this all the time. We look at client data from clinical trials and sometimes there are points that are such extreme outliers that we know something is wrong. Take a height-weight plot, for instance. Enter one person's data in centimeters instead of inches, grams instead of pounds, and suddenly he looks like the largest patient in the world. It's the most basic kind of data collection, but it's absolutely critical. As we dose some medications based on an individual's size, it can be downright dangerous if no one catches the error.

And it's not just numbers we're talking about. We're capturing complex data structures like medical images as well. Imagine the sheer complexity of a single MRI. Each scan is composed of dozens of "slices" (cross-sections of the body), each slice actually the combination and assembly of multiple images. If you've ever taken a high ISO (image sensitivity) photograph with a digital single-lens reflex camera, you are probably familiar with the problem of noise. Static can get in the way of a clear, crisp image. The multiple images that are combined to form each MRI slice are like long-exposure photographs with that same digital camera—they reduce noise.

Of course, digital SLRs are rapidly being replaced by the cameras in our phones, with greater and greater image quality, and increasingly less noise getting in the way. Our phones do it with multiple cameras and computational photography techniques that combine the images from all of them into one. In many ways, it is just like an MRI: all that complexity for a single slice. Then, we can assemble multiple slices into three-dimensional images, or examine them to determine the size of a tumor. Only after all of this image processing does the data from an MRI become useful for diagnosis.

But it's not even useful enough for perfect diagnosis on its own. The MRI is only one test at one point in time that needs to be combined with all of the other data for a particular patient. We need systems that can ingest all of this data, the lab values, the images, the velocity vectors, the DNA sequences, proteomics, the ways we use our phones to check our calendars—all of the varied sources of patient equation inputs that we've talked about already—and manage the analysis, harnessing the bits of information that will help determine where we are in the phase diagrams of health. As we look at more and more complex therapies, and more complex forms of data, we need to take all the raw bits and bytes and turn them into useful information. Data can't analyze itself. The information needs to be demystified, standardized, linked together, and have the right algorithms applied to it. The job of data management done well makes the data complete, clean, and fit for the purposes of what we want that data to help us do.

The Progression to Value

No matter how sophisticated the systems used to model our health and guide our medical care are now or will be in the future, they will at their core be based on statistics and computer science. These are two disciplines where the principle of garbage in/garbage out clearly applies.

We can think of the progression toward the beneficial application of data to a specific problem as a series of steps. David Lee, Medidata's chief data officer, was the first person to teach me about the importance of data standardization and a step-wise approach to creating value from that data. There is an absolutely critical chain of events that needs to unfold before analyses can generate true benefit. Capturing the data is obviously the first step. But disciplined data management that follows the raw capture is critical—and nontrivial—if you want to eventually derive an actual benefit from the information. Figure 10.1 shows graphically how David originally explained it to me.

The captured data must first be cleaned. We need to make sure that units are consistent and that whatever capture and integration systems we have employed (keeping in mind the potential errors from human processes, disconnected systems, and imperfect human programming)

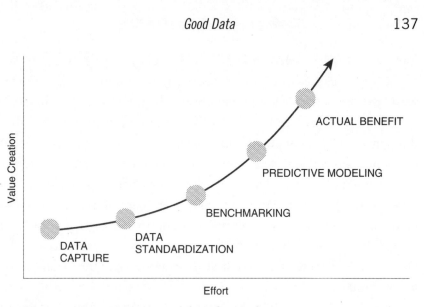

Figure 10.1 Creating value from data

have resulted in a set of data we can feel confident in. Let us not forget the lessons of the Mars Climate Orbiter!

This problem of integrating and cleaning research data in a medically and scientifically rigorous way, incidentally, is what led to the founding of Medidata in the 1990s. Working at Columbia, I saw how difficult it was to both capture and integrate data. I was certainly one of the fallible humans in the system, though I was trying my best. I remember in one case, there were lab and pathology data available in a particular hospital system, but we didn't have a terminal for it in the research building where I worked. My "data capture" process involved two elevators and crossing a street. And a handwritten laboratory notebook, of course.

This may sound like a hyperbolic anecdote from a quarter century ago, but it is still true that there are disconnected systems in our lives, and data sets that don't share a common vocabulary. It is a problem that people like Jerry Lee and so many others are still trying to solve today.

Back then, the deficiencies were even clearer. In 1994, I was sharing a lab bench with Ed Ikeguchi, a resident in the urology department. We became fast friends, sharing common interests in computer science, inventing and making things, and exploring the emerging world of the

Internet. If you have ever worked in a laboratory, or even taken a lab class as part of a chemistry or biology course, you are undoubtedly familiar with how much time you can end up spending with your benchmate.

As we worked on our respective research, spying each other through a wall of test tubes and reagents, we had plenty of time to talk. Inevitably we would find ourselves lamenting the systems used for research, and how much human work was involved in transcribing and transporting data. At the time, virtually every clinical trial in the world used paper—just like my adventure crossing the street to get data and bring it back to my lab. But this was happening on a much larger scale. Data would be copied from medical charts onto paper forms, and those forms would be carried by hand, or sent—sometimes by mail, or in the most "modern" trials in the 1990s, by facsimile machines. It would then be typed into databases—not once, but twice, in an attempt to avoid yet another opportunity for transcription error.

We looked at the world of academic research, as well as industry, and the original glimmer in our eyes that would become Medidata started with a conversation about using the Internet to replace all of that work, and to facilitate far more automated data cleaning and integration. I think the question "If you can buy a book online, why can't we run trials online?" may have started it all.

It would take a few more years for us to meet Tarek Sherif and start Medidata Solutions, Inc. But in the intervening time, we began to build out some rough software ourselves, eventually creating a corporation that would end up as Medidata's precursor, and opening an "office" by moving my bed into my living room—making my one-bedroom apartment into an incredibly small studio living space.

Thinking constantly about online research—and not sure at that point if a life at the lab bench (my original career plan) was the right thing for me—I was incredibly lucky to find an opportunity to work on an electronic medical records project emerging in our department. It was right at the nexus of my interest in computers and my interest in research, and it was there that I learned valuable lessons around the standardization and benchmarking of data—or, more honestly, about the lack of value generated when data is not standardized, making benchmarking impossible.

Carl Olsson, a great mentor and the chair of our department—along with strong support from his team of admirably forward-looking physicians and scientists—wanted to install an electronic medical records system that would allow us to perform research projects much more quickly and effectively than the current system allowed. The grand idea was to connect research data across all of the physicians working in the department.

Unfortunately, the project was a failure. There were issues, as there often are, with technology not working as well as we had hoped, and—albeit at a relatively early point in my career—I take my share of responsibility with regard to how we managed through it. However, the greatest problem we had was with how the various members of the department wanted to record their data. Replacing paper medical charts and dictated notes—with their inherent lack of structure—was an incredibly difficult challenge to overcome. Even technologies today, like Natural Language Processing (NLP), that are meant to find structure in unstructured data (and chart notes are often cited as a perfect use case for them) can't solve some of the problems we saw back then.

Different physicians—in some cases working on the same disease, in the same building, even in the same office—had very different mental models for measuring disease progression in their patients. In theory, we could have built a common data model, but the practical reality was that doctors weren't going to reinvent their thought processes in order to use it.

Compounding the problem was the fact that most electronic health records software systems—and this still applies even today—aren't designed for research, but for the business of practice management and billing. In hindsight, our inability to create that research core was inevitable. Allowing people to record data as they saw fit and were most naturally inclined to do, without common data models and processes, meant that we couldn't easily compare the data from one patient to another. We failed at data standardization. And therefore we couldn't launch into those imagined comparisons across patients and across practices. We couldn't use benchmarks. We couldn't scale research.

As we look back at the progression toward value in Figure 10.1, it really is the case that only after we are satisfied that we have high-quality data, standardized and benchmarked, that we can unlock the higher levels of value creation. Then, finally, we can take that—the "core" we tried to achieve at Columbia—and begin to not just perform more traditional statistical analyses at scale, but also to leverage machine learning and predictive modeling to create actual benefit.

We can start to predict—to rewrite the history of my electronic medical records experience—which patients will benefit the most from which therapies. And we can do that with algorithms built on the fact that we can compare—benchmark—those patients we are trying to predict for against the global set of patients who have been treated before them, and who are like them based on biology, physiology, and behavior.

As you grasp how fundamental this progression is in data science—as fundamental as gravity is to physics—an incredibly important aspect of scaling data science emerges. You can see that the relationship between effort and value is not linear as you advance through the progression of milestones. Cleaning and standardizing data is hard. It took Dr. David Fajgenbaum years to collect data, months for Medidata to work with his team to clean and standardize it, and ultimately just minutes to run the algorithms used to subtype Castleman disease patients. Artificial intelligence algorithms create huge value, they are what will power so much of our future, and they are the part of the process that—if you are a scientist—is truly sexy. But they don't work without tremendous effort to make sure that they are built on the right foundations. Much as we remember the failed Mars probe, the argument can be made that we can see this lesson in the business failure of Watson for cancer treatment recommendations.

Once the data is robust, accurate, and reliable, we can expand our thinking into more creative uses for it, especially as applied specifically to the world of clinical trials, which is where we turn in the next chapter.

As I've learned more and more about what our clients are trying to achieve, I've realized how much more we can do to build upon what a standard clinical trial has looked like for a generation. To take data from one trial and use it in another—synthetic controls—or to adjust trials on the fly based on the results—adaptive trials—can make it orders of magnitude easier (and cheaper) to gain new knowledge.

And, once we incorporate this new clinical trial knowledge with our advancements in understanding behavioral and cognitive phenotypes, as well as all of the other layers of data we've discussed in the book thus far, we can empower the life sciences industry with enough information to create medications and treatments with more and more specificity, and ultimately make real gains for patients, ones that were impossible to envision when I first started on my own data journey a quarter of a century ago.

Notes

1. Ian Steadman, "IBM's Watson Is Better at Diagnosing Cancer than Human Doctors," *Wired UK*, February 11, 2013, https://www.wired.co.uk/article/ibm-watson-medical-doctor.
2. Casey Ross and Ike Swetlitz, "IBM's Watson Supercomputer Recommended 'Unsafe and Incorrect' Cancer Treatments, Internal Documents Show," *STAT*, 2018, https://www.statnews.com/wp-content/uploads/2018/09/IBMs-Watson-recommended-unsafe-and-incorrect-cancer-treatments-STAT.pdf.
3. Julie Spitzer, "IBM's Watson Recommended 'Unsafe and Incorrect' Cancer Treatments, STAT Report Finds," *Becker's Hospital Review*, July 25, 2018, https://www.beckershospitalreview.com/artificial-intelligence/ibm-s-watson-recommended-unsafe-and-incorrect-cancer-treatments-stat-report-finds.html.
4. Heather Landi, "IBM Watson Health Touts Recent Studies Showing AI Improves How Physicians Treat Cancer," FierceHealthcare, June 4, 2019, https://www.fiercehealthcare.com/tech/ibm-watson-health-says-ai-making-progress-clinical-decision-support-for-cancer-care.
5. Eliza Strickland, "How IBM Watson Overpromised and Underdelivered on AI Health Care," *IEEE Spectrum: Technology, Engineering, and Science News*, April 2, 2019, https://spectrum.ieee

.org/biomedical/diagnostics/how-ibm-watson-overpromised-and-underdelivered-on-ai-health-care.

6. Robert Lee Hotz, "Mars Probe Lost Due to Simple Math Error," *Los Angeles Times*, October 1999, https://www.latimes.com/archives/la-xpm-1999-oct-01-mn-17288-story.html.

7. Lisa Grossman, "Nov. 10, 1999: Metric Math Mistake Muffed Mars Meteorology Mission," *Wired*, November 10, 2010), https://www.wired.com/2010/11/1110mars-climate-observer-report/.

8. Robert Lee Hotz, "Mars Probe Lost Due to Simple Math Error."

11

Changing Clinical Trials

The way we run clinical trials hasn't changed significantly in decades. Yes, we're doing things online instead of on paper, and, yes, most organizations are starting to be open to new types of measurements, in the home instead of in the clinic, with wearables and other new-generation devices, and, sure, there is a growing sense that we can enhance the data set with new approaches and ideas.

But it is still early days, and trials are still on the fringes of the data revolution—for now, partly because of the huge expense involved in launching a trial—and thus the fear of taking an expensive risk on the unknown—and partly because there hasn't been much reason or industry impetus to move trial design, trial collection, or trial access forward. That has to change. It's that simple.

To reach the full potential that these new patient equations offer, clinical trials need to evolve. And they need to evolve in three ways. We need to change the way patients find and participate in trials (what people call "access"), we need to become comfortable collecting new kinds of data in new ways (going all the way in terms of scale from DNA to behavior and our environment), and we need to move to new mathematical designs. We need to innovate with new trial frameworks and techniques that will help us more effectively discover the inputs and outputs of the equations that will lead to maximum benefit for patients. In this chapter, we cover all of these issues in depth.

Expanding Access to Trials

According to the *New York Times*, fewer than 5% of adult cancer patients in America enroll in clinical trials, when greater rates would likely save lives—not just the lives of patients who enroll but the lives of future generations who would benefit from the increased research opportunities.[1] And while part of the reason is the necessary eligibility requirements of certain research studies, it is also the case that patients aren't always (or even often) steered toward trials that might benefit them, or made aware that even those who will not receive the study drug will still receive the same standard of care treatment that they would outside the trial—and for free.

The *New York Times* piece pushes for clinical trial navigators to help patients find the trials that might benefit them most—but the education needs to spread throughout the health care system, with many clinicians needing just as much information and guidance as patients. While it is true that trials won't help everyone—another *New York Times* article cites numbers above 90% as the failure rate of precision medicine studies—it's also the case that the patients in these trials are generally the ones whose diseases have proven most resistant to standard treatments—and the only way to improve these numbers is going to be with further trial research.[2]

One advocate who has been fighting for increased trial access for years is T. J. Sharpe, who was diagnosed with stage 4 melanoma in 2012. "I was originally diagnosed with stage 1b melanoma that I had removed when I was 25 years old, and then 12 years later I get diagnosed with stage 4. . . . [M]y son was only 4 weeks old at the time," Sharpe told *CURE* magazine, a consumer publication focused on cancer.[3]

Faced with his diagnosis—and an oncologist telling him he'd be surprised if Sharpe survived even two years—Sharpe sought out immunotherapy trials, and after one failed trial, he tried again—and after years on the drug Keytruda, has been cancer-free since August 2017.[4] I talked to Sharpe, and he emphasized how difficult it still is for patients to even be referred to trials.[5] Since diagnosis, he has worked as a patient advocate and consultant to the research industry, and emphasizes the need for more information—and more tools, for doctors and patients.

Run by the National Institutes of Health (NIH), ClinicalTrials.gov is a publicly available resource that describes itself as "a database of privately and publicly funded clinical studies conducted around the world."[6] I receive emails and calls regularly from those who have received unfortunate diagnoses (or know people who have), and see me as their connection to the clinical trial industry. They have heard about the potential to access cutting-edge therapies through clinical trials, and they want advice about what trials they might be candidates for, and which might be of the highest potential benefit to them. ClinicalTrials.gov is inevitably the tool I use to respond. It is not, however, without its flaws.

"ClinicalTrials.gov is not a user-friendly tool, and wasn't really intended to be," T. J. Sharpe explains. "It was designed to be a repository for results, but it's being used to find trials because right now it's the only way. . . . There often isn't a clear way to find the right trials for the patient, to match their health with the criteria in the database, to evaluate whether it might work well for them."

Sharpe sees three primary problems with the current system: access to general knowledge about clinical trials, access to a useful database that can effectively match the right trial to the right person at the right time, and access to understandable results. "How do you evaluate apples to apples?" he asks. "If you have three different companies announcing trial results that all show efficacy, how can you compare them, when they might all have different endpoints, different populations, and more?"

Recalling our phase-diagram ideal of matching the right patient to the right therapy at the right time, Sharpe is highlighting the problem that there is no view into the available set of clinical trials that gets us anywhere close. There's no way to see where an individual might map across the necessary dimensions to be effectively matched to the selection of therapies that could treat them. Of course, we might not know yet if a particular experimental therapy will work for a given individual. That's why we do the research. However, even seeing where those potential matches might be—in one comprehensive, organized, accessible place—could help trial volunteers have the best possible chance of finding something that might cure or slow the progression of their disease.

It's not just patients who don't have the information they need to compare trials—it's physicians, too. There's no guide to interpretation, no way to separate out subsets of the population so someone can see how a particular trial worked for patients like them—with similar genetics, general health, and comorbidities. There are simply not enough meaningful insights being generated from the data and exposed to either practitioners or patients.

Sharpe sees the patient equation challenge as a big one right now. The data is in many different silos, and the industry isn't as motivated to evolve as he would have hoped. Being patient-centric is a buzzword, he fears, but doesn't actually translate into creating trial designs that let patients compare one drug to another, or figure out what trial might be best. His hope is that the life sciences companies will start to understand this and see that it is better business to get effective and actionable information to patients and doctors, and enable patients to become better advocates for themselves.

What might that translate into, from a practical perspective? Sharpe imagines a trusted source of trial information—far more user-friendly than the ClinicalTrials.gov site—where life sciences companies and other health care providers can contribute to creating a one-stop shop for patients, doctors, and researchers. If someone gets a new diagnosis, they or their doctor could log on and figure out what knowledge is out there, what the latest therapies are, what possible trials exist, and what the results along the range of therapies have been, not just for patients in general but for patients as similar to our new diagnosee as possible.

Pharma's Lack of Connection to Clinical Care

Alicia Staley is Medidata's senior director of patient engagement and a three-time cancer survivor in her thirtieth year of survivorship. Staley was diagnosed with Hodgkin's lymphoma as a young adult, and then breast cancer in both 2004 and 2008. She agrees with T. J. Sharpe's take on the industry, and believes that pharma's lack of connection to clinical care is a primary source of the difficulty.[7] "For too long," Staley says, "pharma has operated in one lane and clinical care in another—with no crossover between the two." This is confusing for patients, Staley argues, and holds back the ability of researchers to recruit patients into trials and then keep them in the clinical research system. It is all transactional—there is no long-term relationship building, not with patients, not with patient advocates, and not with the health care industry at large.

In fact, it's too often the case that even doctors don't really know how clinical trials work. It's simply not relevant to most of their professional lives and what they do day to day. This ought to change if we want true industry collaboration. The current lack of such collaboration plays out at every level, from education to treatment. Staley believes the life sciences industry needs to realize that patient education and the creation of long-term relationships with advocacy groups helps them—not just when it comes to selling them the next blockbuster drug, but for trial recruitment and data collection, and to truly get us on the road toward richer disease models. Just like Sharpe argues, Staley insists the data is far too siloed and that there needs to be cooperation. "The value isn't in data blocking or data hoarding," says Staley, "because data that isn't being analyzed, shared, and used productively has no value. Data without action is valueless."

And yet, Staley sees all kinds of things happening in the world of clinical trials that don't serve patients at all, particularly doctors refusing to share trial opportunities with patients just because they're based at another health system. Clinical trials are operated around physicians who are chosen to be the "investigators" in each individual study. If a physician thinks that a study might help a particular patient, but it's not a study that physician is an investigator in, the process will include a referral to a study investigator. That means the patient's treatment will be with another doctor, possibly at a different facility, and perhaps in a different health care system. The patient may benefit, but the doctor and hospital may lose a paying customer. This can unfortunately create disincentives for referrals out of the system. "You think it's about the loss of a potential revenue stream, but it can actually turn out to be the loss of a life," Staley laments.

Unlike Sharpe, who sees the most promise in a technological solution to educate patients—the perfect trials database—Staley worries that an overreliance on technology can leave out lots of patients, at least right now, who aren't plugged in. "The industry needs to meet the patient where they are," she says. At the same time, she sees a huge place for technology in collecting richer sets of patient data—as long as someone is listening to the signal. To instrument patients, "so that they can walk through life throwing off valuable data nuggets," Staley says, "makes it easier for patients to live their lives, to avoid being constrained by constantly visiting doctors and wasting time."

There's a mindset shift that needs to happen throughout the industry, Staley says, and it's the same kind of shift I talked about earlier, where patient equations can move us from a reactive system to a proactive one. Can we build systems that aren't just addressing things that have already happened, but can in fact educate patients even before there's a diagnosis? Can we instrument people to catch things earlier, when there are more treatment options, or to tell that a patient is becoming refractory to their treatment before it's too late?

"Pharma is still a mature industry that can make a lot of money without changing much," Staley fears, "but they have to realize that by collaborating with patients, with advocates, with the health care industry, and with each other, they can really make a bigger difference in people's lives."

Truly Patient-centric Trials

The frustrations expressed by both Sharpe and Staley—about the difficulties of finding trials and navigating the problem of access—stem from a particular cause: trials are designed around investigators, not around patients. This is not an accusation against those who design, sponsor, and (like me) help to run them. It is a practical limitation, imposed by important scientific and regulatory requirements. Trials are, by definition, experiments. They need to be controlled—by which I'm referring not just to the usual controls where some patients receive a new drug and others receive some standard of care or placebo treatment, but also controlled in terms of consistency.

If some aspect of care is inconsistently handled for different patients in a study, it can create a confounding effect as far as determining whether or not a particular treatment is beneficial. In any good scientific endeavor, it is always easier—and by definition more reliable—to keep as many variables as consistent as possible. The worst case is an inconsistent variable that isn't part of the ultimate analysis. It's just creating the potential for inaccurate results. Keeping a trial limited to a particular set of investigators, through whom you know that the protocol will be executed consistently (meaning that the treatments and tests that define how the therapies will be evaluated for safety, efficacy, and value to the patient will be reliably performed and recorded) is a way to meet our ethical obligation to create a valuable result.

There are also regulatory requirements, sensibly and responsibly imposed by organizations like the FDA, to ensure that the protocol is being followed consistently. Experimental medications can often lead to unknown and dangerous side effects. The data sets that are produced in studies are not only the summation of the outcomes for the volunteer subjects, but they are also the information regulators use to make assessments for approvals.

Imagine a typical phase III trial, comparing a new medicine to the current standard of care, hoping for results that lead to drug approval. Not only are lives at stake for the hundreds of patients in the study, but also for the thousands, tens of thousands, and tens of millions more future patients for whom that drug may or may not be available down the road. Care is absolutely required to ensure the most reliable result, and that care is achieved through the current investigator-centric paradigm.

But that doesn't mean it's the only possible approach. The technologies and connectivity that are enabling so many of the therapeutic breakthroughs and new measurements in today's world might also be able to change the way we structure trials. Perhaps we can flip the current approach on its head and make studies truly patient-centric. Efforts like these are happening as we speak.

Anthony Costello is senior vice president, Mobile Health at Medidata and leads our involvement in the ADAPTABLE trial (Aspirin Dosing: A Patient-Centric Trial Assessing Benefits and Long-Term Effectiveness), a real-world trial that brings the study to the patient instead of the other way around, sponsored by the Patient-Centered Outcomes Research Institute (PCORI). In an interview, Costello talked about the study's transformative approach to recruitment—patients who receive their care at a PCORnet site (The National Patient-Centered Clinical Research Network, covering more than 68 million patients nationwide[8]) are identified through their electronic medical records, and sent an invitation with a code (a "golden ticket") that allows them to log onto the study website and sign up to participate.[9]

This is the beginning of how the study turns on its head the entire idea of how we recruit for trials. Instead of finding investigators who then try to find participants, here the participants are effectively the ones who enroll themselves—and in this case, thanks to the power of a huge network of physicians, they are prescreened in advance to make sure they meet the study criteria, and provided with everything needed for them to enroll and participate. A virtual site is created around them.

ADAPTABLE, and other virtual trials like it, prove that you don't need a site to be the center of recruiting and treatment. These kinds of studies will continue to proliferate and become more of a normal practice in the future—and make everyone in the system better off, thanks to technology.

The patient's burden is lowered, certainly—they don't have to travel to clinics as often, and the study is easier to maintain as part of their daily lives. Anecdotally, ADAPTABLE has surprisingly high engagement rates, with patients compliant with the needs of the study and fewer of them dropping out, a huge problem in many studies. Costello thinks that the reason is at least partly because of how easy it is for patients to participate under this virtual model.

The companies conducting the research (or, in the case of PCORI and ADAPTABLE, the nonprofit organization conducting it) also benefit. Costs for recruiting go down, and time to recruit goes down as well. ADAPTABLE has 15,000 patients participating, a number that would be orders of magnitude harder to achieve in a traditional trial.

The outputs of the study are better as well. It's easier to get the kind of continuous monitoring previously discussed.

But this isn't an all-or-nothing option for conducting studies. Instead of patients having to travel to a physician's office for every data point to be collected in a particular study, they can be given the option to go to a pharmacy with a mini-clinic, or to a local laboratory for a blood draw. Drug supplies can be shipped to their homes. Perhaps they will go to that physician's office for an initial screening, for key check-in points, and to close out their treatment. But any chance to move even part of a study to the virtual environment—and relieve participant burden—should be taken advantage of.

Within the next five years, I expect we'll see almost every clinical trial taking advantage of virtual trial designs. Some trials will be entirely virtual—like ADAPTABLE—but more likely we'll see a bimodal distribution (two prominent peaks, if we were to plot it on a graph) where most trials are either 20% virtual or 80% virtual. The former category will largely be in cases where patients are critically ill, or the therapies are complex to administer. We'll need them to be in the clinic more, and they may even want to be there, but there will be quality-of-life adjustments by using the virtual space to make certain aspects easier.

The 80% peak will be for chronic conditions or for easily administered medications and evaluations of progression. These studies will contain elements that can be performed at home, at pharmacies, or with nurse practitioners visiting people at home, in addition to—as mentioned—perhaps a visit or two to a clinic to screen the patient, enroll and train them on whatever they need to know for the study, and then to close out their participation at the end of their course of therapy.

These kinds of virtual trials are coming at a time when the life sciences industry needs to evolve more than ever. With increasingly precise medicines, the math tells us that the number of patients who will benefit from each medicine goes down. Finding the right patient for a breakthrough precision medicine is harder than finding the right patient for a medication designed to be more broadly administered. Thus, finding the right candidates (able, willing, and appropriate) for research projects becomes an even harder problem to solve.

Accepting New Kinds of Data

The second big piece of the trial discussion is that life sciences companies need to continue moving in the direction of broader data capture, from wearables and mobile devices to genetic sequencing and the retaining of biospecimens. Richer, broader data in trials means better analysis. The more variables there are, the more likely we can find the meaningful ones.

Tarek Sherif, my co-founder and co-CEO at Medidata, talked to *Pharma Times* about this very issue back in 2016. "Historically in clinical trials," he said, "we have collected more or less subjective data through diaries, paper . . . or by getting patients to come in to the clinic and do a test. These supposedly measure the efficacy of a treatment, but you are taking a snapshot in time."[10]

Indeed, those snapshots in time don't come close to the kind of objective data we can now get with better and more advanced patient instrumentation. We can now come closer than ever before to analyzing real-world experience than merely a test result in a clinic. We can see what a patient's mobility is like, changes in step count during a trial, sleep data, and more. And while back in 2016 companies were starting to do electronic clinical trials, few were really committing to the idea of wearable trials.

Things have improved since 2016, but not by enough. And even as we see more and more wearables being incorporated—from Fitbits to Apple Watches—we still don't see sensors in trials across the board. Genetic panels are regularly being utilized in oncology and other therapeutic areas, but we don't see full gene sequencing across all studies, or the kinds of proteomics that proved so powerful for David Fajgenbaum and the Castleman Disease Collaborative Network.

Kara Dennis, Medidata's former managing director of mobile health—and one of the smartest thinkers I know about new technology in clinical trials—spoke to me about her take on these developments early on in the process of conceiving this book. "It will take some time for pharma to move away from the well-validated, well-proven measures that they've used for lots of patients over many years, but we are absolutely seeing the early steps, the process of validating the quality and usefulness of wearable data in studies," Dennis told me.[11]

The biggest challenges with digital data, she explains, are the quality of the sensors themselves, and whether subjects can use them properly. "Even with something as simple as a thermometer, the subjects may not be good enough at using it themselves, and there may be a difference between a clinician taking these measurements and subjects doing it on their own." The other problem is compliance. "What kind of infrastructure do we need?" Dennis asks. "Will patients remember to use the device? Will they leave it on when they're supposed to, charge it, wear it at night if they're supposed to, or in the shower?"

As these issues recede into the background—as wearables are more and more accurate, and function with less and less potential for user error (implantables, etc.)—the hope is that pharma will become more comfortable using them. An industry analyst at Gartner has said, "Seismic shifts in this market will not happen until the pharmaceutical lobby has confidence in the underlying systems supporting wearables, and that means that clinical validation expertise for wearables must improve."[12]

But the digital clinical trial is, fortunately, becoming more of a reality as time passes and knowledge and comfort grow, making trials more accurate, more efficient, and more patient-friendly than ever before. We can use technology to remove physical barriers, geographic barriers, and temporal barriers that all make launching and completing a study more challenging and more expensive. Between video calling to connect patients, doctors, and researchers and the landscape of wearables, patients can be full trial participants without leaving their homes, and researchers can still get complete and accurate information, images, and data.

It's one thing—albeit an important thing, without a doubt—to move trials into the twenty-first century by accepting new technologies and data collection tools. It's an even bigger step to open up trial design itself, take the shackles off traditional mathematical design, and move into new statistical techniques, new ways to compare the safety, efficacy, and value of a therapeutic, and new paradigms through which we can speed up how quickly something can move from the laboratory setting into the market, helping patients far more quickly than ever before.

Unshackling the Clinical Trial

In the life sciences industry, since the days of Lind and his experiments with sailors and scurvy, we are used to having a two-to-one ratio of patients to evidence. We need one patient treated with one medication and one patient treated with another—two people—in order to make a comparison. One patient gets a traditional course of chemotherapy for their cancer, while the other gets an immunotherapy. Or, one sailor gets lime juice to drink, and the other one seawater.

This need is changing. Here in our state of data-driven disease models, as we look for the equations that define the lines between what to treat and what not to treat (or between who to treat with an existing on-market medication and who will be the best candidate for an experimental therapy), we can start to break that two-to-one paradigm and create a more steam table-like view.

With better instrumentation and richer patient data, we can begin to look at measures of safety, efficacy, and value in new ways. We will have to, in order to achieve a future state of precision medicine. If you think of the number of patients in a study—the total number—as the denominator in a fraction (where the numerator is how many of those patients benefit from the treatment), as the treatments get more and more targeted, we will have a harder and harder time finding enough of them to reach statistically-reliable conclusions. We need to get more units of evidence from each patient whose data gets incorporated into research in order to make the research possible in the precise world of tomorrow.

The phrase "digital transformation" is often thrown around by pharmaceutical executives, as they—correctly and with good intent—realize that the infrastructure and processes they use for research and development are begging for modernization. But rethinking trial design (and breaking the two-to-one patient-to-evidence ratio) goes a step further. It's a critical step when we think about the ultimate goal of building disease graphs that can truly empower better prediction and decision-making. To get our treat/don't-treat lines to be as crisp and precise as possible, we need lots more evidence than we are currently generating, lots more data from our trial patients.

It is so easy now to dive in deeper than we used to be able to—to get higher-resolution measurements from sensors, to parse through patient histories, or to use artificial intelligence to find connections that we couldn't identify on our own. We don't have to miss episodes in episodic disease, because we can now gather data in real time, 24/7. We don't just need to draw the binary conclusion of whether, say, lime juice is the right treatment for scurvy. We can go further and try to figure out how much lime juice is the right amount, and whether that changes if you're a man or a woman, a child or an adult, or if you have any number of comorbid conditions. We need this increased data to be able to say with confidence whether to treat a high PSA result or not, whether Keytruda will be better for you than conventional chemotherapy, and whether you are going to have clinical signs of Alzheimer's disease while it still matters, or not until you're projected to be 180 years old. The digital infrastructure makes this possible like never before.

Enter Thomas Bayes

Thomas Bayes was a statistician in the 1700s whose work ultimately led to a split in the world between two schools of statistical methodology: the frequentist and the Bayesian. Put simply, a frequentist approach to determining the chance that a coin toss will result in either heads or tails requires us to decide first on a number of times that we will toss the coin, measure the outcome, and then, finally, calculate our conclusions. A Bayesian approach, alternatively, allows for adjustment on the fly. Our predictions don't need to wait for the full set of data. We can modify our expectations and our hypotheses as we see more and more evidence.

With coin tosses, each toss is a trivial amount of effort—assuming we already have the coin—so deciding to toss a coin 100 times in order to figure out how many heads to expect in the future is a reasonably trivial proposition. But when it comes to patients—real people who are looking to extend their lives or increase the quality of them—it's not trivial at all. One hundred trial subjects—just to form an initial understanding of whether and for whom a treatment works—is a lot of people exposed to something that may not help them.

Using Thomas Bayes' statistical techniques, we can do better. We can expose as few patients as possible to a treatment that won't work and instead give it to the maximum number of people for whom it will. We can get our therapies through the research process more quickly, to make them more generally available. We can learn something about the nature of a coin toss every time we perform one—which means fewer coin tosses are needed to draw a conclusion. In other words, we can break the two-to-one patient-to-evidence ratio requirement.

Don Berry, a professor at the University of Texas M.D. Anderson Cancer Center and the founding chair of its department of biostatistics, is the designer of I–SPY 2, a breast cancer study that marks the largest and arguably most successful use of Bayesian statistics in clinical trials to date. Berry's work on bringing Bayesian statistics into medical science has been pioneering, and it links directly to the ideas we just talked about in the previous section. When you talk to Berry, you realize how applicable Bayesian thinking is to bringing precision medicine to research.[13]

Instead of taking the non–Bayesian frequentist approach—where we need all of a study's data in order to even make an initial estimate of therapeutic value—the Bayesian approach lets us use a probability distribution for that value, based on past knowledge, and then new data can be used to update that probability distribution as the study goes along. Simply put, the probability distribution acts as a function—an equation—that plots the expected outcome of the experiment, and whether a treatment will be effective for a patient.

Thus, rather than starting with an assumption, with no idea if that starting assumption is correct, or how to adjust it along the way if it's not, we can keep learning as a study proceeds. We can't predict perfectly, but we can create better and better estimates based on what we already know about the world, about patients, and about how they respond. We can keep updating predictions, using today's data to figure out with greater likelihood where we will be tomorrow. And, ultimately, we can move patients around during a trial in order to maximize their outcomes, and maximize what we can learn from the trial, without sacrificing the objectivity and statistical value.

Put simply, we learn as we go, explains Berry. And if data from other trials helps us make better inferences about our current one, then we can and should use it to the extent that it is statistically valuable to do so. The I–SPY 2 trial is aimed at finding the best treatments for early breast cancer in high–risk patients, where their cancer has not yet become metastatic disease. What are the best therapies for treating this disease effectively? Figure 11.1 is a graphical representation of the kind of trial design pioneered by studies like I–SPY 2.

If a therapy demonstrates poor results for a particular subtype of patients in the trial, patients with that subtype get a lower and lower

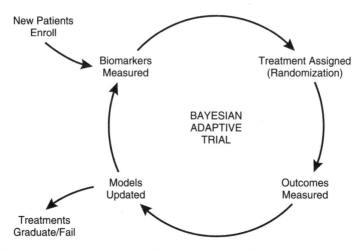

Figure 11.1   Collaborative Bayesian adaptive trials

Trials with multiple drugs in different arms that take advantage of Bayesian adaptive assignment of patients to the drugs most likely to help them all share similar designs. Patients enter the study and data is collected before they are assigned to a treatment. This biomarker profile determines which patients previously enrolled (as well as the patients who will come after them) are "like" them. Patients are randomly assigned to a therapy, but with a bias toward drugs that have helped patients like them in the past. The outcomes are measured, the mathematical models that relate combinations of biomarkers with likely successful and unsuccessful treatments are updated, and this data is used when the next patient enters the study. Note that this is a continuously running cycle, with patients constantly enrolling and models being updated while patients are being treated. Finally, when enough evidence is amassed showing that a particular drug works well for a particular group of patients as defined by their initially-measured biomarkers, it can be "graduated" from the study and moved on for regulatory approval. Similarly, drugs that simply don't work for enough people of any profile are dropped, and room is made for potentially more drugs to become part of the treatment options in the study.

probability of being assigned to that therapy, all the way down to a zero probability if the treatment proves to most likely have no value for such a patient. That is something you can't do in a standard two-arm trial: if a therapy isn't working, the trial is over, and you have failed. But in a multi-arm adaptive trial like I-SPY 2, there are multiple experimental therapy arms (as well as a standard-of-care control arm) and a set of genetic tests that are used to establish which therapies show the best outcomes for patients with particular genetic profiles.

As patients enroll in the study, and new data comes in, more knowledge about which biomarkers are associated with positive or negative outcomes is fed back into the assignment of subsequent patients to particular therapy arms. Instead of performing the statistical equivalent of tossing a coin to decide whether a patient gets the drug on study arm A or B, randomizing them to one of two arms of a study, when a new patient is enrolled in this kind of Bayesian trial, their biomarkers are used as a way to preferentially randomize them to therapies that have already been successful for patients like them.

This should sound familiar. Berry's approach is very much like building a steam table and defining the phase transitions that define what will more likely be a successful treatment for any given individual. The dimensions here are the biomarkers, not temperature and pressure. And although we can't—practically or ethically—test every therapy on every combination of biomarkers (which would be the experimental approach to generating a steam table), we can use Bayesian statistics to start with some assumptions about what those phase transitions look like (the initial probability distribution), and with each patient treated we can refine that function. In other words, we can refine the patient equation represented in the study as we go along.

The phase transition visualization of the way I-SPY 2 works is mine, not Berry's, but the thinking that led to this book truly starts with Don Berry's advocacy and mentorship for this kind of trial design. Even without an appreciation for the mathematical advantages, simply realizing that adaptive designs result in more patients being exposed to therapies that are beneficial to them should be enough to see their advantages. In Berry's words, "You learn and confirm. And you see if your predictions can be reproduced."

Breaking the Barrier

The I-SPY 2 trial doesn't have a fixed set of therapies. There are 19 therapies that have been incorporated so far. Six have "graduated" as of this writing, and more will. Once there is enough data to confirm that a particular drug works well for patients with certain biomarker profiles, that drug is removed from the trial. The company that makes it can use the data generated for regulatory approvals, having gained further ground as far as the precision application of their therapy than would be possible in a traditional phase I–phase II–phase III clinical development program. So not only are there benefits to patients in the trial in terms of having likelier access to better therapies, but those therapies can be brought to market faster to patients waiting for them everywhere.

In the United States, the FDA has been supportive of Bayesian trial designs[14,15]—but there are hurdles because of the inherently (and in many ways responsibly) conservative culture of the pharmaceutical industry, as well as industry incentive structures that are designed to support the machinery of running studies in traditional designs. Plus, there are very practical limitations to this kind of study design. It requires significant coordination and collaboration. Recalling the protocol that describes every aspect of the therapeutic administration, there is the need for a "master protocol" that governs the overall design and operation of the trial. All of the participating companies, and all the organizations with drugs being evaluated in the adaptive design, need to work within that master protocol's framework. The requirements for regulatory and scientific rigor are no different than in a traditional study design, only there are more experimental therapies, more patients, and the trial runs over an even longer time frame. This adds significant complexity. Although it is very difficult to argue against the ethical and financial benefits of adaptive, Bayesian-style trial designs like I-SPY 2, the costs of the individual studies and the complexity of coordinating them remain barriers.

These barriers, however, can, should, and will be overcome, because there is huge benefit. These types of studies break the two-patients-per-unit-of-evidence limitation we've operated with for centuries. In the simplest way, sharing a single control arm across multiple study arms with a range of new drugs means that we're able to reuse those control patients. With seven experimental arms, we effectively have 1.125 patients required per unit of evidence. And that is just the simplest view of a study like I-SPY 2. Arguably, due to the learning nature of the study and the virtuous cycle of its design, we are creating even more evidence per patient.

Ultimately, that increase in evidence-generating power will result in more and more trials like this. GBM AGILE (Glioblastoma Adaptive Global Innovative Learning Environment) is an ambitious new adaptive trial design conceived in 2015 to help speed knowledge about treatments for glioblastoma, an aggressive form of brain cancer responsible for the deaths of Senators Ted Kennedy and John McCain, among many others.[16]

Like I-SPY 2, the GBM AGILE trial is designed to evaluate many therapies at once, with just one control group—meaning patients are more likely to get an experimental therapy, and, even more critically, more likely to get an experimental therapy that is right for them. Columbia University has been among the first institutions to enroll patients in the trial. Their news release explains, "Throughout the trial, tumor tissue from participants will undergo analyses to identify biomarkers that may be associated with a patient's response. As the trial accumulates data, its algorithm refines the randomization process, so that patients have a better chance of getting a treatment that appears to show benefit."[17]

Columbia's Dr. Andrew Lassman, chief of neuro-oncology, says, "This trial design offers a way to lower the cost, time, and number of patients needed to test new therapies for newly diagnosed or recurrent glioblastoma."[18] Given the poor prognosis for patients diagnosed with glioblastoma and the lack of effective treatment options, the need for programs like GBM-AGILE is clear.

Having established the value of collaborative, adaptive designs like I-SPY 2 and GBM-AGILE, we now have to ask whether there are other barriers that can be broken down, or other ways for life science companies to collaborate that can go beyond even these studies in terms of generating evidence, getting safe and effective precision therapies to market more quickly, and creating breakthrough value for patients. I believe there are, and the discussion continues with the idea of synthetic control arms.

Synthetic Control Arms

The idea of a synthetic control was first described in a paper in 1976 by Stuart J. Pocock in the *Journal of Chronic Diseases*. "In many clinical trials the objective is to compare a new treatment with a standard control treatment, the design being to randomize equal numbers of patients onto the two treatments. However, there often exist acceptable historical data on the control treatment," states the article's abstract.[19]

The idea is that we can synthesize historical patient data into a *hypothetical* control group that will function just as well as a randomized control group. As long as these two hypothetical sets of patients are equivalent based on the definition of the study—that is, if they share the same characteristics and meet the right inclusion/exclusion criteria—they should function just the same. The idea isn't dissimilar to sharing patients across the arms of a multi-arm Bayesian design like the I-SPY 2 trial. We have a protocol being rigorously followed by the investigators, and patients who all meet the criteria for being part of the study—should we not be able to reuse the data?

If we are looking for, say, a group of patients with heart disease who will be given a particular study drug, we already have data from many other trials with heart disease patients who have been given the standard-of-care treatment as part of a control group. Why not reuse their results? Or, at the very least, why not reuse the data generated in those previous studies to supplement the new data we're obtaining in the trial? The word "synthetic" can be confusing here. It's not that the control patients are somehow synthesized. These are very real participants in clinical trials, just not the clinical trial currently being performed.

The synthesis is of their experiences as control subjects into a new control cohort, a new arm synthesized from data deriving from other rigorous and scientific clinical trials.

Mathematically, Pocock made the case in his paper that we can—and, from the perspectives of cost, time, and ethics, we should—approach control groups in this way. Think about those two patients, one experimental and one control—tens, hundreds, or thousands of times over—whose data is finally assembled into a data set that shows the difference in outcomes for those who are getting the experimental therapy and those who are not. If we can reuse control patients from previous studies, we should be able to save half the cost. We only need to enroll patients who are to get the experimental therapy, because the control group is already taken care of.

Time becomes an issue here as well. Assuming there are no short-cuts in how long it takes to evaluate whether or not a particular therapy works, the idea of saving time with synthetic controls may seem unintu-itive to those who don't work in clinical research. If it takes 12 months to go through the course of therapy and see if, for instance, a tumor stops growing, we're not going to save any time by reusing data from other trials. However: the number of patients we have to find goes down—in the most extreme example, by half.

The time it takes to recruit patients into a study is typically one of the key rate-limiting parts of the process. Assume we need to enroll 120 patients in a theoretical study, and are able to find 10 participants a month. (Those numbers are reasonable for many studies. In some cases, it can be even harder to recruit, and the trend as we move toward more precise therapies—as we've already discussed—is going to be in that direction.)

Between the time we've enrolled the first and last patients into the study is a full year. Then add a year for the last patient recruited to get through the complete course of therapy, and then the time it takes to evaluate the effectiveness and safety. If we could reduce the number of patients we need to enroll by half, six months in this case gets shaved off the timeline. A regulatory submission could happen six months earlier.

Six additional months of patients diagnosed with the condition the drug addresses could have broad access to the new treatment.

Even if the treatment doesn't work better than the standard of care, we've avoided asking 60 additional patients to take the chance to get randomized to a therapy that isn't going to help them, and give up the opportunity to be enrolled in studies that could serve them better. Particularly in therapeutic areas where there are no effective therapies currently on the market, we've created more chances for success. We've minimized the number of patients exposed to something harmful, and maximized—during and beyond the study—the number of patients who can benefit from more effective medications.

So why—with what appears to be a huge set of advantages—isn't this done more? It's certainly on the radar screen of many. Julian Jenkins—the former GlaxoSmithKline executive who worked on Flumoji—says that pharma is absolutely looking at this. "If I know the old drug worked against a particular target," he says, "then, in looking at whether a new drug is going to work, many companies are trying to use secondary analysis, looking back to test hypotheses, to validate targets. It speeds things up, and is a huge enabler for the industry."[20]

And yet, the standard of care—the gold standard—for clinical evidence is still the randomized, prospectively-controlled trial. Why? The answer is partly because of the conservatism of the life sciences industry (always important to point out that this is a good thing that protects us all), and partly because creating synthetic control arms with previous clinical trial data isn't an easy thing to do. Most trials—virtually all trials, unless they are part of a master protocol like GBM-AGILE or I-SPY 2—have their own unique combination and cadence of visits to the clinic, lab tests, imaging, and so on. The way that studies are designed and run—one at a time, on one particular drug—means that every study's data set has its own unique design and particularities. It's not just a matter of taking data from studies, pooling it, and using it again. We need to ensure that the data is high-quality, standardized properly, and consistent. That consistency across trials isn't always possible to find right now.

Even once the data is standardized, the hard work isn't over. Although we try to eliminate biases from clinical trials, there can still be inherent issues. Take the simple example of age. A clinical trial (and, again, this is a very reasonable example) may have inclusion criteria that patients must be over 18 and under 65. With a standardized data set, it is simple enough to find patients who meet those criteria. But what is the distribution of age across the synthetic controls? Do we use a normal distribution, centered around age 42? Perhaps our synthetic control group skews younger, and perhaps the distribution of ages among the prospectively enrolled patients skews older. Should this matter? Might this create a confounding element in our synthetically controlled study that makes analysis harder, not easier?

The answer in this case is that we don't know, and therefore we must do anything we can to make the characteristics of the patients—at least all of the characteristics that we know about—as consistent as possible with the prospectively enrolled patients. We'd like the inputs of the synthetic controls to look as much like the inputs of prospectively enrolled patients in the study as possible.

The work doesn't end there. The outputs of previous studies need to emerge in a way that is matched to the new study being performed. Raw data collected in the previous trials needs to be recleaned and the results recalculated. And before you even get to all that standardization and cleaning, you need to actually find all of the raw data from those previous studies. This data may be in deeply-buried folders in servers across dozens of pharmaceutical companies. This data may not be well-cataloged or indexed in a way that makes finding all of it possible.

Our Synthetic Control Model

The effort needed to successfully reuse clinical trial data is why, over the four-plus decades since Pocock wrote his article in 1976, the idea of synthetic controls hasn't been scaled. This is where my company, Medidata, comes into the story. Barbara Elashoff, who broke her leg back in Chapter 2, along with her husband Michael Elashoff and their former colleague at the FDA, Ruthanna Davi, all reassembled at Medidata and began to work on the idea of synthetic controls with an advantage that nobody previously had: a platform where clinical trials had been run for over a decade with consistent data definitions, all the data in one place—in the cloud, where the studies themselves were run—and an organization placed centrally and able to ask more than one thousand life sciences companies if they would like to pool their control data for this greater good. Not to mention, we also had a commercially-sustainable business model, where the costs of standardizing data and managing the complexities of synthetic controls would be an incentive, not a disincentive, to make them work at scale.

Every patient who is in the volunteer pool—with consent and permission from the patients and from the companies involved—is treated as equal: as members of one giant clinical trial data set. For any given indication, relevant patients are selected and those exposed to experimental therapies are excluded. Matching algorithms—ways to look at each individual as a matrix of data—are used to ensure that the types of skews present in different variables won't impact downstream analyses, and, ultimately, from a data set synthesized across what is effectively the breadth of the life sciences industry, a synthetic control arm emerges.

It is still, to be sure, not a trivial process. This is another example where the execution of analyses is fast, but there are painstaking months—sometimes years—of necessary preparation and the testing of techniques. However, along with some of the life sciences companies that participate in the project with us, we've paved the way for these data sets to be used—both for planning purposes and as a supplemental data source to benchmark trial results. Soon—perhaps by the time you are reading this book—synthetic controls will be used as part of the statistical package submitted to regulators in the approval process for a new medication.

The inherent, incredible, game-changing value of being able to reuse patient data to create more evidence will probably offer further surprises—in a good way—for those creating therapeutic value for patients, and for the patients waiting to receive it. For a pharmaceutical or biotechnology executive, even if a synthetic control isn't part of the data they submit to a regulator, or used to prove the value of a new therapeutic to a payer or a provider, imagine the value of knowing that your control data "looks" like control data in other studies.

The need to eliminate biases in clinical trials should be clear. A drug that appears to be safe and effective in research, but has had biases introduced into that research, can result in bringing a drug to market with elevated expectations. Whether it's because of the criteria by which patients were selected, the geographies where investigators were chosen, or something else about the investigators or institutions, having elements that skew not the inputs but the outputs of the study—the endpoints related to survival or quality of life—can have tremendous consequences. Comparing a control arm to a synthetic control and seeing that the standard of care or placebo arm in a randomized, controlled trial matches your results will mean more confidence that you have guarded against that risk.

That's just the starting point. The value of generating high-quality evidence faster and more efficiently has been discussed. Once therapies have been approved using synthetic controls as a replacement (or at least as a supplement) for prospectively enrolled control subjects, I expect the life sciences industry to embrace the idea at scale. The current exception—the occasionally-presented idea at scientific meetings—will become the new standard by which therapeutics go from theoretical value in a laboratory to therapies available to the public.

There is precedent for this. There are multiple kinds of synthetic controls, and the ones discussed up to this point—the reuse of data coming from the rigorous scientific and regulatory environment of a trial, albeit a different trial than the one at hand—represent what should become the gold standard moving forward. There is also data from the world of health care outside of clinical development. If we can look at, standardize, and benchmark the data from clinical trials against these other sets of data, the same progression of value should be possible. Using this information to plan studies, estimate the value of therapeutics, mitigate biases that could be introduced in prospective controls, and ultimately supplement or replace the controls necessary for a trial are all steps along the way. Companies like Flatiron Health, for example, which is using real-world data to accelerate cancer research, are proving out this idea—scientifically and as a business model—every day.[21]

Making Every Trial an Adaptive Trial

There is an exciting progression beyond this idea of synthetic controls. If you think about the process for creating synthetic controls as described above, a key step is eliminating the subjects previously exposed to experimental therapies. This makes sense, since we want to compare a new drug to the on-market standard of care. But: imagine a trial where the new drug is better than the standard of care. It should, therefore, be on a track—or at least be a possible candidate—to become the next standard of care. So there can become a virtuous cycle of clinical trial data and synthetic controls. The old experimental cohort is the new control, if the tested therapy turns out to be the new standard. We end up with a self-perpetuating data asset that benefits both patients and the life sciences industry.

Now consider the Bayesian adaptive design, and the advantages already discussed of a trial where we aren't just testing the fitness of a particular drug for a broadly defined set of patients, but creating a learning environment where biomarkers are continually leveraged to pair the best therapy with each patient enrolled. Recall the complexity with administering a process like that, and with creating a master protocol that governs how the trial, across all therapeutics, is run.

How is this Bayesian adaptive environment different from the one we are creating with synthetic controls? My answer is that they aren't different at all. By combining these concepts, the life sciences industry can create a collaborative research environment that involves not just the reuse of controls, but also allows for the continuous learning necessary for the precise pairing of every available drug (on-market and experimental) to every waiting patient in a close approximation—almost a perfect implementation, save the impractical, unethical idea of testing patients and therapies like temperature and pressure in a lab—to the steam table-backed phase diagram vision of the future.

This future is one that colleagues and collaborators both inside and outside of Medidata and I hope to make a reality, ultimately creating a super-sized virtuous cycle, as represented in Figure 11.2.

Patients in previously-run clinical trials for what is the current standard of care become a continuously-refreshed control arm. Standardized data across not just a handful, but tens or hundreds of potential new drugs (or combinations of therapies) can be compared by using the same data cleaning, standardization, and benchmarking techniques already used today for synthetic controls.

Instead of a competitive environment where investigators, or the patients themselves, are recruited into disparate clinical trials, the industry can work together to create a bias—in this case a positive one—where a Bayesian adaptive approach is used to enroll every patient who could

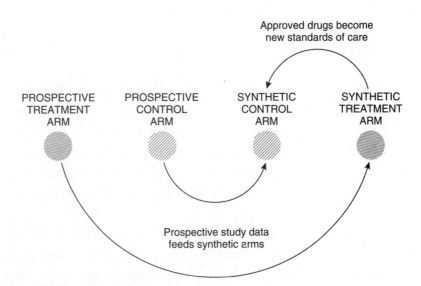

Figure 11.2 The virtuous cycle of synthetic controls, standard of care, and new drugs

benefit from an experimental therapy to the best possible one for them, based on the industry-wide knowledge at the time.

The life sciences industry's commercial architecture is based on the value generated by drugs and devices. The cost savings generated by running more efficient clinical trials, and the revenue opportunity of getting a drug to market faster, are of course hugely valuable to the companies themselves and to patients. But a truly collaborative environment where we preferentially randomize patients to the best available known therapy of any type—for them, at that point in time—creates an unprecedented number of units of evidence per patient in research programs.

A great litmus test for conviction in medicine is whether—just like Dr. David Fajgenbaum—someone is willing to take their own medicine. A collaborative environment where volunteers' biomarkers are measured, where the past experiences of patients like them is available across therapies, and where they can be randomized to an experimental therapy regardless of what company is running a trial (effectively creating an adaptive environment for every drug being tested in it) is the world in which I want to be a patient.

A Stroke of Insight

I was asked not long ago to present ideas about the future of research at a conference on stroke, run by the American Heart Association. The extent of my academic cardiology knowledge is unfortunately limited to an afternoon crash course in interpreting ECGs, so I thought it was best to admit as quickly as possible in my talk that I was thoroughly unqualified to offer any opinions on how cardiology research specifically could or would change in the future.

However, I then explained to them what I would say to a group of oncologists: If you are looking to build a mathematical model for early diagnosis in oncology—asking what biomarkers can be measured as early indicators that a patient will be diagnosed with cancer—and you are only looking at oncology research, you've made the problem much harder than necessary, if not impossible to solve.

All of the patients in the oncology data sets have already been diagnosed with cancer. On the other hand, virtually all research projects—whether academic or funded by industry—that enroll patients prospectively include a medical history, patients' vital signs, standard blood labs, an extensive list of prescription and nonprescription medication being taken, and a list of "adverse events"—severe, life-threatening ones like cardiac arrest, as well as less severe (but not necessarily less important) ones like headaches.

If we were to look at a cardiology study instead of one in the oncology space—which might have thousands or tens of thousands of patients in it—we should be able to see which patients manifested comorbidities (like a cancer diagnosis) based on adverse events, medications taken, having to be dropped out of the study, or even death. We have a run-up to that diagnosis or death that includes a set of medical data far more extensive, and more exquisitely curated, than we would find in any integrated health system's medical record, in our personal health records, or even combinations of the data sets that governments, academic institutions, and companies around the world are trying to create. (Not that these data sets from outside of research aren't worthy endeavors. They are.)

Figuring out how to get unexpected evidence from the data collected in a research project is the ultimate manifestation of the strategies presented here. Making cardiology research data a valuable synthetic asset for oncology studies—or the converse, seeding models for heart failure or stroke with data from oncology, diabetes, or other studies—will unlock and fuel the virtuous cycle of precision medicine research even more. We can find clues that add huge insights to our patient equations from the records of patients who just so happen to be diagnosed with new conditions while they are being closely monitored.

Adaptive trial designs offer huge potential as we go forward in a world rich with data, and where we need better ways to test hypotheses quickly and accurately. But we don't just need to rethink our approach at the front end of the clinical trial pipeline. We also need to reinvent our relationship with patients at the other end in order to get the right treatments out to the public and truly make an impact.

In the next chapter, we'll turn our attention to the patient-facing piece of the data revolution: disease-management platforms and around-the-pill apps that can motivate and change behavior, measure outcomes, and match patient to treatment in ways that we haven't ever been able to do before smartphones and wearables. Not everyone will be part of a clinical trial at some point in their patient journey, but everyone has the chance to be impacted by apps and other interactive programs that bring trial results to light, and get people to care about their health and take the right actions for their future.

Notes

1. Susan Gubar, "The Need for Clinical Trial Navigators," *New York Times*, June 20, 2019, https://www.nytimes.com/2019/06/20/well/live/the-need-for-clinical-trial-navigators.html.
2. Liz Szabo, "Opinion | Are We Being Misled About Precision Medicine?," *New York Times*, September 11, 2018, https://www.nytimes.com/2018/09/11/opinion/cancer-genetic-testing-precision-medicine.html.
3. Meeri Kim, "The Jury Is Out," *CURE*, June 19, 2018, https://www.curetoday.com/publications/cure/2018/immunotherapy-special-issue/the-jury-is-out.
4. Ibid.
5. T. J. Sharpe, interview for *The Patient Equation*, interview by Glen de Vries and Jeremy Blachman, July 1, 2019.
6. U.S. National Library of Medicine, home page of ClinicalTrials.Gov, 2019, https://clinicaltrials.gov.
7. Alicia Staley, interview for *The Patient Equation*, interview by Glen de Vries and Jeremy Blachman, July 1, 2019.
8. "PCORnet®, The National Patient-Centered Clinical Research Network," Patient-Centered Outcomes Research Institute, July 30, 2014, https://www.pcori.org/research-results/pcornet%C2%AE-national-patient-centered-clinical-research-network.

9. Anthony Costello, interview for *The Patient Equation*, interview by Glen de Vries and Jeremy Blachman, December 2, 2019.

10. George Underwood, "The Clinical Trial of the Future," *PharmaTimes*, September 23, 2016, http://www.pharmatimes.com/ magazine/2016/october/the_clinical_trial_of_the_future.

11. Kara Dennis, interview for *The Patient Equation*, interview by Glen de Vries and Jeremy Blachman, February 24, 2017.

12. Eric Wicklund, "Gartner Analyst: Healthcare Isn't Ready for Wearables Just Yet," *mHealthIntelligence*, November 19, 2015, http:// mhealthintelligence.com/news/gartner-analyst-healthcare-isnt-ready-for-wearables-just-yet.

13. Don Berry, interview for *The Patient Equation*, interview by Glen de Vries and Jeremy Blachman, May 2, 2019.

14. Center for Biologics Evaluation and Research, "Interacting with the FDA on Complex Innovative Trial Designs for Drugs and Biological Products," U.S. Food and Drug Administration, 2019, https://www .fda.gov/regulatory-information/search-fda-guidance-documents/ interacting-fda-complex-innovative-trial-designs-drugs-and-biological-products.

15. Janet Woodcock and Lisa M. LaVange, "Master Protocols to Study Multiple Therapies, Multiple Diseases, or Both," ed. Jeffrey M. Drazen et al., *New England Journal of Medicine* 377, no. 1 (July 6, 2017): 62–70, https://doi.org/10.1056/nejmra1510062.

16. "Introduction to GBM AGILE: A Unique Approach to Clinical Trials," *Trial Site News*, May 3, 2019, https://www.trialsitenews .com/introduction-to-gbm-agile-a-unique-approach-to-clinical-trials/.

17. Andrew Lassman, "Smarter Brain Cancer Trial Comes to Columbia," Columbia University Irving Medical Center, April 24, 2019, https://www.cuimc.columbia.edu/news/smarter-brain-cancer-trial-comes-columbia.

18. Ibid.

19. Stuart J. Pocock, "The Combination of Randomized and Historical Controls in Clinical Trials," *Journal of Chronic Diseases* 29, no. 3 (March 1976): 175–188, https://doi.org/10.1016/0021-9681(76)90044-8.

20. Julian Jenkins, interview for *The Patient Equation*, interview by Glen de Vries and Jeremy Blachman, March 24, 2017.

21. "About Us," Flatiron Health, 2019, https://flatiron.com/about-us/.

12 | Disease Management Platforms

There's an app for everything, or so it seems these days. For every One-Drop, which has a carefully defined mission and proven clinical effectiveness, there are dozens of others with spurious value, whether calorie counters or fitness trackers or mood detectors or, recently found on a list of "best" health apps, Waterlogged, which reminds you throughout the day to drink more water.[1] Not to say that drinking more water isn't likely a smart call for many of us, or that an app can't engage us and help make sure we do, but when these apps are marketed to literally billions of people with smartphones, even a subscription price tag of a few U.S. dollars creates an attractive enough incentive to envision a new digital snake oil economy.

Atul Gawande has criticized wearables for not being "integrated into the practice of medicine in a really critical way . . . demonstrating major improvements in people's outcomes," and the same criticism can apply to most apps.[2] They are standalone patches that purport to diagnose a problem or help to treat one, but they're not necessarily clinically validated, or part of a larger platform, or integrated into patients' lives such that they actually get used consistently, produce actionable information, and ultimately make a difference. Is all of this digital infrastructure, from apps to the proliferation of sensors around, attached to, and even inside us destined to be an ineffective fad? Clearly I don't think so, but acknowledging these criticisms as valid and relevant is an important step toward making the digital ecosystem an effective part of health care, and a valuable lever for us as individuals to manage our well-being.

Kara Dennis, formerly managing director of mobile health at Medidata, says that one of the biggest challenges with apps is retention, getting patients to be bothered to consistently log in and enter data, whatever kind of data it might be. I haven't tried the aforementioned Waterlogged app, but I can certainly report my own lack of compliance after deciding to measure my coffee intake with Apple HealthKit. Even my own strong curiosity around quantifying another measure about myself wasn't enough to keep me tapping a button on my phone's home screen every time I indulged in an espresso for more than a couple of days.

This chapter is about how we overcome these issues. How do we make apps relevant, and how do we make sure we remove users' needs to manually manage devices and data? We've already covered how the data itself isn't useful without the right algorithms behind the scenes converting it into something clinically relevant—something actually connected to and affecting our biology—but how do we design the apps, wearables, and the larger platforms around them so that they will actually, in the end, matter?

The Promise of Mobile Apps

When things work, it all sounds easy. A study presented at a recent meeting of the American Society of Clinical Oncology discussed an app used by lung cancer patients that improved overall survival time by seven months compared to the average. According to *FiercePharma*, the app, MoovCare, collected a set of data and alerted physicians when anomalies were detected by the AI algorithm behind the scenes.[3] Doctors could then follow up with their patients, address problems sooner, and, ultimately, keep them alive longer.

Another study looked at whether mobile apps are able to improve medication adherence—showing that an augmented version of a medication reminder app for patients on antiretroviral therapy was able to reduce errors, improve adherence, and in fact decrease viral load.[4] Groove Health is one company combining data from a mobile app with existing health care data to better understand patients and improve adherence.[5] "The complex nature of medication adherence demands solutions that are more innovative than simple medication reminders," Groove's founder and CEO Andrew Hourani told *MobiHealthNews*. The app attempts to identify each patient's reason for nonadherence and to intervene appropriately by providing medication information, encouragement, dosing help, or directions to a nearby pharmacy.[6] Janssen, the pharmaceutical division of Johnson & Johnson, has also released tools to help improve adherence, including smart blister packs for medication and electronic drug labels.[7]

These examples only begin to scratch the surface of what a digital health management platform can do. Beyond just warning doctors about suspect data anomalies or reminding patients to take their pills, we can broaden our thinking to truly integrated digital solutions—digital therapeutics. BlueStar is an app that provides in-the-moment guidance for patients, telling them when to check their blood sugar, and collecting information on diet, activity, medication dosing, symptoms, lab results and more—and sending that information to their doctors.[8] BlueStar has been clinically shown to lower hemoglobin A1c values by 1.7–2.0%.[9] This is just one of a bunch of approaches. Pear Therapeutics has partnered with a division of Novartis to develop an app called reSET that delivers cognitive behavioral therapy for substance-abuse disorder.[10] Proteus Digital Health has developed an ingestible sensor that can be embedded into an oral medication and record if and when someone has taken their pills.[11]

Novartis recognizing the powerful future of digital therapies is commendable, and Proteus is a substantive platform that can objectively, quantitatively monitor and enhance compliance with sensors and digital technology. But the fact is that pharmaceutical companies and digital therapy developers are working separately, and, considering the value they create as individual companies, not as partners. Pharmaceutical companies are being left out of most of these patient platforms—and they shouldn't be.

If we accept that the ultimate litmus test for the worthiness of a digital intervention is a biological change in the user—that is, a change in behavior, cognition, or physiology—then there is not a divide between drugs, devices, and digital. Digital is certainly a newer tool for health care providers. But digital therapeutics should not be thought of any differently than a molecule in terms of whether and when to use them. The same rules—and the same measures of success through outcomes—should apply.

Thinking about all of these alternatives simply as tools for health care leads to an important way of thinking. Whether or not a life sciences company is successful can be defined by one simple idea: are they providing better tools to health care providers than the tools they currently have? Full stop. If a pharmaceutical company makes a drug that is more effective or safer (and ideally it's both) than what's on the market today, they will be successful. The drug will provide more value to patients than the current standard of care, providers will want to prescribe it, payers will see value in reimbursing for it, and the pharma company's revenue will cover the cost of R&D, allow the company to invest in new therapies, and return value to shareholders.

Everyone wins when better tools are created. If the same theoretical drug isn't a better tool for treating patients, then no one will want to take it out of the toolbox. And room will be made for the next life sciences company to try to improve on the current toolset.

Once we abstract everything to this idea of tools—molecules, medical devices, wearables, and apps—the competitive landscape becomes clear. Pharma companies may see digital therapeutics potentially taking away market share from them. But if you look at companies like Proteus, partnering with Otsuka to deliver drugs on digital and device platforms, or at the use of drug-eluting stents (medical devices used to hold arteries open while releasing drugs into nearby tissue—which began to be deployed almost 20 years ago), some of the most ingenious and valuable developments have come not from one category of therapeutic, but from the combination of multiple modalities.

The pharma and biotech industries have every incentive to find ways to track patients who are actually taking their drugs, make sure they are taking them optimally, and leverage patient engagement and behavior change to create the greatest possible biological effect. If you're a pharma executive, you should want to know that your patients are actually taking the medication they've been prescribed. You should want to have patients tuned to the right dosage. You should want them to exercise, eat, and act in ways that increase the efficacy and safety of your therapeutic. If you aren't doing that, it doesn't mean that your drug isn't spectacularly valuable on its own. But you do run the risk that a competitor will create a better tool—in combination with digital technologies—than your drug alone.

You should also want to use these technologies to get patients who are not responding off the drugs as quickly as possible. Whether related to reimbursement models (which we'll talk about more in Chapter 14) or simply to show that your drugs are working for patients and providing them with the best possible treatment, you should want to measure whether therapies are working and, at the same time, if they are, to properly motivate and incent patients to use them. There are huge costs to drugs not being effective—certainly in a value-based care scenario but also simply in marketing and word-of-mouth effects. It is not good for anyone to have drugs out in the world that are not helping patients.

As one example, one of the biggest problems for pharmaceutical companies is that patients don't finish the full course of their medication—and outcomes suffer. If apps can help address this problem, that is potentially huge. There is useful information to be discovered here. Are patients stopping the medication because of side effects?

Because of an inconvenient dosing schedule? Because symptoms have resolved and they just don't finish the course? The answers to these questions can shape future development, without a doubt.

Digital from the Beginning

For the life sciences companies who do leverage digital to supplement the measurable biological outcomes their products deliver, I believe the next biggest mistake is waiting until the end of the traditional drug development process to think about them.

Consider the relatively simple problem (though without a simple solution) of medication adherence. A Proteus-style digestible to measure whether a pill has been swallowed could certainly be part of a solution, but it's not the only option. Other engagement apps are possible, or wearables that measure effects, something that reminds the patient to take the pill, or alerts a provider that it's not being taken. Imagine, as in Figure 12.1, that the pharmaceutical company—forward-thinking in today's market, at least—starts to think about a digital engagement and compliance measurement platform around the time that their drug is approved by the FDA.

There is some inherent value in the drug itself, marked by the horizontal line A. The development process can obviously increase that value, through the kinds of precision targeting we've already discussed—but for this example, we'll assume the value stays constant. Let's also assume that the company is successful in being able to engage patients, increase their adherence, and change their behaviors in meaningful ways for the disease being treated. (We will attack that assumption shortly, though!)

As the company develops and delivers this digital companion to the drug, it increases the therapeutic value (see line B). The better that engagement strategy gets—and we know that more and more data can improve engagement, as we saw with examples like OneDrop—there is additional patient value generated.

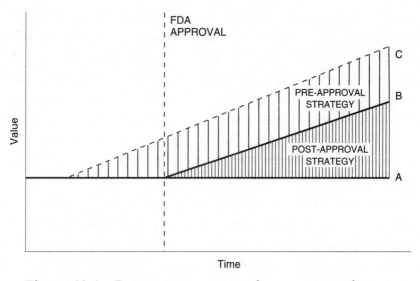

Figure 12.1 Pre- versus post-regulatory approval engagement strategies

But, if the company began to develop that engagement strategy during the drug development process rather than waiting until release (line C), we can see an even greater amount of value generated over time (the total area between A and C). Patients benefit more as individuals, and more of them benefit.

Moreover, the total patient value—literally the sum of all positive biological effect for the drug and the engagement platform—is greater at the time of drug approval than it would be without having plugged in that engagement strategy in advance. This may or may not be relevant to a regulatory agency. Perhaps there are no competing products for the indication. But if there are, anything that can be proven to increase safety, efficacy, or patient value is relevant. That additional value might make the difference.

Plus, the pricing of the drug is going to be coincident—or at least will track with, potentially up to a year later in some parts of Europe—the regulatory approval. The more demonstrable benefit that is shown, the easier it will be to justify a higher price.

Of course, we can challenge the underlying assumption that this theoretical company will be successful in creating a worthwhile digital strategy. Apropos to our discussion of digital snake oil, not every app, and not every engagement strategy—just like not every drug—will successfully create a positive effect. What better time for testing could there be, if a company wants to have a disciplined, scientific approach to ensuring that their engagement strategy will be successful, than when they are already working in the disciplined, scientific framework of drug development?

Patients will be instrumented far more during development than during the commercial life of the drug, and there is the opportunity to control variables—to tune the dial on engagement the same way we might tune the dial to find the right dosage of the molecule.

Digital strategies are at their most valuable when they are not just add-ons, but integral pieces of the development process—not just a go-to-market strategy. Virtually every pharmaceutical company should be thinking about a digital companion to the medicines they are developing. And if they aren't thinking about it now, it may be too late.

The development of the digital companion to the drug could even make its way to more customized drug labels. Just as unexpected biochemical or genetic biomarkers may have an effect on efficacy or safety, there may be cognitive or behavioral responses—measured explicitly, or the byproducts of digital strategy research and development—that can be triggered by some aspect of the labeling.

But It's Not That Easy

Laying out this idea—"digital from the beginning"—makes it seem like it's a no-brainer, and that every drug company should have figured this out already. But there's a reason they haven't. Building an effective digital product is hard. For every Twitter and Facebook—undeniably sticky technological applications—a thousand social media companies died along the way, unable to engage people enough to make a viable business. It is naïve to think that creating these apps is easy. In the end, it's not so different from evaluating a hundred compounds to try to find the one drug that works.

Stan Kachnowski, professor at Columbia Business School and chair of HITLAB—the Healthcare Innovation and Technology Lab—sees data in action every day, and what it takes to get new technologies into the marketplace. In talking to him, he characterizes one of the biggest challenges as diffusion—can a particular platform make its way into the population, become a trusted part of a patient's everyday life, and actually be used to effect change?[12]

On the one hand, Kachnowski sees a lot of tools rapidly expanding into health care and changing what we do as life sciences companies, as doctors, and as patients—but on the other hand, he also sees a lot of mistakes, and a lot of assumptions about diffusion that are simply incorrect. Diffusion—more than sales, more than profitability, more than press coverage, more than even results—is what matters, Kachnowski insists. The diffusion of apps into the patient population, or of digital systems by clinical trial sponsors, investigators, and subjects, has been considerably slower and more fraught than may have been expected a decade ago.

"It is difficult to predict diffusion," Kachnowski says. "We try to do it at HITLAB by doing very early testing, but when something is on the cusp, figuring out which way it's going to tip is hard." He has seen things like online consultations and physicians being paid to write emails come into the world and not get nearly the traction he predicted. "I thought for sure that would be widely adopted . . . and it's not. I get it wrong a lot of the time."

Kachnowski has seen failures like a Harvard attempt to integrate payers and providers, which required the support of too many large stakeholders to truly take off. He hasn't seen an app for health that has picked up more than 10% diffusion into the population, not a single health care app with more than 3–4% engaged users over the course of a year, millions of dollars being put into these apps with very little to show for it.

Pharma has such powerful incentives to get people to use apps—the kinds of engagement, tracking, and subsetting that we've already discussed—and the money to develop and distribute anything they want to put their energy behind. But Kachnowski doesn't see it happening. Instead, he sees regulation getting in the way—pharma companies legally can't see much of the data, they can't collect identifiable patient data, they can't really collect anything right now that they can use to help their adherence models. I'm less skeptical than he is—I think there are ways to work around this challenge, to stay within the regulations and still learn plenty from the data. But he is undeniably right that the amount of effort that the biggest pharmaceutical companies have put around initiatives like these is limited.

In Kachnowski's mind, it's payers who will have to lead the digital revolution. Yet they are also bewildered by how little adoption they have seen with the apps out there. He has been involved in the development of CardioNet, a company providing ambulatory ECG monitoring to detect and treat arrhythmias, and he believes it has saved a very significant number of lives—but patients were never going to pay out of pocket for it, and it had to go through the payers. It has disrupted the industry—hospitals have lost tons of money from patients who used to be admitted for a week to monitor them in-house and now they just get sent home with a CardioNet device—but it took the payers insisting that this was going to be the new standard of care in order to gain any traction in the market.

Kachnowski sees the same thing happening with sleep. Home-based sleep kits are hard to sell directly to patients, but a substantial fraction of payers now require a home sleep test before they will reimburse for a stay at an in-person sleep center. So the number of patients being directed to sleep centers has fallen precipitously, and it's almost becoming a business of the past. Kachnowski says that Columbia's sleep wing used to be 5,000 square feet, is now 500 square feet, and is inching closer to no longer being a viable investment of resources.

On the pharma end, he sees the money being spent on the wrong technologies. Not that many people are going to sign into standalone apps and do anything with them consistently. The value has to be obvious—and especially with many patients not wanting to face the fact that they have a particular disease, and not wanting to engage with their health any more than they have to, it is a huge challenge. He calculates that $15–$20 billion has been lost in the development of beyond-the-pill apps over the past decade, a ton of energy and zero return because patients simply won't engage consistently enough to produce useful data. And that even in the world of wearables, too many consumers don't want to wear them, they don't like the way they look, they don't understand them, they don't fit, and there's a social stigma. "What 85-year-old woman with thin wrists, and maybe not a great understanding of the value, is going to wear an activity tracker?" he asks.

There are two saving graces Kachnowski points to. One is that, more and more, we have devices to collect data passively, which don't require people to log in, enter data, or do anything that might stand in the way of diffusion. The other is that when apps or wearables are deployed in clinical trials, compliance is virtually 100%—and it becomes a game changer. "When the physician goes to the subject and says 'you have to wear this, it is vital for the study,' they do it," Kachnowski says. "They will wear it 24/7 because their physician is the one person on the planet they trust."

But Kachnowski has confidence that more companies will figure it out and that more will solve the diffusion problem and help carry digital health to the next level. The economic incentives for the successful development of digital engagement strategies and companion digital therapeutics are undeniable. It is a huge area of opportunity for life sciences companies, big enough for them to want to continue to try to tackle the problem, even after so many failures.

Thinking about that future—the competitive landscape of pharma companies not transforming themselves into digital therapeutics companies, but incorporating digital into the fabric of the molecular products they development—I am optimistic. There will be winners and there will be losers, but progress will be made.

Where That Leaves Us

If there's one lesson I want readers to take from this chapter, it's that the life sciences industry going forward isn't and can't just be about drugs and physical devices. It is also about digital diagnostics, companion apps, and platforms that we use to manage diseases that include drugs—not merely drugs that have simple around-the-pill apps that don't create biologically-based and measurable outcomes. This is something everyone in life sciences needs to be thinking about—even though these digital solutions are expensive to develop and successes have been hard to come by as yet. As *MedCityNews* writes, "diagnostics have been a tough sell. While they're necessary to fulfill precision medicine's promise, no one really wants to pay for them."[13]

Yet, diagnostics are what will elevate us from the cusp of the data revolution into a world of fully-developed patient equations. They are going to tell us who is going to best benefit from the hugely-valuable drugs being developed. Ultimately, apps and diagnostics need to end up being a part of the standard workflow for treating patients. Instead of a patient presenting with a particular indication and being prescribed a drug, we need built-in intelligence to tell us whether that particular patient should get drug x or drug y, and then to track their response so that if it's not working, we can switch them as quickly as possible to something that will. An around-the-pill platform that incorporates this from the start—that subsets patients from the very beginning so that only the right ones even start down this course of therapy—is going to find itself hugely valuable.

We need to think about the right platforms for managing dosing—for antibiotics, for infusion therapies, for everything. We can predict the curves for a particular patient as far as blood percentage concentration over time, and just like the OneDrop app, alert patients for their next dose.

And, finally, we need to make sure sensible regulations are in place. Not just to address Stan Kachnowski's point that pharma needs to have permission to collect the data they need in order to sensibly expect they will make the investments needed to wade into this area in a serious way, but also to make sure that patients are protected from apps that don't actually do what they claim to do, or what they intend. We have regulations for things we ingest or implant, but we don't think about them in the same way when we're talking about a digital device of some kind, or particularly just a smartphone app. But if a cardiac monitor is connected to an app that is producing recommendations about heart medication, or there is a system telling you how much of a drug to take and when, these need to be accurate, or they're dangerous. We need disciplined research to connect the inputs to the outputs. We can't have an app telling us that if we eat one more cheeseburger, we're going to have a heart attack—unless we've somehow validated that the prediction is likely to be correct.

The endgame is pretty clear to me, even though it's obviously at least a generation away. Someday these systems—apps, wearable sensors, ingestibles, and implantables—are all going to work together to create an amazing synergy of health, lifestyle, and behavior. We'll be prescribing games for patients to play in order to determine whether they need a particular drug, when they need it, and how much they need. Or the patient's performance on the game will change the drug that comes with it, and then a sensor in the body will send data into the cloud that will change the game to better help us the next time it's played. We'll be printing pills at home that will give us the right dosage of everything we need for that day, based on our stool sample, our activity level, all the measurements being passively collected from our bodies. Or maybe we won't actually print the pill—it'll all be blended into a cookie, delivered via Amazon to our door, as part of our dinner. And when we open the package, it will have a sensor inside measuring our grip strength, which will serve as one more input into tomorrow's cookie.

Clearly if the future is going to look like this, collaboration is critical. Incentives have to be properly aligned, new payment models have to be put into place, every piece of the system has to be restructured in such a way that we can reach the full potential of the data. That is what the final section of the book will look at: how can we move from each of us creating and deploying our own patient equations to a world that is effectively powered by them, providing patients with everything they need to optimize their health and providing us with the business incentives to keep moving in the right direction, working together, and improving lives? We'll start with collaboration in the next chapter, and then move to payment models and incentive alignment in the chapters that follow before we address the COVID-19 pandemic and then reach the conclusion of the patient equation story.

Notes

1. Jignesh Padhiyar, "Best Health Apps for IPhone in 2019 You Shouldn't Miss Out," Igeeksblog.com, January 17, 2019, https://www.igeeksblog.com/best-iphone-health-apps/.

2. Mercatus Center, "Atul Gawande on Priorities, Big and Small (Ep. 26)," Medium (*Conversations with Tyler*, July 19, 2017), https://medium.com/conversations-with-tyler/atul-gawande-checklist-books-tyler-cowen-d8268b8dfe53.

3. Beth Snyder Bulik, "Payers Say They'll Cover Pharma's beyond-the-Pill Offerings. They Just Want Proof First," *FiercePharma*, August 24, 2016, http://www.fiercepharma.com/marketing/payers-want-more-info-pharma-and-healthcare-digital-health-technologies-according-to.

4. Jing Zhao, Becky Freeman, and Mu Li, "Can Mobile Phone Apps Influence People's Health Behavior Change? An Evidence Review," *Journal of Medical Internet Research* 18, no. 11 (November 2, 2016): e287, https://doi.org/10.2196/jmir.5692.

5. Jeff Lagasse, "Groove Health Gets $1.6M for Analytics Platform Focused on Medication Adherence," *MobiHealthNews*, August 8, 2017, https://www.mobihealthnews.com/content/groove-health-gets-16m-analytics-platform-focused-medication-adherence.

6. "Maxwell: AI-Powered Patient Engagement," Groove Health, 2019, https://groovehealthrx.com/AI.

7. Stephanie Baum, "Janssen Develops Mobile Clinical Trials Platform to Reduce Drug Development Costs, Improve Adherence," *MedCity News*, October 14, 2017, https://medcitynews.com/2017/10/janssen-develops-mobile-clinical-trials-platform/.

8. "A New Sort of Health App Can Do the Job of Drugs," *The Economist*, February 2018, https://www.economist.com/business/2018/02/01/a-new-sort-of-health-app-can-do-the-job-of-drugs.

9. "Scaling Impactful Digital Heath," Welldoc, Inc., July 8, 2019, https://www.welldoc.com/outcomes/clinical-outcomes/.

10. Simon Makin, "The Emerging World of Digital Therapeutics," *Nature* 573, no. 7775 (September 25, 2019): S106–S109, https://doi.org/10.1038/d41586-019-02873-1.

11. Ibid.

12. Stan Kachnowski, interview for *The Patient Equation*, interview by Glen de Vries and Jeremy Blachman, February 10, 2017.

13. Josh Baxt, "To Elevate Diagnostics, the Unloved Stepchild of Precision Medicine, Educate, Educate and Educate," *MedCity News*, August 29, 2017, https://medcitynews.com/2017/08/teaching-payers-pharma-physicians-patients-investors-diagnostics/.

Scaling Progress to the World

13 | The Importance of Collaboration

You can't do it alone. For us to scale progress to the world, companies in health care simply can't remain in their individual silos. Data needs to be combined to realize its full potential, which means players across the spectrum must work together. Finding, developing, testing, and marketing the right treatments for patients requires a coordinated effort. Companies must share data, talk to each other, and collaborate in order to thrive.

Take an eye drop developer, for instance. In the past, that company needed only to be concerned about eye drops, to some extent at least. Now, that same company ought to be sharing data with ophthalmologists and endocrinologists, with chronic care diabetes drug manufacturers, with players across the spectrum. Easier said than done, of course. We talked already about good data versus bad data—one principle of having good data is that it's in a form that's able to be shared in the first place. Standardizing data is obviously of key importance for collaboration, because we can't join forces if our information can't interconnect. But data standardization isn't enough. We need the willingness to share—and not just the willingness, but the realization that it is an imperative, and that cooperation will lift us all to greater heights in our quest to help patients and to create solutions that drive our organizations forward.

We need each other's data in order to enrich our models, to understand how our products and solutions are impacting patients in the world, and to fill in the gaps in our own views of patients as individuals, within populations for the modeling of disease, and across researchers who are working to manage and cure them.

Cancer treatment, for example, has been compared to a game of whack-a-mole. As soon as you bop one enemy on the head—you cut off a pathway gone awry, making cells in a tumor proliferate without control—another pathway will break down or compensate somewhere else. Working together, across silos, is just like a cocktail of medications, meant to bop all of the moles on the head at the same time.

William Carson, the recently retired CEO of Otsuka Pharmaceutical and chairman of the company's board, gave me a wonderful analogy for collaboration.[1] Imagine that each pharmaceutical company working to cure a particular cancer is one person in a room. There is one door. If everyone tries to get out the door at the same time, not only will it take a long time, but it will be a congested, chaotic mess. If the people line up before they walk out the door—if the pharma companies in the metaphor work together to figure out which therapy should be first in line, second in line, and so forth—then everyone gets through the door faster. The patients we are all working to serve get their treatments—their cures—as effectively and quickly as possible.

This isn't just a pharma problem, though. We are all collecting data across the continuum of care, and its fullest power is unleashed when we fit it all together.

A Tiny Island or a Larger Ecosystem

It doesn't take much looking back to remember a time when people signed up for email-only web services like Geocities and Hotmail. But almost as soon as it launched, Gmail became king—because it was integrated with the entire suite of Google products, and enabled data to be shared across a whole range of applications. Similarly, Jawbone fitness trackers didn't integrate their data into the giants like Apple and Google—and after being valued at as much as $1.5 billion in 2012, by 2017 they were liquidating their assets.[2] You can try to be a tiny island, with one crop, cut off from the larger mainland—but evidence shows that it is ultimately almost impossible to survive in the tech space without being part of a bigger ecosystem, and without integrating with large, platform players.

Apple has built a tremendous ecosystem around its devices, particularly the iPhone and Apple Watch. Through its ResearchKit, developers can create powerful research apps, and get them in front of possible participants through the App Store. They have even entered into agreements with large-scale health care players (starting with Aetna, to look at instrumenting their health insurance customers).[3] A joint Aetna-Apple app known as Attain offers health recommendations based on Aetna records, including vaccinations, medication refills, and information about lower-cost lab test options. It is a small step in the direction of digital medicine, but shows the potential.

The Economist has written about Apple, Amazon, Facebook, and Google's Verily diving into health care, trying to be the connective tissue that can bring everything together.[4] Apple is exploring sensors that measure stress and blood oxygenation, and trying to find ways to measure blood glucose with the Apple Watch. Verily is building surgical robots, and in 2017 launched Project Baseline, an effort to collect comprehensive health data to be deployed in exactly the ways we've discussed in this book. "Change doesn't happen in a silo," says the Project Baseline website.[5] "Through Project Baseline, Verily is building a connected ecosystem, engaging partners across healthcare, life sciences, and technology." Facebook is using artificial intelligence to monitor posts and find users who might be depressed, so that it can potentially intervene.[6] These big tech players will likely do whatever they can to find inroads into health care and do what they can to make themselves critical parts of the future, however it unfolds.

And they ought to. The future that we're envisioning—at least the one I want to be a patient in—requires connective tissue that acquires and transports data, and that can support businesses and market infrastructure as well as apps and data flows. These digital infrastructure giants are the organizations that can make sure the right incentives are cleverly and seamlessly integrated into patients' lives in order to make our patient equations work. They are the ones who can develop activity tracker batteries that last for a year and don't need to be recharged.

It's hard to get useful wearable data when there is any responsibility to manage infrastructure on the patient's end—when devices need to be taken off, or batteries recharged, for example. That's why ingestibles and implantables are so exciting. Of course, even they require connectivity, a digital fabric that brings all that data together. Between our phones, glasses, rings (and perhaps even cars), these companies are—or at the very least are among—the global players who will provide that network of connectivity.

We talked in Chapter 11 about adaptive clinical trials—but the possibilities don't stop just with individual organizations. Institutions can learn even more by collaborating with their peers—especially as medicine gets more and more precise. The traditional clinical trial model was based in part on the idea that any medical center would have exposure to lots of different patients, enough to populate a trial for most reasonably common conditions. But in the new model, we are looking to develop not just drugs for a wide swath of the population, but for very specific subsets—highly-specific cancers, for instance.

There may be only a very small group of patients nationwide—let alone at one particular institution. Siloed data may not slow you down if you are developing a statin, but as the inclusion and exclusion criteria lists get longer and longer, and trials get more and more specific, it becomes likely that even the largest and most prominent academic medical centers might see only a few relevant patients per year—which is neither cost-effective nor time-effective from any research perspective.

In Don Berry's I-SPY 2 trial, companies are working together in order to increase the chance that the study can find drugs that work in a more cost-effective, speedy way. Every individual life science company doesn't need to enroll control patients, and doesn't need to organize a giant new trial for one drug when instead they can all be combined under one organization. (It is also better from an ethical perspective, because fewer patients will be exposed to a placebo and the chance for great care will be maximized.) Using the I-SPY 2 model, having a site with just one patient ends up being workable—especially as we move more of the trial to the digital realm—because costs are more limited. And, as we explored, the adaptive trials of today can lead to broader industry collaborations as we as an industry—not just one medical center, company, or country—climb the data value chain toward more and more valuable and actionable insights.

How Data Collaboration Can Change the Game

All projects in life—not just in life sciences—have limits on resources: money, people, and time. We inevitably need to think about timelines and budgets at the same time as we think about rigorous science. But data collaboration can help us accelerate value and mitigate risk by centralizing and concentrating certain core research needs. Companies can get drugs approved and go to market more quickly, if they don't each design their clinical trial data systems and instead use one from a cloud software vendor.

This is an idea proven to be effective thanks to not just my company, but to the electronic trial industry that has attracted players as diverse as startups, database giants, and companies ostensibly in salesforce automation. We can confirm that there is a valuable drug response using synthetic control arms, and we can use integrated data across molecular to global scales to see which patients have the best chance of responding in order to seek them out, or the highest risks of adverse reactions in order to exclude them from trials. We can deliver the most valuable therapies to patients throughout the therapeutic life cycle, from the first time it is used in humans, to the moment the drug has been approved, to the last time it is prescribed before being replaced by a "better tool." (And using the platforms we just discussed in Chapter 12, we can account for the drug's value in all of those patients' lives more easily and accurately.)

The use of synthetic controls becomes a self-perpetuating business model if all data is pooled, as the data for new drugs today becomes tomorrow's control data. As we discussed in Chapter 11, if patients are getting a drug in one arm of a study—today's experimental therapy—those patients can become tomorrow's control patients, as the new standard of care. This applies across drug companies. If company A is testing a new drug for a particular condition, then as soon as that drug is approved, the patients in that trial can become part of the synthetic control group for company B's new trial of their next-generation drug, attempting to further the state-of-the-art therapy for the same condition. This saves immense amounts of time and money, and creates huge value by continually making the advancement forward less burdensome for patient volunteers in research, and faster to arrive for patients outside of trials.

You can also aggregate patients across trials and across drug companies into an experimental comparator group. A client can come to a company like Medidata and say it wants to launch a trial for, say, breast cancer with a particular set of markers over a particular period of time. Instead of the drug company needing to find 50 patients for this trial, Medidata can go into its storehouse of patient records and do that work. In the traditional model, of course doctors who are prominent in their fields and who actively participate in research can quickly help patients get access to trials. However, in models built around data sharing, with intermediaries and aggregators doing the work of connecting patients to research projects, identifying which patients will likely be the best responders (and matching them to the right trials) can be scaled beyond the connections and experience of individual investigators. We can build massively scaled adaptive trials, build synthetic control arms, and build up data in the process about people on experimental therapies for a particular disease—which all ends up enriching the next study, and the one after that, and the one after that.

Every time we get an outcome, we can look at patients through a range of different lenses, help drug developers figure out which biomarkers matter most for their new therapies, which biomarkers matter for another company's therapies, and predict which drugs help different subpopulations the most. And, we can do all of this while constantly comparing outcomes to the current standard of care and to previous trials across life sciences and health care. We can offer the benefits of enrolling as many patients as possible, but at the same time also limit the sample to the patients most likely to be good responders. By targeting the drug more closely to likely responders, its value proposition grows. The evidence for a payer or regulator to look at becomes much stronger, and the preference for a particular treatment by a patient or by a physician (as well as the willingness to approve and reimburse for it) all go up.

Demonstrating that value proposition more quickly—proving the drug works, even for a smaller subset of patients than originally hoped for as biomarkers are discovered and target populations narrow—still creates huge economic value. Selecting for better outcomes is better for drug companies, for payers, and for patients. Everyone ends up a winner. It's not the traditional model, but it's a disruptive way to take advantage of the promise of data and the hope of collaboration. Too often, I see companies running out of money before they find that value proposition—and then no patients end up benefiting. We can do better. Data collaboration can help us do better.

Put another way, making every patient across massively scaled research a potential participant in a single denominator—not trying to create evidence-based conclusions from data solely in single research projects, but across them—changes the equation (the business equation) around return on investment in research and development, and absolutely revolutionizes life sciences.

Alas, good intentions regarding data collaboration aren't enough to make it all happen—and, frankly, good intentions around any of these new data-driven technologies aren't enough to move forward at the pace at which effective change ought to progress.

There is a naïve view that cooperation in efforts like data sharing can be sustained entirely through altruism, even if commercial factors don't support it. I think there is substantial evidence to prove otherwise (for example, the lack of progress along these lines by not-for-profit industry endeavors like TransCelerate BioPharma), and sufficient reason not to rely on good intentions to be the only fuel that can propel us to these incredible possibilities.

The data in collaborations is no different than data in a single study—or in plotting the course of a single Mars probe. It must be cleaned, standardized, and made interoperable and fit-for-purpose for the analyses that create new comparators like synthetic controls and enable the discovery of new biomarkers and subtypes of diseases. All of that—just like every step in a laboratory, where a new molecule is synthesized and tested to see if it has the potential to become a new medication—takes time and money. Sustainable commercial business models need to be created that make this future state feasible. Incentives for the companies that create this research fabric to power innovation are just as necessary as they are in the world of smartphones and operating systems.

And then, of course, these innovations must be brought to patients at scale. One of the biggest things standing in the way of that progress is the need for new reimbursement models that truly incentivize the right behaviors and investment in the right initiatives across the landscape of precision medicine. The way we get there is by keeping our eye on the big picture—and tying our compensation to those big-picture results. It's about reimbursing life sciences companies and health care organizations based not on what we do but on the outcomes of what we do.

There has been a trend toward value-based reimbursement, but we are still in the relatively early days, and only a small percentage of what we do is successfully compensated under these new models. As an industry, we need to encourage the move toward value-based reimbursement models, and as a society we need to understand where we have the technology and data to measure value. To align incentives, we need to move closer to a system of outcome-based rewards. The next chapter will explore this issue more fully as we drive toward a better understanding of how to move the world toward a patient equation–driven future.

Notes

1. Courtesy of William Carson.
2. Wikipedia Contributors, "Jawbone (Company)," Wikipedia, October 1, 2019, https://en.wikipedia.org/wiki/Jawbone_ (company).
3. Jonathan Shieber, "Apple Partners with Aetna to Launch Health App Leveraging Apple Watch Data," *TechCrunch*, January 29, 2019, https://techcrunch.com/2019/01/29/apple-partners-with-aetna-to-launch-health-app-leveraging-apple-watch-data/.
4. "Apple and Amazon's Moves in Health Signal a Coming Transformation," *The Economist*, February 3, 2018, https://www.economist.com/business/2018/02/03/apple-and-amazons-moves-in-health-signal-a-coming-transformation.
5. "Project Baseline," Verily Life Sciences, 2017, https://www.projectbaseline.com.
6. "Apple and Amazon's Moves in Health Signal a Coming Transformation."

14 | Value-based Reimbursement

For too long, our reimbursement systems have been driven by what we do, what we make, and what we sell—and not whether a treatment works, or how effective it turns out to be. The truth is—and you probably realize this by this point in the book—our ability to measure value in health care has been limited until recently. We could track gross measures like survival rates across populations, but there's a big difference between surviving in a hospital room, with limited quality of life, and surviving at the baseline level established before an illness hit. We could also track individual patient outcomes in detail, but that data remained trapped within each individual's chart, not connected to or compatible with an integrated view of outcomes for patients like them.

The future of medical reimbursement is all about value—from a broader perspective than just survival—hinging on the integration of the details of individuals. Incentives for pharmaceutical companies and device manufacturers are changing as we realize we can measure more. We can measure whether something is working for each patient, and how much it is working—and we can move patients from treatments that don't work to treatments that do.

Moreover, in a value-based world, the calculations can go far beyond each individual. Data can give us the ability to make convincing arguments for regulators to let our drugs and devices enter new markets, give us new paths to approval, and new ways to value the work we do that isn't just based on how much cost we incur developing our treatments—but based instead on how much improvement these treatments bring to our patients and to the world.

These new therapies may be more expensive than the broad-audience drugs of the present, but their costs will be justified based on realized value—not just theoretical improvements to quality of life and longevity. The alignment of incentives across health care delivery and the research and development of better tools for health care will change the business equations. This will be thanks to focusing on patient equations, and on investing and delivering a better future for patients as individuals, and as populations—regardless of whether the population size is in the billions or perhaps just dozens with a particular rare disease.

Beyond Survival

Improving survival rates is terrific, there's no doubt. But—looking back at the discussion of the territory algorithm in Chapter 2—is survival the only measure we should value? We have the capability to show the economic impact that survival has on society and on each individual in a quantitative way. We can measure—or at least start to measure—how much quality of life is included in an extra 18 months of survival for a patient, as well as how much increase in GDP those extra 18 months might lead to for a government or society. We could never do this before, but with cognitive, behavioral, and nontraditional physiological inputs, we now can. We can present to regulators not just those traditional survival numbers, but more—to make the case that our drugs and devices are of real value across new dimensions.

Regulators are conservative. They should be. Their job is not to enthusiastically trust, but to skeptically question the evidence presented to them. Let's turn back to the idea of territory as a proxy for overall health. Maybe it will prove to be a surrogate measure for how much someone is able to work. Maybe we can use it as a quantitative input that helps estimate how much someone is contributing to GDP—a proxy endpoint for socioeconomic engagement and output. If that's true, it can help justify our entering a market and asking for a certain price on our product.

In a truly value-based world, if territory turns out to be a quantitatively valuable predictor, it could be used to justify a life sciences company being paid a certain percentage of the increased GDP their product leads to. If my drug causes 10 million people who would have otherwise died to each contribute $10,000 a year to the world, that's $100 billion in value per year. Is that worth $1 billion, $10 billion, or more to the pharma company that generated it? The answer to that question lies in economics and the negotiations of payers and consumers. But the ability to make that case—responsibly, reliably, and objectively—lies with the life sciences industry. And our regulators are the best starting point to make sure the evidence for such a case is sound.

Take gastric bypass surgery, for instance. It's not just about the success or failure of the procedure. People end up changing their diet, exercising more, and living fuller lives. Does that translate into more productivity at work? They lower their risk of sleep apnea and diabetes, adding years of life—higher-quality, more productive life. Or at least the patients with good follow-up care have all of these spillover returns. So if we base payment at least in part on these other measures, we not only incentivize performing a successful procedure, but we also incentivize good follow-up care—which is what we should want our system to do.

Another example: physical therapy always matters post-surgery for musculoskeletal procedures, but a surgeon's compensation isn't affected by the outcomes of the PT. Doctors perform amazing surgeries, and then give someone a Xeroxed copy of a 20-year-old sheet of paper explaining what they should do in physical therapy. This doesn't make sense in an outcome-based world. Whether or not I recover well from surgery depends as much if not more on my PT than on the surgery itself. We can measure mobility and overall activity before and after surgery and compare.

Financial success ought to mean getting patients as close to their before-condition numbers as we can—and, even better, financial success ought to mean preventing problems in the first place. If I'm a doctor and I intervene to stop you from ever needing diabetes medication, why shouldn't I make more money than the doctor who ignores you until he has to treat you for the diabetes he didn't help prevent—and why shouldn't that doctor make more money than the doctor who treats you for diabetes, but does a lousy job and your hemoglobin A1c gets worse? Doctors ought to be incentivized to actually care about the follow-up and the long-term outcome just as much as they care about making diagnoses and performing procedures. This is what will actually make a difference for patients.

These examples are simple to write, but hard to implement. The physicians and surgeons here suddenly have their compensation tied to things beyond their control—the patient's discipline in diet and exercise, or a physical therapist's ability to motivate. But it's even bigger than that. This isn't an exercise in changing the incentives and compensation for just one part of the value chain. The manufacturer of an implant, the surgeon, the physical therapist—the entire health care system ultimately responsible for delivering an outcome (in this case, an individual who can move around, enjoy life, and be productive at work) needs to be accountable as a team to deliver that outcome.

At the front end, that means we incentivize only offering the procedure to the people who will most benefit from it. Perhaps there are other therapeutic choices for a particular patient that would potentially have better outcomes. If we know that a patient is unlikely to follow post-surgery guidelines, perhaps they need to be incentivized or engaged differently as well. Limited resources—time and money—are unavoidable. So we need to figure out how to best drive outcomes along every step of the value chain, and to make sure we start every patient down what we predict will be the most productive path. This is how we figure out how to give the most effective treatments to the patients who will benefit from them the most.

John Kuelper, writing for the publication *STAT*, explains this issue about as well as anyone I've seen: "Today's insurance models are designed around the 'average' patient.... If every patient with X type of cancer gets Y drug, we will see better outcomes on average, so we encourage all patients with X type of cancer to get Y drug."[1] But that approach doesn't work for targeted, personalized treatments. "[E]ven if 95 percent of patients would see no improvement with the drug," Kuelper writes, "identifying the 5 percent who would have a profoundly beneficial response makes it possible to economically justify a price point that looks high on its surface."[2]

The (Mathematical) Fountain of Youth

For Alzheimer's disease and other neurodegenerative disorders, even if we do a great job as a society of keeping people alive longer, we need to make sure we are also keeping them productive. Again, the incentive has to be something more than just years of survival.

If we graph quality of life against years alive—see Figure 14.1—we want to maximize the area under the curve.

Regardless of how "quality of life" is defined on the y-axis, it is something that every stakeholder along the reimbursement value chain—not to mention the patient—should be able to align on. Note that the graph makes an important distinction between value and time. Quality of life and duration of life are perpendicular dimensions. Quality could mean socioeconomic engagement, or it could be measured by territory, or it could be anything that is valued by the patient or by society—or it could be proxies for any of those values. The integral of that value over time, from birth to death (point A) is the summation of that value over a lifetime. The shaded area is what we seek to maximize.

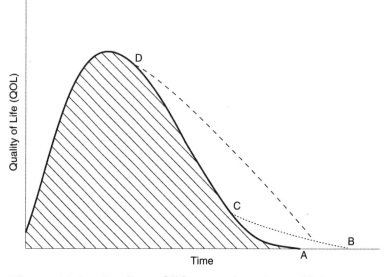

Figure 14.1   Quality of life over duration of life

So what is the most effective way to maximize it? At least in this theoretical illustration—and I think by general consensus—there is a time when quality of life declines, as we get closer to death. Unless unexpected or accidental, the course of most fatal illnesses leads to limited activity, consciousness, and—simply put—lower value for a period of time.

This is getting to the point of the difference between keeping people alive longer and keeping them productively alive. If we extend the point of death (point B) out from an already declining point in quality of life (QOL) (point C), there is an increase in the total value under the curve. However, that increase is relatively small. If we can instead alter the trajectory of decline in QOL at an earlier point (point D)—change the arc of decline more fundamentally—there is a much greater effect on the total area, even with no or close to no extension of life.

What is the result of drinking from the mythical fountain of youth? To live forever from point C on this chart? I think I'd pass. But if it results in the extension of the peak of the curve—literally, in this example, the top of the curve—as long as possible, creating a substantial change in the total area, then sign me up on the quest to find it!

This is exactly how I think about our jobs in life sciences. The example may be hyperbolic, but the result is literally what motivates so many of us in health care.

There is a case study in rheumatoid arthritis (RA) that illustrates how this theory can meet a practical, patient equation-based reality. Full credit goes to GlaxoSmithKline's work on the PARADE study (Patient Rheumatoid Arthritis Data from the Real World), which we were lucky enough at Medidata to provide some of the technology to help run (along with Apple via HealthKit). In advanced RA, patients spend a lot of time managing their joints (for example, wrapping them in hot towels—or, rather, having them wrapped for them—before getting out of bed in the morning). Yet RA disease progression has often been quantified with measures in a clinic—like counting the number of swollen joints on a patient's hands.

PARADE was an endeavor to deploy sensors and an easy-to-use app—a virtual trial brought to the patient, instead of bringing the patient into a clinic—to explore what really matters to patients, so that new baselines could be established for what "good" looks like in RA therapy. GSK focused on establishing new ways to look at value and exploring digital means to measure them. Instead of counting swollen joints in the clinic, perhaps we could measure how long it took patients to actually get out of bed in the morning. Perhaps instead of having to put patients physically in front of health care professionals to measure how well they could move their wrist, we could take those measurements with the accelerometers in their phones (which, yes, we were able to do, with reliable, quantitative results from the real world).

Ultimately, the results of PARADE and studies like it are destined to be used to demonstrate value and create measurements that truly matter to patients. We can then align them to incentives for providers, payers, and pharma.

Quality of life may look different for everyone. The point is not that the same measure will work for every patient. It certainly won't work for every condition. But we need to figure out what makes a difference so that it's not just about incentivizing survival, but quality survival. If drug A extends life by 18 months spent in a bed, and drug B extends life by just 12 months, but those months can be spent running on a beach, not every patient might make the same choice. Does a patient want to live to see his grandchild graduate from college, no matter the quality of those months or years? Is the goal one final road trip? Is it worth it to trade cheeseburgers and milkshakes for salads and kale juice? We may have the ability to extend our lives by minutes, months, or years, but with what pain and what cost (monetary and otherwise) to those around us and to society at large?

The curve is probably different for everyone, although the mathematics of decreasing returns inevitably applies to us all. There is no right or wrong answer. The point is that information can be generated from objective data, and reliable predictive models can be created based on what matters to individuals—so that patients and their caregivers can make informed choices. Data can give us all more control over expected outcomes and let people decide based on their own preferences.

Money-back Guarantee

We are seeing the beginnings of value-based reimbursement take hold in pharma. We talked already about Novartis's Kymriah, where a rebate returns the cost to payers when patients don't respond to therapy. Or at least that's the idea in principle—actual outcomes-based contracts are more complex, and, for now with Kymriah, limited to just its use in acute lymphoblastic leukemia (ALL) and not its more recent approval for B-cell lymphomas.[3]

Perhaps surprisingly, payers have not been fully supportive of outcomes-based contracts (OBCs) for drug therapies, at least not yet. Part of the problem is that the contracts as written right now cover only the actual cost of the medication and not all of the ancillary costs associated with treatment—care regimens to get the patient ready to receive the drug, for example—and so it is still a huge expense even if the drug itself is free. Part of the problem is that the current measurement—success at 30 days post-treatment, in the case of Kymriah—may not actually reflect long-term success. And part of the problem, at least in the United States, is navigating privacy laws that can get in the way of hospitals sharing treatment results with payers. According to an article in *Pharmaceutical Technology*, "There does not seem to be a specific push from private payers for treatment centres to enter into OBCs."[4] Again, we need to create aligned incentives across all participants in the delivery of therapeutic value, and systems that can support the objective measurement of that value.

Nevertheless, Kymriah is not the only example of experimentation with payment models along these lines. The weight loss and diabetes prevention app Noom—an app-based diet and life coaching tool, effectively a digital therapeutic—offers itself to employers on an outcome-based model. If a user doesn't lose 5% of his or her body weight while using the app, there is no charge.[5] Omada Health, which makes a digital diabetes prevention app, works similarly. According to *Vator News*, Omada gets paid based on the amount of weight the user loses. "[I]f the user has lost 2 percent of their weight, Omada charges 2x its fee; if they have lost 4 percent, then the company charges 4x, and so on."[6] (The base fee, according to the article, might be something on the order of $10 per user.)

An article recently appeared in *The Atlantic* about Bluebird Bio, a company developing a gene therapy for thalassemia, a blood disorder that leads to low hemoglobin, affecting approximately 100,000 babies born each year.[7] Bluebird's therapy will cost approximately $2 million, split into five yearly installments—but if the patient doesn't improve, only the first installment will need to be paid by the patient's insurer.[8]

The problem, Peter Bach of Memorial Sloan Kettering Cancer Center tells *The Atlantic*, is that value-based agreements make it easier for companies to charge exorbitantly high prices in the first place. "When Bluebird says, 'We've got a $2 million therapy,' they just made that up," Bach told *The Atlantic*. "Markets should set prices—not financing mechanisms."[9]

Making Value-based Care the Future

Peter Bach's concern is legitimate—but it just means that we need better pricing standards, not that outcomes-based reimbursement is the wrong way to go. The value—and the efficacy—of the therapy may be up for debate, but the model is a step in the right direction for value-based care. The challenge is that we simply aren't there yet as far as the data—we don't yet agree on what we should be pegging reimbursement against and how to move an entire legacy industry toward a new financial model.

Therefore, my advice to companies that come to me right now, in the course of developing the next great pharmaceutical, is to think about socioeconomic value in their therapeutics as quickly as possible while developing them. Put activity trackers on patients, leverage ideas like territory, record a breadth of digital data on everyone in their trials, whether or not they think it matters today. They will collect an interesting biospecimen that could enable the creation of a richer disease model to help subset patients, even if it is not part of the evidence used for demonstrating why the price point for their medication makes sense.

They might also expose inconsistencies not just in the patients themselves, but in their environments. We don't know the formulas yet, but I am convinced there are ways that measurements like territory or other high-resolution behavioral markers will contribute to models of disease progression. How someone is moving around the planet or interacting on social media might—and I believe should and will—contribute to our ability to detect whether or not they are responding to treatment, or whether (in oncology cases particularly) they need a new therapy. There will be other behavioral or cognitive biomarkers we've yet to even think of that will be additive to predictions. The information is out there, and we have the ability to collect it, even the obligation to collect it, and use it to help us create better disease models—because that is the road to better outcomes.

We talked about my Alzheimer's graph way back in Chapter 2, the cone of possibilities for my future. If a doctor can change my trajectory, move me from someone who appears as if he will need treatment in the future to someone who likely won't, then in a perfect outcomes-based world, that doctor should be compensated. There is a modern statistic in baseball called win probability added (WPA), the change in a team's win expectancy for a particular game based on the actions of each player. If it's the bottom of the ninth inning with two outs and your team is losing by a run, the chance of you winning that game is just 4%.[10] But if you hit a home run, the odds of victory jump to 56%. Your action is responsible for that rise from 4% to 56%, and in a world of outcomes-based reimbursement in baseball, you would be paid whatever that half a win might be worth. We can't be quite so precise in medicine (at least not yet), but prescribing you a statin may increase your odds of surviving another decade by a few percentage points. The doctor who makes that decision should get paid more than the one who doesn't.

That's at the individual level. At the population level, in most countries, regulatory approval of a drug just means that it is safe enough from a medical perspective. But we can also consider economic approval. Is the drug safe and effective enough from the perspective of economic returns? If we can use our new streams of knowledge to get patients off drugs that aren't working and onto new ones faster than before, there's economic value if the patients are quicker to contribute to society again. We don't want to give a drug to eight billion people. We want to give it to the ones for whom it will make a difference, where it will meaningfully affect their odds in a positive way. The endgame is being able to demonstrate this, and that's why the new tools are so critical. Giving the wrong treatment costs money. Using the wrong app, one that doesn't produce the actionable advice it claims to, also costs money. We want to spend our limited pool of money on effective therapies, not ineffective ones. We need our breakthroughs to reach as many people as possible—and wasting money on cases where they won't be of benefit doesn't help anyone. This is a case of money as a limited resource—but it is really an argument about opportunity cost. We could have used those resources on efforts that drive outcomes. Why are these aligned incentives and value-based systems so important? Because they reduce waste.

I spoke to a class of Columbia Business School students getting a certificate in digital health, and many of the questions were about value-based contracts. To those students, I explained that you need to worry about three things when considering a value-based approach that we just don't pay enough attention to today.

First, consider who should take your drug. "Take it if you have this mutation, but not that other one. Not if you have a previous history of heart disease. Not if you're under 18." These are natural ways life scientists think about medication, inclusion and exclusion criteria in clinical trials, and drug labels that are approved when we make medications available to the public. We can get even more specific as we refine our patient equations. Take it if you're at least this active in a typical day. Take it if you can also avoid these three foods. Take it if you combine it with these exercises, these other medications, and fall in a particular range based on this wearable sensor. Maybe it's a binary yes/no decision that we end up producing, or maybe it's a weighted score of how well we expect you to respond. But in any case, there is a patient equation that can predict who will benefit, and we should continue to refine it to figure out who the target patient population is, as precisely as possible.

Second, how do we prove the drug is working? This is a newer idea in life sciences, particularly in the commercial part of a drug's life cycle—but even in the research and development phase, from the perspective of not just the entire population, but individual patients and what really matters to them. What aspects of physiology, cognition, and behavior can we measure that track with effectiveness and safety? How do we measure them, and what can we do to enable that measurement—or find proxies for it—at scale? This is the argument for tracking behavior in all clinical trials. If we're not keeping these measurements in mind while evaluating our drug physiologically, we've missed a huge opportunity to relate physiology to behavior in our modeling of disease as it responds to a new therapy. Figuring out how you engage with a patient in that process goes right along with the measurements. Are there things you need to do (think back to our disease management platforms in Chapter 12) to get the best outcome with your drug in each individual?

Third, make sure you know when you should stop the patient from using your therapy. This third consideration in value-based environments is antithetical to how most life sciences companies have traditionally operated. Yet it is just as important as the first two—if not the most important in eliminating waste in a value-based system. What will be the signals that come out of the data you are collecting that indicate a patient isn't benefiting from the drug? How will you feed that information back into the criteria for who should take it? What will you do to help everyone across the value chain—including the patient—realize as quickly as possible that the therapy is failing, and how can you facilitate the transition to an alternative (even competitive—see, I told you it would be antithetical!) therapy? Every time a patient takes a pill after the point where we could have known it's not working is wasting the patient's time, decreasing the area under their QOL value curve, and degrading your margin in a value-based world.

Managing all three of these concepts is a difficult task for the life sciences industry. But if it was easy, everyone would do it. The companies that embrace this thinking, understand how patient equations are the key to getting there, and manage to execute will be the winners—both financially and in terms of bringing the most value to patients.

Value-based care absolutely requires something different from fee-for-service. It's a huge change to the traditional business model, and requires new ways of thinking. We need to be able to predict outcomes and trajectories. And we also need to effectively measure the outputs that we decide matter. But it's not science fiction. We are on a path to value-based care.

But this isn't enough. We can change the way payers are reimbursed and how drugs are valued, but that doesn't get us to systemic change in every aspect of the health care system. We haven't spent much time in the book talking about two huge stakeholders in the future of medicine: doctors and patients. Doctors need to come on board the data revolution in order to propagate these technologies to the world, and patients need to understand how all of this is set to make radical improvements to their health.

In the next chapter, I talk to internist and cardiologist—and my own physician—Dr. Dan Yadegar, and patient advocate Robin Farmanfarmaian about where doctors and patients fit into a patient equation–powered world, and how we can make sure incentives are aligned for the betterment of individuals and of society.

Notes

1. John Kuelper, "Community Providers Will Help Drive the Future of Precision Medicine," *STAT*, February 23, 2018, https://www .statnews.com/2018/02/23/precision-medicine-community-providers/.
2. Ibid.
3. Manasi Vaidya, "Outcome-Based Contracts Viable for Kymriah, but US Payers Still Unsure," *Pharmaceutical Technology*, July 30, 2018, https://www.pharmaceutical-technology.com/comment/outcome-based-contracts-kymriah/.
4. Ibid.
5. "Noom—The Anthology of Bright Spots," The diaTribe Foundation, 2016, https://anthology.diatribe.org/programs/noom/.
6. Steven Loeb, "How Does Omada Health Make Money?," *VatorNews*, February 3, 2017, https://vator.tv/news/2017-02-03-how-does-omada-health-make-money.
7. Suzanne Falck, "Thalassemia: Types, Symptoms, and Treatment," *Medical News Today*, January 10, 2018, https://www .medicalnewstoday.com/articles/263489.php.
8. Sarah Elizabeth Richards, "Pharma Should Pay for Drugs That Don't Work," *The Atlantic*, April 22, 2019, https://www.theatlantic.com/ideas/archive/2019/04/pharma-should-pay-drugs-dont-work/587104/.
9. Ibid.
10. Greg Stoll, "Win Expectancy Finder," Gregstoll.com, 2018, https://gregstoll.com/~gregstoll/baseball/stats.html#H.0.9.2.1.

15 | Aligning Incentives

To get the most out of a patient equation–powered world, lots of pieces we've discussed already need to come together. Data needs to be integrated across health care in much more complete ways than it is now. Pharmaceutical companies need to embrace the power of sensors and adaptive trial designs, and bring clinical trials into the twenty-first century. Best practices for disease management apps need to be developed and tested. Companies and organizations across life sciences and health care need to think about how they can use new streams of data to provide better and more actionable insights to patients who use their products and services. Reimbursement models need to move in the direction of value-based care. And, finally, doctors and patients need to come fully on board.

It is far too easy to put doctors and patients to the side when we talk about the patient equation-driven future. After all, they aren't the ones developing the products, launching the clinical trials, deciding on reimbursement models, or looking at the big picture of the life sciences industry. They aren't dealing with FDA regulations, or, in most cases, spending much energy thinking about the business side of medicine beyond their own practices or experiences.

And yet, doctors and patients will determine the success or failure of the data revolution. If doctors aren't on board with recommending and prescribing smart devices to their patients, diffusion won't be achieved. If doctors aren't at the forefront of data collection and sharing, looking for insights into the useful biomarkers of the future, we won't be able to move our knowledge forward. If patients don't understand how these technologies can help them, and how data can make their lives better, healthier, longer, and more productive, they won't engage, they won't help generate the information we need, and they ultimately won't see the benefits.

It is critical that doctors and patients are not only engaged and well-informed, but that their incentives are fully aligned with the rest of the industry. In this chapter, we look at the patient equation future from the perspectives of doctors, and then patients, in order to figure out how we can best effect change across the care continuum, and make the biggest impact on our businesses.

Human Doctors, Digital Doctors

It is not hard to see how doctors could get fully on board with the ideas in this book. Doctors unquestionably want rich sets of good data. They want information on their patients just like pilots want maintenance records on the aircraft they fly. Better, more complete data means doctors can work more effectively on more valuable interventions and preventative measures during patient encounters. The information streams that sensors provide can help establish useful baselines and let doctors move from being purely reactive to being able to work proactively and prevent problems down the line. I am not a physician, but it would be hard to convince me that doctors who are not on board with this vision are capable of practicing good medicine in the world of digitization and data sophistication that we live in. It's as simple as that.

At the same time, some doctors may be worried that these tools are going to automate them out of existence. Who needs a doctor if an app can tell you what illness you have and how to treat it? The answer, of course, goes back to the failures of IBM's Watson in making smart recommendations for cancer treatment: computers aren't always right. Artificial intelligence can do a lot for us, but it can't replace human judgment, human experience, and complex human decision-making. Garbage-in/garbage-out applies to data as well as to assumptions for what a desired outcome might be.

We talked in the previous chapter about the difference between mere survival and quality of life. When faced with that trade-off—do you want to live more years in a hospital room, or fewer years outside in the world?—there is not necessarily a right answer or a wrong one. Different patients might have different preferences. A computer can't help us make those decisions; a doctor can. Artificial intelligence can replace rote tasks like measuring blood glucose, injecting us with insulin at the right time and in the right dose—things we can get bored by, lose track of, or make a mistake with. But that doesn't replace the doctor. Instead, it frees the doctor to think, to strategize, and to do the higher-order work that robots and predictive models can't.

What we're talking about is expanding the doctor's toolkit. Just like some products—think wearables like Ava—expand the ability of patients to exert control, we have more and more ways for doctors to have increased information, or at least the possibility of it. What do they want their patients to be wearing, tracking, or reporting? What data is going to help fuel better medical decisions and more productive appointments? What should be measured more accurately than what a patient is normally able to report? In what situations is objective data going to potentially change treatment?

The line of thinking that says technology will inevitably mean a loss of power for doctors is something I strenuously disagree with. The new technologies aren't taking away but giving more—more power to effect change and to identify and deliver better treatments to improve lives. Yes, automation eliminates rote tasks. Robots can replace humans on an assembly line. But the human body is incredibly complex, we live in even more complex changing environmental conditions, and knowledge of disease and health continually evolves. New tools to manage us are constantly being invented. Someone who wants to follow procedures by rote as prescribed by what they learned back in medical school, and not be an active participant in the patient equation-driven world, should absolutely be worried about being replaced by an algorithm or robot. But the kind of physician I want to be in the care of has nothing to worry about.

Dr. Daniel Yadegar is a cardiologist in New York City, with an undergraduate degree from Harvard and a medical degree from Cornell. He has worked at some of the city's top institutions. He's also my own personal internist. I chose to interview him for this book because rather than being afraid of the future, Dr. Dan—as I have come to affectionately refer to him—has embraced it. He believes, as we all ought to, that the new technologies aren't setting us up to replace doctors but that they are hugely powerful tools to help doctors manage their patients' health and help them live longer, better lives.

Dr. Dan wants to use these new tools to be able to diagnose heart disease and catch cancers before clinical symptoms ever manifest. To that end, he's changed the entire way he operates as a doctor. Unlike traditional physicians, Dr. Dan doesn't just want to see his patients once a year to gather some isolated data points—he wants to see a far richer picture than that. He has patients constantly monitoring their blood pressure, tracking sleep data, heart rate variability, stress markers, and more. And he puts all this data together to augment his understanding of the patient and make better and smarter decisions. He sees the practice of medicine on a path toward greater information, a greater set of tools, from drugs and devices alone to drugs and devices supplemented by digital systems that incorporate trackers, mathematical models, and more.

When I first went to Dr. Dan—for what was technically a checkup—he wanted what felt like about two liters of blood. I tell people that and they're surprised, but in Dr. Dan's words, "I wanted as much information as I could get, objective and subjective. So many of the recommendations for how we manage patients are based on population-level stats, data about cost-efficient recommendations based on someone turning a certain age, but what's missed are the individual blueprints."[1] He wanted to know not just how old I was, but who I was, from every perspective we're able to assess. "Especially with advancements like biomarkers, genomics, proteomics, every patient is different. We need to look at what's specifically going on with each individual."

Dr. Dan looks at a patient's coronary calcium score as a measure of risk stratifying: are they more likely to have a heart condition that needs medication? He looks at sleep—"having good objective measures of sleep would be great," he says—and diet and exercise. He looks at blood pressure variability—at a continuous measure of blood pressure instead of the staccato points of measurement in his office. "Having these additional points of data is always helpful," Dr. Dan says. "They let me make better decisions about a patient's health care. Is a patient a 'dipper,' whose blood pressure drops every night, for example?"

"One of the biggest health care problems out there is heart failure," Dr. Dan explains. "Trying to decrease heart failure readmissions to the hospital is so important, from a patient health perspective and also a cost perspective. One device out there uses impedance. When impedance decreases, it shows that heart failure is right around the corner. The patient hasn't manifested symptoms yet, but if a pacemaker or other device is showing that impedance is decreasing, I double up on the medication so the patient doesn't have to go to the ER. I can see it in the numbers before it happens."

Seeing it in the numbers before it happens is exactly what patient equations are all about. And Dr. Dan wants as many useful numbers as he can get. "If there could be a composite set of data to tell me the continuous heart rate variability, the number of cigarettes smoked, the peaks and valleys in blood pressure, the patient's surrogate stress markers, the amount of mindfulness during the day, how much protected time someone has to not do anything . . . objective data about diet and nutrition and exercise, amount of REM sleep . . . the kind of information I could wish for to optimize patient care is endless. It would all absolutely influence my dialogue with every patient."

Even better, he says, would be if insurance companies were measuring these numbers too, and paying him based on how much he was able to help his patients' data get better. "We have aligned interests," he insists.

Dr. Dan is emphatically not scared of the data replacing him and his function. "The art of medicine is taking those data points, objective and subjective, and trying to optimize them—how do you use resources, in terms of approach and quality? It's not just a formula. My patients want more than the standard of care. They want to feel good, and if they are living longer, they want their cognitive faculties, they want their independence, but to make those decisions takes more than just the numbers. It takes looking beyond them."

And to truly effect change with most patients takes more than just a data printout. The doctor-patient relationship is also so important—and that's something the data can't re-create on their own. "One of the things missing with technology," says Dr. Dan, "is that doctor-patient bond. I am afraid we will get good at diagnosing and preventing disease but not as good at taking care of the illness as far as actually treating the patient. Our role is to anticipate what might happen and have useful, meaningful discussions that might prevent it from happening in the first place. The data can't do that."

Respecting the Unquantifiable

Indeed, as Dr. Dan says, doctors need to go beyond the data. Effective physicians in a patient equation-powered world won't just be treating discrete episodes of illness—they'll be partnering with patients to manage their health and optimize their lives. They will be monitoring our trajectories as we move along the lines defined by patient equations in the multidimensional phase diagrams we've already discussed. The pitfall is relying too much on the data alone.

"Let's not confuse the exchange of data with the exchange of knowledge," Michael Hodgkins, chief medical information officer at the American Medical Association, told an audience of medical leaders, at a 2017 conference reported on by *MedCityNews*.[2] "In chronic disease, if we don't solve the problem of how to adapt these tools to clinical practice and patient care, we're not going to make much progress," he said. It can be too much. The data alone only gets us so far.

But it can change the paradigm. Imagine a doctor's office of the future, as Glen Tullman, executive chairman of consumer digital health company Livongo, does in an article in *Forbes*. "Imagine receiving a suggestion on your smartphone," he writes, "that your doctor would like to see you to determine whether that nagging cough is seasonal asthma or an exacerbation of your congestive heart failure."[3] The doctor of the future can order labs in advance, deploy a range of home-based tests (perhaps through apps on the patient's phone or other devices) and collect whatever data is necessary to make the in-person conversation more fruitful and productive.

Data, in the future, will be already loaded and ready to apply. It's an unreasonable expectation that a doctor can do everything in one office visit when they often start with nothing. The baseline will change. The expectations will change. And a side benefit: for better or worse (and, of course, when it comes to actually helping doctors make choices that improve our health, it's definitely for better), we can't lie to our digital doctors. The sensors know whether we exercised, what we ate, if we took our pills. The guarantee of objective honesty alone will enable huge amounts of progress in patient care.

Dr. Rajesh Pahwa at the University of Kansas Medical Center told *mHealthIntelligence* about how wearables, like a smartphone or smartwatch, can help him treat his Parkinson's patients: "[Pahwa] can track body movements over a period of several days, charting the instances and severity of tremors, and correlate those movements with the patient's prescribed treatment of L-DOPA, a medication usually taken every four hours."[4] The digital device helps him refine the treatment, and improve life for his patients.

But Dr. Pahwa's clinical judgment is still critical in the process, and that's what we can't forget. There's an example from outside of health care that crystallized this idea for me. On September 26, 1983, Stanislav Petrov, a lieutenant colonel in the Soviet Union military, was on overnight duty monitoring early-warning nuclear satellites. Suddenly, according to the *Washington Post*'s account of the situation, "sirens began blaring. A red button on the panel in front of him flashed the word 'Start.' On a computer screen was the word 'Launch,' in red, bold letters." The technology was telling him that the United States had just launched a nuclear strike.[5]

Five missiles were launched, according to the warning system. Petrov had to decide whether to tell his commanders to strike back or tell them the system was wrong. His gut told him the system was wrong. And that's what he told his commanders. "I had a funny feeling in my gut," Petrov told the *Post*. "I didn't want to make a mistake. I made a decision, and that was it."[6]

He was right, even though the machine was saying otherwise. Technology, whether in a potential nuclear war or in the doctor's office, is not always foolproof. It does not always have the answers. But it can certainly help doctors make better decisions, empower them in ways we couldn't even imagine a few years ago. Doctors like Dr. Dan, who embrace these new data sources, will thrive. Others will be left behind, particularly by patients who choose to take it upon themselves to get the most that they can from the new technologies.

Empowered Patients

The publication *Elemental* writes about entrepreneur Julia Cheek. "In 2017, [she] broke a record on ABC's *Shark Tank*: The show's judges awarded her a $1 million deal for her company, EverlyWell, marking the largest investment a solo female entrepreneur had received in the show's history."[7] EverlyWell sells at-home medical tests, of the same quality that would be used in a medical lab or doctor's office, for conditions and measurements ranging from Lyme disease to cholesterol to sexually transmitted diseases. Cheek's company is just one of many new entrants in the space. It's not that the technology they are selling is new—but the impulse for patients to be more involved in the kinds of information gathering they would typically see as exclusively owned by the health care system is tied inextricably to the topics we've been talking about in this book. Patients are able to do more for themselves—and so they are.

It comes back to the late Jack Whelan, the self-tracking cancer patient and advocate I talked about in the Introduction—one of my first inspirations in thinking about patient equations as he showed me graphs of his biomarkers in Microsoft Excel. With the tools to track, patients can be part of their care, more than ever before. Jack knew as much about the clinical trial landscape as his doctors did, and as much about his own biomarkers. In fact, he probably knew more. He felt that his care would be better if he was at least partly at the wheel—and technology made that possible. The efforts to move patient equation–type thinking into the mainstream will only be helped by patients who understand the power of data and take it as seriously as their health care providers do.

Patients don't all need to be Jack Whelan, instrumenting themselves and tracking their biomarkers at home, but they do need to be willing to leverage their data, or willing to wear a device (or multiple devices) and engage through the digital world in their health care. They need education—and the pharmaceutical industry can certainly help here—about how apps and wearables can be combined with pills and procedures, and should be taken just as seriously. They need to understand that in the new world of health care, information is power, and information can help them. It can help them stay healthy between appointments, it can help them partner with the health care system to find the best treatments for whatever ails them, and it can ultimately help them live longer and healthier lives. And they also need to be scientifically skeptical. They need to understand and want measurable, objective outcomes. And they need to know the difference between those objective science-tested facts and the promises of snake oil.

Patient advocate, entrepreneur, and author Robin Farmanfarmaian talks about the patient as the "CEO" of his or her health care team—bringing together doctors, devices, apps, and more to optimize their health and their lives. "The amount of information we have as patients now is staggering," she told me in an interview.[8] "We can wear a clinical-grade EKG monitor that connects to our iPhone and sends the information into the cloud. Contact lenses can track our glaucoma progression, socks can measure our gait, subcutaneous sensors can measure glucose, and epidermal sensors can measure UV radiation. I don't want the raw data, but if the AI can produce a dashboard with actionable items for me to deal with—should I drink eight ounces of water because I'm dehydrated?—then I can go out and hire a doctor or other health care professional when I have a problem that benefits from their input, and otherwise I can be in charge myself."

For Robin, the technology provides freedom and power. "It's not necessarily the doctor's fault if the outcome turns out badly," she says. "Doctors are traditionally siloed in their home health care systems. If they work at, say, Stanford, they don't necessarily know anything outside of those four walls, they don't know about all of the devices, medications, and technologies available in the world, purely because there is too much information coming out every day." Which means it's incumbent on us as patients to take charge. Scary, perhaps—but also reassuring in that it means that we can have more control over our own medical destinies. (And payers ought to be willing to incentivize patients to take as much control as they can, to track, to listen, to be fully engaged—because healthier patients are going to mean lower costs at all points along the way.)

A column in *MedCityNews* by Jeff Margolis, chairman and CEO of WellTok, a consumer health software company, puts this issue about as well as anyone: imagine two different tubes of health care data, he writes. The first concerns what doctors should do to "fix" their patients. The second is about what patients can do themselves "to achieve their highest health status in the context of their daily lives. . . . We've spent decades working to perfect the first tube," Margolis writes, "but what about the second?"[9] We can't ignore patients, and, in fact, we need to embrace the opportunities that technology gives us to touch them directly and help them manage their medical lives.

Glen Tullman's company Livongo, in fact, is already doing this—in the area of diabetes now, with plans to expand elsewhere in the future.[10] He started Livongo believing that health care should be following the same path toward reduced complexity through technology as almost every other industry has over the past generation. "It's so much easier to ticket a flight than it used to be, for instance," he told me in an interview, "and yet health care has become more confusing, more complex, and more costly." Everything has become more consumer-focused except health care, Tullman realized. Since that epiphany, he has been investing through his venture fund in companies that seek to create more intelligent, informed, and connected health consumers. He wants to use data to keep consumers out of the health care system and treat them as people, not patients.

"We believe people will make good decisions," he says. "We just need to make it easy and cost-effective. No one wants to be sick or get bad care. It's just too complex. We have to make it simpler to make the right decision." With Livongo, he works with existing players in health care—insurers and employers—to get to their members and employees and give them data tools to improve behavior and decision-making. In the area of diabetes, he is disrupting the traditional model by making money by providing actionable advice instead of by selling blood sugar test strips for exorbitant rates to patients who desperately need them. Livongo provides the test strips for free, with the confidence that patients aren't checking their blood sugar more than they need to, and that he needs to partner with them for health instead of fighting them every step of the way.

"Everything we do is about our members," he says. "If you have a question, you touch the screen [on our app] and someone calls you, 24/7, within 60 to 90 seconds." This keeps people out of the hospital, and it keeps them happy. He charges employers based only on whether the members use the system, so that if Livongo is not providing value, the employer doesn't pay. As the company realized that 70% of people with diabetes also suffered from hypertension, Livongo expanded into that domain as well, providing an integrated experience—one platform with advice for patients to stay healthy, manage their diabetes and hypertension, manage their weight, and manage their mental health. The company collects data—it has amassed the largest database of blood glucose information in the world—and uses predictive data-driven science to figure out what information it needs to provide to patients to help them better manage their health, telling them when to check their blood sugar, when to eat something, when to drink more water, and more. The result has been a cost savings of more than $1,000 a year per user, with measurable improvements in hemoglobin A1c and other indicators of health.

It's not an artificial pancreas, but it's an end result far easier than wearing a clunky or invasive device that patients may never comply with—it's data, applied as intelligently as possible (Livongo calls it Applied Health Signals) toward improving health, in the patient's home and in the patient's pocket.

At the end of 2019, that left us in a place where the pieces were beginning to come together—collaborations to share data, reimbursement models beginning to reflect the advantages of a data-driven system, and doctors and patients coming on board to help lead the charge toward more robust patient equations. And then, COVID-19 emerged, and changed everything. We'll talk in the final chapter about how the ideas we've just spent the past 15 chapters discussing have become even more critical in the context of a pandemic-scale infectious disease, and what we need to know to navigate a post-pandemic world.

Notes

1. Daniel Yadegar, interview for *The Patient Equation*, interview by Glen de Vries and Jeremy Blachman, February 7, 2017.
2. Josh Baxt, "Data, Data Everywhere, Not a Drop of Insight to Glean?," *MedCity News*, August 25, 2017, https://medcitynews.com/2017/08/data-data-everywhere-not-drop-insight-glean/.
3. Glen Tullman, "Health Care Doesn't Need Innovation—It Needs Transformation," *Forbes*, December 21, 2016, http://www.forbes.com/sites/glentullman/2016/12/21/health-care-doesnt-need-innovation-it-needs-transformation/#7e9623525a4f.
4. Eric Wicklund, "A Parkinson's Doctor Explains How MHealth Is Changing Patient Care," mHealthIntelligence, October 2, 2017, https://mhealthintelligence.com/news/a-parkinsons-doctor-explains-how-mhealth-is-changing-patient-care.
5. David Hoffman, "'I Had A Funny Feeling in My Gut,'" *Washington Post*, February 10, 1999, https://www.washingtonpost.com/wp-srv/inatl/longterm/coldwar/soviet10.htm.
6. Ibid.
7. Erin Schumaker, "What's Driving the Boom in At-Home Medical Tests?," Medium (*Elemental*), May 15, 2019, https://elemental.medium.com/whats-driving-the-boom-in-at-home-medical-tests-2e9812e38a16.
8. Robin Farmanfarmaian, interview for *The Patient Equation*, interview by Glen de Vries and Jeremy Blachman, February 22, 2017.
9. Jeff Margolis, "How Consumer Data (Not More Clinical Data) Will Fix Healthcare," *MedCity News*, April 9, 2018, https://medcitynews.com/2018/04/consumer-data-not-clinical-data-will-fix-healthcare/.
10. Glen Tullman, interview for *The Patient Equation*, interview by Glen de Vries and Jeremy Blachman, September 3, 2019.

16 | And Then, a Pandemic

The most astonishing thing about the pandemic was the complete mystery which surrounded it. Nobody seemed to know what the disease was, where it came from or how to stop it. Anxious minds are inquiring to-day whether another wave of it will come again . . . [1]

While it sounds like that could have been written in 2020, as COVID-19 outbreaks spread around the world, it was actually written more than a hundred years ago, in the wake of the 1918 Spanish flu pandemic. It's from an article in the journal *Science* that was sent to me for some historical perspective by a friend and kindred spirit in biology and statistics, Dr. Rebecca Doerge, dean of the Mellon College of Science at Carnegie Mellon.

The piece was written by civil engineer George Soper, who initially gained fame by identifying "Typhoid Mary" as the source of the typhoid fever epidemic in New York City in 1906. "Until [the mass of statistical data is studied]," Soper wrote, "it will be impossible to give the number of persons attacked, their age, sex, condition and race, the complications and sequelae of the disease, much less the relations which these facts bear to the preventive measures."[2]

Alas, in the setting of COVID-19, it appears that not much has changed—or at least not changed enough—when it comes to our ability to understand and prevent this kind of pandemic. Of course our medical knowledge has increased dramatically over the past hundred years, as have the tools available for diagnoses and treatments. On top of that, the world is connected by a technology fabric that couldn't have even been dreamed of a century ago. And yet the advice to prevent the illness's spread sounds very much the same. Again from Soper:

> There is one and only one way to absolutely prevent it and that is by establishing absolute isolation. It is necessary to shut off those who are capable of giving off the virus from those who are capable of being infected, or vice versa.[3]

I found it astonishing to read this, when you consider the break-throughs in medicine and technology that have occurred since 1918, as well as so many on the horizon, as discussed in the preceding chapters. Indeed, it is sobering to realize how close we still are to the thinking of a hundred years ago. But it is also galvanizing and inspiring to think that the ideas in the first 15 chapters of this book might be ones that finally lead to change.

The spread of COVID-19 around the planet, and the damage it has inflicted on the world, will likely be a subject of historical and scientific investigation for decades. But looking at the pandemic even today already highlights how important and useful some of the concepts in this book can be. What can we do as professionals in life sciences and medicine (and what can we understand as individuals) to speed our recovery from this pandemic, to lessen the negative effects it will have on human health, and to make the next pandemic—whether a hundred years or a hundred days from now—play out differently? How can we limit the damage ranging from the direct impact of the virus to the more indirect impacts from people postponing medical treatment, from clinical trials being canceled or delayed, and from hospital bed and staffing shortages affecting patients with illnesses unrelated to COVID-19? What lessons are applicable to the management of diseases, across the entire range from infectious to hereditary?

Phase Diagrams Revisited

I had an eye-opening moment just a couple of weeks into the COVID-19 outbreak in the New York area. A friend—relatively young and to the best of my knowledge otherwise healthy—died quickly and unexpectedly from the virus. At the time, the prevailing assumption was that the most important COVID-19 risk factors—the individual variables that were inputs as to whether a person was likely to have a life-threatening case of the illness—were age and immune status. People were thought likely to merely experience flu-like symptoms (if experiencing any symptoms at all) if they were under 60 and had normal, robust immune systems. We now know that assumption was wrong.

It may have simply been that my friend was on the wrong side of the odds. But perhaps not. There were increasing reports at the time of young, otherwise-healthy victims from Asia and Europe—and then more from closer to home. Whether other factors could have helped (and can still help) predict disease severity in COVID-19 patients became critical to the concept of giving the right treatment to the right patient at the right time. We often think of precision medicine as it applies to rare diseases or cancers, but it is no less applicable in the case of infectious disease, as this historic event—and the untimely demise of so many, including my friend—so poignantly illustrates.

Looking back at the phase diagrams we discussed in Chapter 9, we can think of age and immune response, instead of temperature and pressure, as our initial—although likely incorrect, or at least insufficient—axes. Imagine the x-axis starting with a healthy immune system at the origin of the graph, getting more compromised (e.g., if someone is immunocompromised from cancer therapy) as you move along the axis to the right, and the y-axis defined by increasing age. That simplistic view would mean that the closer someone was to the origin of the graph, the less likely they would be to develop and suffer from COVID-19 (the disease) based on exposure to SARS-CoV-2 (the virus itself).

But in the case of my friend—and many others, of course—those two variables were not enough. They do not appear to provide a sufficient mathematical model to predict who needs treatment, and who might not. So what inputs were we missing at the time, or may still be missing as we attempt to better understand the disease?

Much like the multidimensional models we have already discussed, we need to stack as much data as possible, to create steam table–like views of the patients who did and didn't suffer from COVID-19. Ideally, we would have a complete view of every patient around the world: who was exposed to the virus, who presented with COVID-19, how long it took before they got sick, what treatments they received, and how long did they take to recover (if they recovered at all)?

However, just like when it comes to other diseases, the disjointed nature of medical systems around the world as well as the nature of the pandemic itself make it impractical to generate that kind of exhaustive view. Not to mention, we'd need to find patients across all combinations of possible underlying risk factors and then treat them with every plausible therapy to see their outcomes in the platonic steam table model. That literal generation of a steam table–style view of data is not just impractical, but unethical and ultimately impossible. But that doesn't mean we can't try to do as best we can.

We can apply the phase diagram model to the data we do have available, exactly in the same way that Dr. Jerry Lee first described it to me. Doing so would allow us to formulate and test hypothetical equations to predict which patients need what treatments (and at what points in time) once we know they have been exposed to SARS-CoV-2—at least while we wait for a safe, effective, and widely available vaccine.

To do this, we need to look at the additional data available about patients who have and haven't suffered from the illness: for instance, body mass indexes, medical histories, and possibly even genes. We can then begin to find groups of patients with associated factors that match different treatments and favorable outcomes. We can create equations that show the phase shifts—the relationships of the input variables to a prediction of how to best treat these patients.

In phase diagram–style we can plot those equations and visualize the progression of the disease (for example, the amount of virus present in a patient's body—their viral load) against time, just as we did earlier with Alzheimer's disease. The combination of phase diagrams and thinking about disease progression—all based on the inspiration of Jack Whelan tracking his heroic battle with cancer that this book started with—can give us the start to the mathematical roadmap we need to efficiently and effectively manage COVID-19. Or at least manage it better than we managed Spanish flu.

Even the analyses discussed around Castleman disease in Chapter 8 are relevant. It already appears, at the time of this writing, that there are multiple manifestations of disease that occur due to SARS-CoV-2 exposure. What was first called COVID-19 may be an umbrella over all of them, or just one of several syndromes that the virus can cause. For example, an inflammatory syndrome, similar to Kawasaki disease, recently started being reported in children. There are also signs that damage to tissues in several organs may be related to COVID-19. This damage could itself be a critical input in finding patient equations for other diseases. Time will tell what the relationship of these conditions are to the pandemic and how best to manage them. But the idea of subtyping COVID-19 across many dimensions is exactly how precision medicine is just as relevant here, or in the context of any pandemic infectious disease, as it has been in the previous examples in the book.

Steam Tables, Sensors, and Early Warning Systems

How can we collect the necessary data for equation generation (or at least some of it), while hospitals are overrun and patients may be unable or unwilling to go to their physicians? Once again, at least some answers lie within previous chapters. The fabric of mobile devices and sensors that exist in our world—and that has been a theme throughout so much of this book—provides a source that doesn't require any interaction between patients and caregivers. These devices and sensors can provide rich streams of data for both generating and testing hypotheses about important factors in COVID-19 patient equations.

In Chapter 4, we looked at Ava, the ovulation-detecting wearable device aimed at helping women become pregnant. Ava uses a set of inputs—temperature, respiration rate, resting pulse rate, perfusion, and heart rate variability—to predict fertility cycles. But what if those same variables could be used to predict worsening COVID-19 symptoms, and help determine—sooner than we would otherwise know—who needs to be treated and who doesn't. Could we build out our map with more measurable dimensions, figure out which are associated with the transition from recovering-at-home to needs-hospital-intervention, and make better decisions that could save patients' lives?

These questions aren't merely theoretical. I caught up with Ava co-founder Pascal Koenig after learning that Ava is being used in a study in Liechtenstein in which 2,000 individuals are being monitored in order to determine whether the measurements tracked by Ava can detect COVID-19 infection more quickly than other means—an early warning system.[4]

"The underlying hypothesis," Ava's press release announced, "is that this will allow the creation of a new algorithm that enables identification of Covid-19 at an early stage even when no typical disease symptoms are present."[5] A new algorithm? Sounds an awful lot like a patient equation.

But the vision for the research goes beyond early detection. As the press release asks, "What if, for example, health professionals could access data on patients' vital parameters for the past few weeks and months?

Alternatively, the study could probe the utility of the Ava bracelet as a remote continuous measuring device for high-risk groups that have to stay in self-isolation at home or in a care setting."[6]

The idea that we could use a device intended for one purpose—tracking fertility—for another—identifying and managing COVID-19—is one we have covered already in this book in a different context. Recall the stroke conference where I said that if we wanted to look for a model for diagnosing cancer, we should look at data in cardiology studies, and vice versa—the incidental data being collected from patients with one condition who happen to develop another is hugely valuable for looking back and testing hypotheses.

We don't know what phenotypes—vital signs, or behavioral or cognitive measures—might have value to add in a COVID-19 context. Do slight variations—temperature beginning to increase outside of the normal cycles each of us experience, for instance—indicate trouble to come? What can we detect 24, 48, or 72 hours before someone needs to be treated? Can we determine the best treatment among multiple options by adding that data in as a factor? Might we, similar to how we discussed cancer therapy, use these slight variations as additional inputs that give us a higher-resolution view of how well a patient is responding to a therapy?

In addition to a wearable on an individual, there are sensing mechanisms whose scope goes beyond a single patient. For illustrative purposes, the number of cars, the number of people, and the noise levels in Manhattan, where I've been during the pandemic, have felt palpably different than they did before. Any given taxi or person might seem the same, if observed without the greater context, but looking at the entire population, the difference is obvious—there are so many fewer of us on the street and on the roads.

If you knew that nonessential businesses were closed, and that people were social distancing, that observation would be expected. But what if you didn't know that? The collective sensory inputs would still exist. If you walked the streets of New York City knowing nothing about COVID-19, it would be clear that something was amiss.

To be entirely candid, that example is a metaphor for how I think the life sciences industry—myself included—completely blew a tremendous opportunity here. We could have made a huge difference helping to manage, and perhaps even contain, COVID-19, and yet we weren't able to. This is an unfortunate product of how little data is shared today, and an illustration of the power of the ideas from the stroke conference and the kind of data pooling discussed in Chapter 11.

The life sciences industry has thousands upon thousands of research studies running around the world, with millions of patients actively participating in them. These studies contain patients with some of the most exquisitely curated data sets in the world of medicine—their histories, their vital signs on a more frequent basis than almost anywhere, often their gene sequences, and samples from virtually every scale of information shown in Figure 1.1 from the first chapter of the book. We also know every medication these patients are taking, their comorbidities, and adverse events, sometimes almost instantaneously as they occur. And yet these clinical trials only look at the indication that the trial is studying, in the context of the therapeutic options being evaluated in the research.

How much steam table data could be filled in if we knew which patients taking part in clinical trials—regardless of therapeutic area—came down with COVID-19? How much more would we know about possible treatments and outcomes? If we had a way to view that data in the context of COVID-19, looking for signs and symptoms, testing hypotheses once the very first patients were diagnosed, then we would have not just a potential early warning system, but the ability to build at least some draft phase diagrams, to figure out what really matters when diagnosing patients and selecting therapies.

I hope the pandemic serves as a call to action in our industry, to figure out how to use this data so that next time we are better prepared. Not only can we help contain the spread of future infections, but we can discover so much more about the management of health across broad populations, thanks to the high-fidelity and high-resolution view of individuals. We need a better way to look at research data through a broader lens and to connect with patients who are volunteering to participate in research beyond the confines of the research itself.

This relates in a broad sense to what the Flumoji effort discussed in Chapter 6 aimed to do for the flu. Flumoji wasn't looking at clinical trial data—it was looking at patient reports and online activity. But there's no reason we can't bring those factors into play here as well. What if, on top of our clinical trial data, we add new layers: what are patients searching for online, and how are they self-reporting their symptoms? Does a rise in temperature combined with a decline in social media activity, email checking, or movement in the world mean something more than the temperature rise alone? Does it indicate that a patient feels sicker, more tired, symptomatic even before the feelings register as illness? We don't know until we test it, until we look at the data.

This also takes us back to the kinds of new measures we talked about in Chapter 2, where I introduced the idea of territory as an input that could tell us more about our health than we realize—how we are moving through the world as a proxy for how we feel. Along similar lines, we are now hearing more and more about contact tracing—looking at our motion through the environment as a way to figure out who has been exposed to COVID-19, potentially giving us insight into what to do about our behavior to either avoid being exposed or take action if we might have been exposed unknowingly.

The effect of our behavior as we travel through our day is highly salient when thinking about COVID-19. It may even turn out to be that exposure isn't a yes/no variable when it comes to our risk of developing the COVID-19 illness. It could turn out that the amount of virus we're exposed to—as well as the timing of repeated, early exposures—is a significant factor in determining risks and therapeutic options. Again, time will tell if this is an important measure. But there may be some predictive value—beyond all of the other factors worth considering—to whether or not we are, for example, working in a hospital. It certainly seems to me, at least anecdotally among friends and colleagues, that there are a large number of otherwise-healthy, relatively young people working in health care who are suffering from COVID-19 when a prediction based merely on age and immune status would assume they would be fine.

It may also turn out to be very important to understand the effect of asymptomatic carriers, and the amount of virus they are shedding compared to what we understand in other illnesses, like the flu. The *New England Journal of Medicine* has already written about asymptomatic spread as the "Achilles' heel of current strategies to control COVID-19."[7] This may be a big part of why it took us so long as a society to realize that the virus was everywhere, and that we needed to lock down the world in order to control it. Contact tracing (and sufficient testing to make that tracing meaningful, of course) could rapidly bring the economy back to life without enduring waves of recurrences.

To get to a point where contact tracing is reliable and ubiquitous will be challenging, but it is made easier by the willingness of companies to share data and collaborate on finding the best path forward. Apple and Google unveiled in April 2020 what *Bloomberg* called a "rare partnership" to add technology to iPhones and Android phones to track location and notify people who came into contact with phone users who are later infected with the virus.[8] "All of us at Apple and Google believe there has never been a more important moment to work together to solve one of the world's most pressing problems," the companies said.[9]

It is way too soon to know what the impact of these efforts will turn out to be, but it is unquestionable that to transform COVID-19 data into actionable, useful, safe, and valuable equations, we must have a broader view of it, across patients, across populations, across research, across medicine, across the technologies that surround us, and across all the scales at which we can measure aspects of health. At the time of this writing, we don't know when the first COVID-19 case in the United States actually occurred. We don't know how widespread the antibodies are, or how quickly the virus is making its way through the population. A rich steam table view could tell us so much more. We have to work to build it—using every data source we have access to, making connections that go beyond the obvious and the easily visible. We need to focus on the underlying patient equations, to look not just at what's in front of us but what the data is telling us that we can't immediately see.

Putting a Spotlight on the Fragility of Our System

It's not just COVID-19 patients we've had to worry about as the pandemic has unfolded. It's been everybody, at every point in our health care system. Whether a patient is in a clinical trial, or just trying to get a regular checkup, our health system is based on the physical co-location of a patient and a practitioner. It is a debilitating weakness. So much so that it's surprising that it took a global pandemic to make it so painfully obvious. People haven't been able to get to the doctor—whether for a broken leg, or a mild heart attack, or for their ongoing cancer treatment—and they certainly haven't been able to get to their clinical trials. Despite so much technology available to us, we still expect and require patients to be physically present in front of a health care practitioner in order to get their care.

Whether it's moving patients to practitioners or moving practitioners to patients, the system simply falls apart when transportation isn't available, if hospitals and clinics are overcrowded, or if they aren't safe (or perceived not to be safe). And the overtaxing of the system creates even more complexity when doctors are expected to be in multiple places at once, when protective equipment is scarce, and when even simple things like picking up medication at a local pharmacy become impossible for a patient. It turns out that the capacity and access we assume under normal circumstances isn't a given when the world shuts down. The way we practice medicine (and certainly the research process, though I'll get to that more in a moment) falls apart when people either don't want to or simply can't easily move around—even if we have the early warning systems and better decision-making that sophisticated disease models can give us.

As we emerge from the pandemic, we are inevitably going to see a backlog of bad outcomes across all therapeutic areas. We're going to see what amounts to an unhealthier population across the board—not just because of COVID-19, but because of all of the routine and not-so-routine care that was skipped, postponed, or forgotten during the crisis. This includes cancer screenings, diabetes maintenance, medication adjustments, chest pain workups, annual physicals, ongoing treatments, and more—medical care that, when delayed, allows for diseases to progress unchecked. Even if hospitals are open and doctors are working (neither a given), people—especially the immunocompromised patients most at risk—can't show up when people with a highly-infectious disease may very well be sitting in the lobby.

These downstream effects are already becoming clear at the time of this writing. A new study in *Gastroenterology* reports on the effects of the pandemic on outcomes for New York City patients admitted to the hospital with gastrointestinal bleeding, finding that patients admitted with GI bleeds presented with lower hemoglobin and platelet counts than before the pandemic (meaning they were staying home longer before showing up for treatment), staying in the hospital longer, and much more likely to require a transfusion.[10] Across a whole range of conditions, I expect we will see these types of findings—patients waiting longer, presenting in worse shape, and needing more interventions to recover, with a higher percentage of patients who ultimately do poorly because of the impact of COVID-19.

It's inevitable that this aspect of our health care system will change because of COVID-19. I hesitate to call it a silver lining, but we are seeing—and will continue to see—the growth of telemedicine and virtual care. In the emergency setting of the pandemic, many doctors and hospitals have attempted to serve patients virtually as well as they can, with doctors moving quickly to phone calls and video visits. Some of that will surely stick, but beyond that, there is no doubt that the issues raised during this crisis will prompt new thinking about how we can reduce the need for patients to be physically present with medical professionals in order to receive care.

Of course there will be certain things that people must go to the hospital for—surgeries, certain types of scans, complex infusion therapies—but we have seen throughout this book the idea that we can combine medical devices with drugs and enable more automated, remote care (as in the case of diabetes management), and there is no question that the move toward this model will become more aggressive. Not only can we move the observation or measurement of a patient to a remote setting, but more and more therapies that are considered complex can perhaps be provided at home if they are conceived in a slightly different way. I suspect we'll see an acceleration of medical device and drug combinations, for example, that allow for this.

Patient equations are critical here—the more we learn about what works and what doesn't, which measurements matter and which don't, the more we can create safe, tailored treatments that serve the patient's condition without needing to put them in front of a physician. In fact, the ability to provide infusion therapies more dynamically and more consistently may result in even more effective disease management—imagine an artificial pancreas–like device in a nondiabetic function, infusing precise doses of a missing critical enzyme for a patient with a rare disease.

With the feedback loop from remote diagnosis and treatment, refining the process to be as effective as possible, we change the typical limits on patients we can treat. Instead of a scale defined by the number of waiting rooms, treatment rooms, and doctors, it's about the availability of sensors and the treatments themselves. Here it's not just a silver lining, but a much-needed societal advancement, post-COVID-19, where these technologies can be deployed not just in cases like diabetes but throughout the health care ecosystem.

A Speedier Road to Modernized Trial Design

When we talk about removing the need for patients to appear physically in the health care setting, it's not just about treatments—it's also about clinical trials. In the setting of COVID-19, there has been a dramatic reduction in the number of people enrolling in new trials, or continuing in trials they were previously part of. Whether for life-threatening diseases or chronic conditions, the research process has come to a virtual halt during this time. According to Medidata's own research, comparing numbers from March 2019 and March 2020 showed a global drop of more than 60% in trial enrollment, hitting every disease area (with life-threatening diseases like cancer down by half, and research in more chronic conditions like diabetes down by up to 80%).[11]

Trial sponsors became immediately concerned about their ability to enroll and recruit patients, and about the financial implications of delayed milestones and cancelled studies. In response to the pandemic, the life sciences industry found itself engaged in some combination of halting new patient recruitment for ongoing trials, delaying studies, extending patient study visit windows, and amending study protocols.[12]

We also found that a significant number of research sites were switching patients to virtual/telemedicine, and here's where we can find some optimism for the future.[13] I talked extensively in Chapter 11 about the need for virtual trials, and the pandemic only highlights the need to move faster and faster in that direction. Talking to *Clinical Leader*, Craig Lipset, founder of the research advisory firm Clinical Innovation Partners, said, "We are certainly seeing dramatic changes happening in both research and healthcare right now . . . When the pandemic is behind us, we will see whether innovation can outlast the crisis."[14]

Indeed, Vas Narasimhan, CEO of pharmaceutical giant Novartis, similarly said, on a recent radio broadcast for the UK publication *Monocle*, "the pandemic has been a huge accelerator on multiple dimensions . . . scaling up telemedicine . . . [with] more patients online."[15]

Without this shift to virtual trials—and maybe even with it, unfortunately—we are going to see a tremendous delay in getting drugs approved. If COVID-19 slows down trials as much as early indications show, without new thinking the approval of life-saving drugs could be pushed for years. There should be a sense of urgency to allow for that necessary new thinking, and to use alternative methodologies to get new therapies to patients who are waiting for them. And, fortunately, we see regulators being particularly vocal about their openness to precisely that.

For example, the FDA is expressing openness to the kind of modernization I've already written about—virtual trials, adaptive studies, and opening up trial design with new thinking and new technologies. Dr. Janet Woodcock, the director of the Center for Drug Evaluation and Research at the FDA, has said, according to *Business Insider*, that the current trial system must change.[16] "This crisis underlies and points out the need to have a better clinical trial infrastructure in place."[17]

Woodcock is open to more adaptive trials like the ones discussed in Chapter 11, including REMAP-CAP, a new COVID-19 study attempting to use artificial intelligence to find effective treatments for the virus, testing multiple therapies at once through data from more than 50 hospitals.[18] "The study is designed to randomize patients with severe pneumonia caused by the coronavirus to receive different treatments within four categories: antibiotics, antiviral therapy for influenza, steroids, and a class of antibiotic called macrolides that are often used to treat patients with skin and respiratory infections," writes Casey Ross in *STAT*.[19]

As with the I SPY-2 breast cancer trial, more and more patients will be assigned to the more promising regimens as the trial continues. The trial, according to *STAT*, "will also seek to evaluate different strategies for delivering oxygen and mechanical ventilation; the primary outcome being measured is 90-day mortality."[20]

Once again, perhaps a potential silver lining from the pandemic will be a faster move to new trial designs, a quicker acceptance of adaptive trials and virtual data collection, and, ultimately, better treatments available sooner to patients. We will need to conduct innovative research to counteract the backlog that we are already seeing in drug development, to cope with the patients whose therapies have been paused, and to help patients who are now in more need of new therapies because their conditions weren't addressed during the outbreak—whether chronic conditions, cancers, or untreated heart attacks and strokes. I fear that the number of patients who will need not just therapies, but innovative therapies—from COVID-19 or due to downstream effects—is going to overwhelm our fragile system again, unless changes are made.

The Next Hundred Years

All of this gets us back to 1919, and the phase diagram view of the pandemic that we didn't have then—and still don't have now. Hopefully, we can put everything together—new phenotypes, virtual medicine reducing the fragility of our system, better trial designs, stronger data collaboration—to emerge from this pandemic with a better plan for the future, and the pieces in place so that the next time pandemic illness strikes, we have more tools, more information, and more ability to get on top of it and stop things from turning out as badly as they did in 2020. Hopefully, we might one day look back on this as the inflection point where we were all finally moved to solve these issues and create a better health care system moving forward.

Of course, the pandemic doesn't change the urgency of the developments described throughout this book. In the Conclusion, I'll talk about how our future state—with or without the cloud of COVID-19 hanging over us—has the potential to be so much richer and better for patients than our current model, and how we can start to take concrete steps toward making it a reality.

Notes

1. George A. Soper, "The Lessons of the Pandemic," *Science* 49, no. 1274 (May 30, 1919): 501–506, https://doi.org/10.1126/science.49.1274.501.
2. Ibid.
3. Ibid.
4. "Liechtenstein Study Aims to Help Combat Coronavirus Pandemic," Ava, April 15, 2020, https://www.avawomen.com/press/liechtenstein-study-aims-to-help-combat-coronavirus-pandemic/.
5. Ibid.
6. Ibid.
7. Monica Gandhi, Deborah S. Yokoe, and Diane V. Havlir, "Asymptomatic Transmission, the Achilles' Heel of Current Strategies to Control Covid-19," *New England Journal of Medicine*, April 24, 2020, https://doi.org/10.1056/nejme2009758.

8. Mark Gurman, "Apple, Google Bring Covid-19 Contact-Tracing to 3 Billion People," *Bloomberg*, April 10, 2020, https://www.bloomberg.com/news/articles/2020-04-10/apple-google-bring-covid-19-contact-tracing-to-3-billion-people?srnd=premium.

9. Ibid.

10. Judith Kim, John B. Doyle, John W. Blackett, Benjamin May, Chin Hur, and Benjamin Lebwohl, on behalf of HIRE study group, "Effect of the COVID-19 Pandemic on Outcomes for Patients Admitted with Gastrointestinal Bleeding in New York City," *Gastroenterology*, May 2020, https://doi.org/10.1053/j.gastro.2020.05.031.

11. Mark Terry, "Clinical Catch-Up: April 6-10," BioSpace, April 13, 2020, https://www.biospace.com/article/clinical-catch-up-april-6-10/?s=69.

12. "COVID 19 and Clinical Trials: The Medidata Perspective," https://www.medidata.com/wp-content/uploads/2020/05/COVID19-Response4.0_Clinical-Trials_2020504_v3.pdf, May 4, 2020.

13. Ibid.

14. Ed Miseta, "Covid-19 Hastens Embrace Of Virtual Trials," *Clinical Leader*, March 30, 2020, https://www.clinicalleader.com/doc/covid-hastens-embrace-of-virtual-trials-0001.

15. Tyler Brûlé, "The Big Interview," radio broadcast (*Monocle*, May 8, 2020), https://monocle.com/radio/shows/the-big-interview/114/?

16. Andrew Dunn, "There Are Already 72 Drugs in Human Trials for Coronavirus in the US. With Hundreds More on the Way, a Top Drug Regulator Warns We Could Run Out of Researchers to Test Them All.," *Business Insider*, April 2020, https://www.businessinsider.com/fda-woodcock-overwhelming-amount-of-coronavirus-drugs-in-the-works-2020-4.

17. Ibid.

18. Casey Ross, "Global Trial Uses AI to Rapidly Identify Optimal Covid-19 Treatments," *STAT*, April 9, 2020, https://www.statnews.com/2020/04/09/coronavirus-trial-uses-ai-to-rapidly-identify-optimal-treatments/.

19. Ibid.

20. Ibid.

Conclusion

If there's one lesson to take from this book, it's this: our health follows paths, paths that are the summation of everything from our DNA to the ways we interact with the world and the effects of the environment on us. Like a trail through the woods, we can observe where we came from. But imagine those paths meandering—not through a forest, but through a multidimensional space encompassing all of the things we might, now or in the future, have the ability to measure: our genes (and which of those genes are on or off), our blood chemistry, blood pressure, the function of our organs, the way we think, the manifestation of those thoughts in our behavior, and so much more.

A map of a forest is two-dimensional. A rocket in space traces a path through three dimensions. To envision the paths in the n-dimensional space of every aspect of our biology, at every scale, is a staggeringly overwhelming problem. But the paths exist. And we have new tools by which we can trace them and predict where they will go.

We can supplement all of our traditional medical knowledge with the digital trails we leave behind us every day. We can use the phenomenal connectivity and computational power available today to figure out what dimensions of information are relevant and predictive of our health futures. We can simplify the problem of trying to measure and comprehend it all. We can combine the known paths for patients, both in and outside of research programs, into a map—a multidimensional map, to be sure, but one with borders, with lines that delineate when and how health can be maintained, and diseases managed or cured.

These paths, these maps, are patient equations. The digital ways we create, harvest, and combine data at scales never seen before in the history of medicine will help us discover them, and will help us reverse-engineer them. Perhaps not perfectly right away, and not in a way that will automate every decision we make for our care—but certainly in a way that is additive to our quality of life, and to our longevity.

All of this presents incredible opportunities for improving our health as individuals, and for unleashing a new era in the practice and the business of life sciences and medicine.

Professor Michael Snyder, director of Stanford's Center for Genomics and Personalized Medicine, has been called "the world's most bio-tracked man."[1] He has spent the past few years wearing devices that measure everything about him and his environment. In the course of doing so, he diagnosed his own Lyme disease from an algorithm that saw an infection hiding within his data.[2] He believes that combining genetic information with our exposome—the chemicals and organisms we encounter every day in our environment—have so much more to tell us than we've let them. "We now think we can tell when you get sick before you realize it," he says.[3]

Snyder and others, according to the *New York Times*, envision doctors doing more than running lab tests and checking vital signs. "They will scrutinize your genome for risk factors and track tens of thousands of molecules active in your body. By doing so, the doctors of the future will identify diseases, and treat them, long before symptoms appear."[4] It's those layers in our layer cake, all making themselves known. Snyder ran a study that found that 53 of 109 subjects discovered something meaningful about their health—undiagnosed diabetes, heart disease, and more—from being tracked.

"We were able to go back and see molecules that were clearly starting to rise months before the diagnosis and then dropped with treatment," the lead author of the study, Sophia Miryam Schüssler-Fiorenza Rose, told the *Times*.[5] "We think these might be very valuable early markers of disease," she said. One person in the study "learned they had early-stage lymphoma before they showed symptoms . . . [from] a test of the person's immunome, which measures levels of immune chemicals in the blood."[6]

Cue Health is developing a "miniature medical lab for the home,"[7] which would collect saliva, blood, or a nasal swab, test for illness, and make actionable recommendations. Alphabet and Apple are developing new health capabilities in their watches with every release. There are, by one report, 17 diseases with biomarkers to be found in human breath.[8] Thirty-eight of the companies listed in the *Fortune* 50 have some kind of digital health care offering.[9] The question is: can yours beat them?

There are pitfalls as we move forward, of course. There is a naiveté right now in the business world that big data and machine learning produce magic,[10] but it's not magic at all. These are merely new technologies that happen to be so much more advanced than the ways we used to think about these problems. They can seem like magic, sometimes. But digital technology, data science, and artificial intelligence are not immune to the real-world requirements of proving therapies to be safe, effective, and reliable.

Whether the therapy in question is a molecule or medical device, or if it is digital, taking advantage of a patient equation-based view of the world allows us to prove that safety, efficacy, and value in more precise ways than ever before.

Companies that already play in the life sciences space are the most well-equipped to lead this revolution. They have the expertise in evidence generation, with techniques that aren't necessarily new. What's new is the relevant scale of evidence generation, from populations down to individuals down to cells—which means that new entrants to the health care ecosystem may be required to bring the massive connectivity and processing power needed to the patients, providers, regulators, and payers involved. But, make no mistake, the life sciences industry has to lead the way.

Privacy and Transparency

I've spent almost no space in this book talking about an issue that trips a lot of us up when we attempt to go to market with data-driven products and services in medicine: privacy. And while it's true that there may be a learning curve for patients (and doctors) to trust algorithms with their health data, at the end of the day, I've largely ignored the issue because I think it's one that's worth putting to the side.

Not because it isn't incredibly important. There are laws and ethical considerations that should be and must be adhered to and thoroughly considered. But if the end product of creating a patient equation-powered future will benefit people and society as much as I believe it will, mechanisms can and will inevitably be created to protect our data and the information generated by it in order to realize the full societal benefit.

Notably, issues of consent must be respected. The standard ethics of clinical research applies, and we shouldn't be leveraging data about someone without their permission—the same way we can't experiment on someone unless they agree to be experimented on. But the technology, to be quite honest, cannot be contained. And the benefits to individuals will doubtlessly motivate consent, as well as incentivize governments, regulators, and corporations to come up with solutions to privacy issues that are reliable, transparent, and auditable.

The reality is that while many of us may not feel comfortable signing a piece of paper saying that our insurance company can see our data—we don't want them to have the power to raise our premiums because they find out we eat horribly and could be blamed for, say, our recent cardiac incident—we probably post enough on our social media pages for them to figure it out anyway. The data we give off each day, those digital trails, are too numerous to control, and attempts to wall them off are destined to fail, just like the containment of the dinosaurs in *Jurassic Park*. Unless someone is willing to go completely off the grid, not use a cell phone, a computer, a credit card, an electronic bus ticket, or ride through a city armed with cameras on stoplights, their data is out there and will find ways to escape.

The even larger truth is that we shouldn't care, because in a patient equation-powered world, the more data that is out there, the more we are helped. The more doctors and researchers learn about us, the better they can find the right treatments at the right time for whatever condition we are faced with. In the movie *Gattaca*, people are placed in a caste in life based on their DNA—so there's an incentive to pass off someone else's genetic code as your own. But if this book has shown anything, it's that genes are only a small piece of the puzzle. Genotype is dwarfed by phenotype. Predictions from genetics alone are just a tiny, tiny piece of the overall picture.

Incentives really are ultimately aligned—government and industry do better when citizens and customers are healthy. Like it or not, even your employer and insurer are on the side of your health. You are a more profitable subscriber and a higher-revenue-generating employee if you are well. It's not just that I believe everyone in every business has the right intentions—although in life sciences and health care, I mostly do (there are easier industries to act badly in). But, if you'll allow me to leave questions of overpopulation and the environment in the same pile as privacy for the moment—in the pile of things that are incredibly important, but not relevant to realizing the value of patient equations—it's economically sensible for them to keep everyone alive and healthy for as long as possible. And that's especially true in a world of value-based care, where the physician, the physical therapist, the pharma company, and everyone in the health care value chain is compensated based on positive outcomes and effective prevention.

So What's Next?

Regardless of your particular role in health care, perhaps entirely confined to wanting your own health to be cared for, I hope this book has been a call to action. The power of predicting the health of an individual through generating consistent maps of population health is spectacular. Plotting the equations in the multidimensional space discussed will require industrial investment, academic contributions, and the consent of individuals. Everyone has an important part to play—contributing data, funding investments, and producing and practicing medicine, all centered around patient equations.

This is not meant to be a definitive work on the subject. The interviews, anecdotes, and ideas presented are like the digital trail of one person's health—interesting, hopefully useful, but limited to who I am and what I've experienced. My hope is that the extraordinary seat that I've had for over 25 years—at the center of the digital revolution in clinical research and its connected ecosystem of health care—and the insights of those interviewed for the book provide perspective that can be turned into action.

Today, we are curing diseases recently thought incurable, and turning previously fatal diseases into manageable, chronic conditions. We are targeting molecules once thought impossible to interact with through medicine, creating medical devices that seem imported directly from 1960s science fiction movies like *Fantastic Voyage*, and accessing computational power and the kinds of data that would be unimaginable when I was doing my first laboratory research a quarter of a century ago.

Of course, an easy argument can be made that health care and life sciences aren't "well." Providing everyone with access to the highest-quality care is a problem we have barely chipped away at in most countries, let alone on a global scale. The costs for developing new drugs and medical devices, and the incentive systems for effectively deploying them to patients, are headwinds—strong ones—blocking forward motion in medical innovation. Clearly, we were unprepared for a pandemic illness like COVID-19. How much more could we be advancing the state of the art in health care tools if we were able to turn them into tailwinds, powering us toward progress, supported by the digital power and biological innovations sitting in data centers and laboratories around the world?

We must work together to make that turnaround happen. Hopefully this book helps us all think about new ways to harness these revolutionary techniques and technologies along a path to some of the lofty future possibilities described in these pages.

This book comes at an interesting time not just in the world at large but in my professional life as well. Shortly before completing the manuscript, Medidata was purchased by Dassault Systèmes, a company whose software has literally transformed the way planes, automobiles, and probably many—if not most—of the products and services that are involved in the "stuff" around you are designed and manufactured (just take a look around whatever room you are in, and think about all of the design and manufacturing that has gone into creating it).

As a product life cycle management platform, Dassault Systèmes—just like Medidata aimed to do before the acquisition—wanted to bring the incredible power of their platform to the world of designing and delivering drugs and medical devices. Now, post-acquisition, Medidata and my own personal ambitions in that regard haven't changed. However, our plans to bring to life a platform that spans dimensions from molecular to individual to population-level modeling and research for life sciences certainly got a lot more credible. And now, with a larger sandbox and more computational toys around me, if I'm to take my own call to action and act on it, I'm realizing clearly what prompted Dassault Systèmes to start poking around Medidata in the first place: that in addition to thinking about platforms, data, and the artificial intelligence on top of it, simulations will play an incredible part in the future of research, medicine, and patient equations.

Bernard Charlès, Dassault Systèmes' CEO and vice chairman, speaks about the importance of the "virtual twin," not just in health care, but based on his experience with simulated versions of what is being created in reality across other industries. In life sciences, we're used to a tiny fraction of drugs—as few as 1 in 10—that enter clinical trials making it all the way through the process to become drugs on the market. Imagine that ratio when it comes to passenger aircraft (the same order of magnitude, and actually more expensive to create than a drug development program). Would the industry function if they only flew 10% of the time once manufactured? Of course not. They fly 100% of the time.

Is the analogy a perfect one? Far from it. But are there lessons to be learned and ways to think about how industries like aerospace can develop incredibly complex products at a staggeringly more reliable rate of success than we do in life sciences? I think that answer is an obvious yes. So as we—the combined Medidata and Dassault Systèmes—pursue some of the ideas in this book, the continuation of the past 20 years of work at Medidata-standalone, you can expect the appearance of virtual twins at every scale. Drugs. Cells. Organs. Patients.

I am convinced that they will be another dimension by which we can multiply the evidence we are able to factor out of every individual unit of patient data gathered. My patient equation work will continue—hand in hand with patient simulations—and I hope and expect it will intersect with everyone's efforts as discussed in, and happening around, this book.

Notes

1. Dana G. Smith, "Meet the World's Most Bio-Tracked Man," Medium (*OneZero*), May 8, 2019, https://onezero.medium.com/meet-the-worlds-most-bio-tracked-man-2077758cf5a2.
2. Veronique Greenwood, "The Next Big Thing in Health Is Your Exposome," Medium (*Elemental*), November 5, 2018, https://medium.com/s/thenewnew/the-exposome-is-the-new-frontier-e5bb8b1360da.
3. Ibid.
4. Carl Zimmer, "In This Doctor's Office, a Physical Exam Like No Other," *New York Times*, May 8, 2019, https://www.nytimes.com/2019/05/08/science/precision-medicine-overtreatment.html.
5. Ibid.
6. Dana G. Smith, "Meet the World's Most Bio-Tracked Man.".
7. "Cue Is a Miniature Medical Lab for the Home," Cloud9Smart, May 20, 2014, https://www.cloud9smart.com/cue_health_tracker.

8. Amanda Hoh, "How a Breath Test Could Reveal What Disease You Have," *ABC News*, July 31, 2017, http://www.abc.net.au/news/2017-07-31/detecting-disease-in-breath-with-world-smallest-breathalyser/8759050?pfmredir=sm.
9. Don Jones, "Conference Talk at Medidata NEXT Event" (October 2016).
10. Wikipedia Contributors, "Clarke's Three Laws," Wikipedia, February 1, 2019, https://en.wikipedia.org/wiki/Clarke%27s_three_laws.

Acknowledgments

Writing this book has been an incredible process, providing an excuse to reach out to people across health care—in some cases people I've had the pleasure of working with, and in other cases people whose work I've admired from afar. Huge thanks to everyone who gave their time to talk through the issues and ideas in this book, and allowed me to share their perspectives: Dr. Don Berry, Anthony Costello, Kara Dennis, Dr. David Fajgenbaum, Robin Farmanfarmaian, Dr. Graham Hatfull, Jamie Heywood, Dr. Julian Jenkins, Dr. Stan Kachnowski, Pascal Koenig, Dr. Jerry Lee, Dr. Veena Misra, T. J. Sharpe, Alicia Staley, Glen Tullman, and Dr. Daniel Yadegar.

I will never be able to repay my literary debt to Jeremy Blachman, my extraordinary co-author. Without his perception, partnership, and persistence this book would not exist.

I want to thank my Medidata colleagues, past, present, and future as part of Dassault Systèmes. Some of them appear in the book by name, but I am equally thankful to all of them. The work we've done together is quite literally this book's foundation. A particular thanks to Nicole Pariser, who was instrumental in turning the idea into a plan—and in giving it a title! Special thanks as well to the tireless Dana Suchow, who made sure all of the conversations, approvals, and endless logistics necessary for the book came together. Thanks also to Medidata's marketing team, particularly Jenni Li, who turned slides, sketches, and pictures of whiteboards into the graphics in the book, and Dianne Yurek, who orchestrated bringing the book across the finish line and into readers' hands. And of course to my friends and co-founders Tarek Sherif and Dr. Edward Ikeguchi. This book scratches at the surface of a journey we began over 20 years ago, an incredible experience, the enormity of which I find it hard to even put into words.

To the faculty and my friends at Carnegie Mellon University, New York University, and Columbia University: the privilege you have extended to me, allowing me to teach and to collaborate far beyond my academic credentials, is one of my greatest pleasures, and has forged much of the content in this book.

Thank you to my parents, Madeline, Alan, Judy, and Ian, whose inspiration, influence, and voices all exist herein.

Finally, to my friends, and to my fiercely loyal sisters, who have tolerated and encouraged my attention to science, technology, and Medidata for all these years: Katie Sue, Jesse, Uri, Mike, Adam, Steve, Andy, Michael, Yukiyo, Seijiro, Valéry, Maria, Padma, Katie, and Lizzy (and again to Tarek, who I have now shared an office and a business with for over 20 years): I love you guys!

About the Authors

Glen de Vries

Glen is the co-CEO and co-founder of Medidata Solutions, a Dassault Systèmes brand, the leading cloud platform for life sciences research. He has been driving Medidata's mission of powering smarter treatments and healthier people since the company's inception in 1999. He received his undergraduate degree in molecular biology and genetics from Carnegie Mellon University, worked as a research scientist at the Columbia Presbyterian Medical Center, and studied computer science at New York University's Courant Institute of Mathematics. Glen's publications have appeared in *Applied Clinical Trials*, *Cancer*, *The Journal of Urology*, *Molecular Diagnostics*, *STAT*, *Urologic Clinics of North America*, and *TechCrunch*. Glen is a trustee of Carnegie Mellon University, a Columbia HITLAB Fellow, and a member of the Healthcare Businesswomen's Association European Advisory Board. Follow Glen on social media at @CaptainClinical.

Jeremy Blachman

Jeremy Blachman is a writer who works with leaders across industries on getting their ideas out to the world. A graduate of Princeton

University and Harvard Law School, he is also a twice-published novelist—*Anonymous Lawyer* (Henry Holt) and *The Curve* (Ankerwycke, co-authored with Cameron Stracher)—and screenwriter, having developed both of his novels as television pilots for NBC. His writing has appeared in the *New York Times*, the *Wall Street Journal*, and many other publications. Visit his website at jeremyblachman.com.

Index

Page references followed by *fig* indicate an illustrated figure.